GUIDE TO
TV MOVIES

by
Roger Morrison

SANTA MONICA PRESS
P.O. Box 1076
Santa Monica, CA 90406-1076
Printed in the United States
All Rights Reserved

INTRODUCTION

Welcome, movie-lover! Please allow me a few words to explain the contents of this guide to you.

To begin with, you will not find every movie ever made inside the covers of this book. Instead, I have included a selection of movies that are extremely popular, or that have unusual artistic merit. There are no bombs here. A one star review does not denote a turkey, but rather a movie that is enjoyable, but also of the average, run-of-the-mill variety. It is most likely included in this guide because of its extreme (and, perhaps, inexplicable) popularity.

The aim of the *Guide to TV Movies* is to provide you with a list of films that have been universally applauded either by the movie-going public at the box office or by critics because of their high artistic value. I have included a wide variety of films, from musicals to drama, from family entertainment movies to films with themes and stories more suited to adult audiences. The vast majority of these movies are shown regularly on television, and nearly all are available at your local video store.

It is my hope that this guide will open your eyes to films that you have never seen before, as well as start a few arguments about the merit of a particular work. Certainly, I expect that you will disagree with quite a few of my opinions; after all, my reviews are highly subjective, and my tastes will not always be in line with yours. I don't claim to be the final authority on movies, but rather an informed film buff with an extensive knowledge of the history of cinema who is able to bring a fair amount of perspective to a particular work.

The capsule reviews contain everything from plot summaries to information about cinematic techniques to listings of the major Academy Awards the film may have won. In addition to the capsule reviews, I have included the running time of the film (this will help you if the movie is on television and you would like to tape it), its rating, the director and principal stars (you'll be surprised to find many of your favorite actors and actresses in films you've never heard of), and a rating system of one to four stars.

Here are the definitions for these ratings:

**** A certifiable classic. Not to be missed.

*** An excellent film, certainly worth watching, but falling just short of the classic category.

** An enjoyable movie that is most likely highly entertaining, but that does not contain the artistry of a three or four star film.

* An average film that will provide some degree of entertainment despite its obvious flaws. It is most likely included here because of its overwhelming popularity.

Happy viewing!

Roger Morrison

A

ABOVE THE LAW (1988)
** R 1:39
DIR: *Andrew Davis* **CAST:** *Steven Seagal, Pam Grier, Sharon Stone, Henry Silva, Daniel Faraldo*
Seagal stars as a world-weary Chicago cop with a shadowy past—he was a Special Operations agent in Vietnam. The plot, which involves a conspiracy among corrupt government officials and drug dealers, gives Seagal ample opportunity to demonstrate his martial arts skills by beating up bad guys. The film, as predictable and heavy-handed as it is, has some terrific action sequences. It also made Seagal a star.

ABSENCE OF MALICE (1981)
*** PG 1:56
DIR: *Sydney Pollack* **CAST:** *Paul Newman, Sally Field, Melinda Dillon, Bob Balaban, Wilford Brimley, Barry Primus, Luther Adler, John Harkins, Don Hood*
An absorbing drama of governmental manipulation and sloppy journalism. Newman stars as an honest businessman who is framed by the government in order to nail a mobster. Field is the reporter who prints the government version, thereby implicating Newman in a crime he did not commit. Even as she defends her reporting, Newman finds a way to clear his name and bring down those who conspired against him.

THE ABYSS (1989)
** PG-13 2:25

DIR: *James Cameron* **CAST:** *Ed Harris, Mary Elizabeth Mastrantonio, Michael Biehn, Chris Elliott, Todd Graff, Leo Burmester*

A futuristic sci-fi adventure involving the crew of an underwater oil rig fending off a psycho Navy officer, a nuclear bomb, and translucent sea beings. Some of the action is harrowing, especially a claustrophobic submarine accident. The special effects, from George Lucas' Industrial Light and Magic, are top rate. But the over-cooked story and hoaky ending involving underwater aliens diminish the film's quality. The visual effects earned an Oscar. Nominations for Best Sound, Cinematography, and Art Direction.

THE ACCIDENTAL TOURIST (1988)
*** PG 2:02

DIR: *Lawrence Kasdan* **CAST:** *William Hurt, Geena Davis, Kathleen Turner, Ed Begley, Jr , David Ogden Stiers, Amy Wright*

Hurt plays a divorced man who makes a living writing cynical travel guides for those who, like himself, hate to travel. Davis plays a sweet, unsophisticated dog trainer and mother of a sickly little boy. The two are from different worlds, but somehow manage to find each other in this bittersweet adaptation of Anne Tyler's best-selling novel about love and loss. Director Kasdan, better known for slam-bang action, has a fine touch with these quirky characters, including Stiers and Begley as Hurt's stuffy, obsessive brothers. Davis won a Best Supporting Actress Oscar for her poignant performance. Nominations for Best Picture, Director and Frank Galati for Best Adapted Screenplay.

THE ACCUSED (1988)
*** R 1:50
DIR: *Jonathan Kaplan* CAST: *Jodie Foster, Kelly McGillis, Bernie Coulson, Leo Rossi*
A gripping film based on the true story of a Massachusetts woman raped in a neighborhood tavern as spectators jeered on the attackers. Foster won an Oscar for her portrayal of the victim, a working-class woman whose foul mouth and sordid lifestyle made her an unsympathetic victim. McGillis plays an idealistic prosecutor who takes on the case against those who cheered during the gang rape. This is a riveting courtroom drama about the injustices perpetrated on rape victims.

ADAM'S RIB (1949)
**** NR 1:41
DIR: *George Cukor* CAST: *Spencer Tracy, Katherine Hepburn, Judy Holliday, Tom Ewell, David Wayne, Jean Hagen*
One of the best and funniest of the Tracy/Hepburn films. The two play husband and wife attorneys

battling on opposite ends of the same murder trial of a woman (Holliday) accused of shooting her husband (Ewell). The razor-sharp, sophisticated script by Ruth Gordon and Garson Kanin transforms the naturally combative courtroom milieu into a hilarious battleground between the sexes. To top it all off, there's even a Cole Porter song, "Farewell Amanda."

THE ADDAMS FAMILY (1991)
*** PG-13 1:41
DIR: *Barry Sonnenfeld* CAST: *Raul Julia, Angelica Huston, Christopher Lloyd, Dan Hedaya, Elizabeth Wilson, Carel Struycken, Judith Malina*
A dark, macabre comedy that stays loyal to the Charles Addam's cartoons upon which the film is based. Julia and Huston were born to play Gomez and Morticia Addams, the amorous, kind-hearted ghoul tycoons who head up a bizarre household populated by a lone hand who scampers up and down the halls. The plot revolves around a conspiracy by Gomez' crooked attorney (Hedaya) to embezzle the family millions by claiming to have found Gomez' long-lost brother (Lloyd). But the story is secondary to the wonderful characters and sight gags that abound in this film. It's like visiting an old friend who you haven't seen in a while because he's been in the attic. Fun for the whole family, both living and departed.

THE ADVENTURES OF BARON MUNCHAUSEN (1989)
*** PG 2:06

DIR: *Terry Gilliam* **CAST:** *John Neville, Eric Idle, Robin Williams, Oliver Reed, Winston Dennis, Uma Thurman*

From the wonderful, warped mind of ex-Monty Python member Gilliam (*Brazil, Time Bandits*) comes this fantasy about the exaggerated recollections of an 18th-century nobleman. Neville is charming as the ancient aristocrat who tells of going to the moon, riding cannon balls, and residing inside the belly of a whale. Gilliam's remarkable, surreal vision makes this fantasy come to life. Williams has a funny cameo as an amorous moon man. Oscar nominations for Art Direction, Costume Design, Makeup, and Visual Effects

THE ADVENTURES OF ROBIN HOOD (1938)
*** NR 1:46

DIR: *Michael Curtiz* **CAST:** *Errol Flynn, William Keighley, Olivia de Havilland, Basil Rathbone, Claud Rains, Alan Hale*

The swashbuckler film that has it all. Robin Hood (Flynn), the legendary hero who robs from the rich and gives to the poor, dashes around Sherwood Forest and Nottingham Castle saving damsels in distress (de Havilland), crossing swords with wicked princes (Rains) and foiling the dastardly plots of evil malcontents (Rathbone).

The Art Direction, Editing and Erich Wolfgang Korngold's rousing score all won Oscars. Filmed in gorgeous Technicolor.

THE AFRICAN QUEEN (1951)
**** NR 1:43
DIR: *John Huston* **CAST:** *Katharine Hepburn, Humphrey Bogart, Robert Morley, Theodore Bikel*
Unbeatable combination of Bogart (in an Oscar-winning role) as crotchety, boozy sea captain Charlie Allnut, and Hepburn as the straightlaced English missionary he ferries up the Congo river just as World War I hits Africa. Along the way, the two match wits and courage with wild animals, the jungle, Nazis and each other. Houston's direction, James Agee's script and Jack Cardiff's cinematography are all first-rate.

AFTER DARK, MY SWEET (1990)
*** R 1:54
DIR: *James Foley* **CAST:** *Rachel Ward, Jason Patric, Bruce Dern, James Cotton, George Dickerson*
A mentally damaged prize fighter (Patric) stumbles into a rough California desert town only to find himself involved in crime and betrayal. Ward plays a seductive alcoholic who embroils the vulnerable boxer in a scheme to kidnap the child of wealthy parents. Her accomplice is a sleazy ex-cop (Dern) whose paranoia and manipulation catch Patric off-guard. This is a first-

rate *film noir* adaptation of Jim Thompson's
hardboiled 1955 novel.

AFTER HOURS (1985)
***R 1:37
Dir: *Martin Scorsese* **CAST:** *Griffin Dunne, Rosanna
Arquette, Thomas Chong, Teri Garr, John Heard,
Verna Bloom*
Dunne stars as a very normal computer program-
mer in this funny, bizarre journey through a very
strange Manhattan night. Stepping out for a cup
of coffee, Dunne meets a beautiful, spacey girl
(Arquette) who sets him off on a series of subculture adventures among New York's avant
garde. Unable to return to his apartment because
he's lost his wallet and keys, Dunne finds himself
mistaken for a burglar, pursued by a highly neurotic woman (Garr), and encased in plaster of
Paris. Scorsese never lets the action wane in this
Kafka-esque comedy.

AIRPLANE! (1980)
*** PG 1:28
DIR: *Jim Abrahams, David Zucker, Jerry Zucker*
CAST: *Robert Hays, Leslie Nielsen, Julie Hagerty,
Robert Stack, Lloyd Bridges, Peter Graves, Kareem
Abdul-Jabbar*
From the jokers that went on to make the *Naked
Gun* films comes this mercilessly funny parody of
nearly every Hollywood disaster film ever made.

Top-heavy with goofy sight gags, deadpan puns and lots of just plain silliness, this movie uses a tommy-gun style of comedy, and most of the jokes stick. Stack, Bridges, Graves and Nielsen all have a ball lampooning the kind of melodramatic fluff that made Irwin Allen famous.

ALICE DOESN'T LIVE HERE ANYMORE (1974)
**** PG 1:53
DIR: *Martin Scorsese* **CAST:** *Ellen Burstyn, Kris Kristofferson, Diane Ladd, Jodie Foster, Alfred Lutter*
Burstyn took home an Oscar for her fine performance as a widow and mother of a young son who must learn to survive alone while holding on to her dream of fame as a singer. She finds a job at a restaurant populated by off-beat staff and patrons. Ladd has a memorable role as a fellow waitress with a mouth like a Teamster. Kristofferson, in an unpretentious performance, plays the new man in her life. Scorsese's direction is uncharacteristically low-key in this warm, poignant film. Nominations for Ladd and Robert Getchell for his screenplay.

ALICE IN WONDERLAND (1951)
** G 1:15
DIR: *Clyde Geronimi, Hamilton Luske, Wilfred Jackson* **CAST:** *Voices of Kathryn Beaumont, Ed Wynn, Richard Haydn, Sterling Holloway, Jerry Colonna,*

Verna Felton, Bill Thompson
Animated Disney version of Lewis Carroll's classic absurdist allegories *Alice in Wonderland* and *Through the Looking Glass* is uneven, but has some entertaining sequences. It's strictly family fare (with none of the sly political allusions and mathematical trickery of Carroll's books) and is fun on a purely visual level. The Cheshire Cat, the Mad Hatter's Tea Party and the Queen of Hearts make this well worth a trip down the rabbit hole.

ALIEN (1979)
** R 1:57
DIR: *Ridley Scott* **CAST:** *Sigourney Weaver, Tom Skerritt, John Hurt, Ian Holm, Harry Dean Stanton*
In the film that made Sigourney Weaver famous, a motley band of space explorers and scientists stumble across a seemingly dead planet that turns out to be host (literally) to a nearly unstoppable alien monster. One by one, the crew falls prey to the alien, until the final, rousing showdown with Weaver. The Oscar-winning alien special effects are graphic and truly horrific and the film is relentlessly suspenseful, although somewhat one-dimensional.

ALIENS (1986)
*** R 2:17
DIR: *James Cameron* **CAST:** *Sigourney Weaver, Carrie Henn, Michael Biehn, Paul Reiser, Bill Paxton*

13

Weaver, as the lone survivor from the first film, returns with a squadron of battle-hungry, but doomed, space Marines to fight the mysterious alien once again. This time, however, there's more than one of the deadly creatures and the action and suspense of the first film is jacked up accordingly. After a relatively calm introduction, the film takes off like a runaway roller-coaster on greased tracks. The film's special effects won an Oscar.

ALL ABOUT EVE (1950)
**** NR 2:18
DIR: *Joseph L Mankiewicz* **CAST:** *Bette Davis, Anne Baxter, George Sanders, Celeste Holm, Gary Merrill, Thelma Ritter, Marilyn Monroe*
Bette Davis shines as Margo Channing, a cynical, aging star of the theater who takes a worshipping fan (Baxter) under her wing, only to find Baxter's fanaticism dominates her life. The wonderful cast really sink their collective teeth into this funny, sophisticated, but jaundiced look at the world behind the footlights. Marilyn Monroe has a small but memorable part as a chirpy young starlet on the make. Winner of six Oscars, including Best Picture, Director and Screenplay.

ALL OF ME (1984)
** PG 1:33
DIR: *Carl Reiner* **CAST:** *Steve Martin, Lily Tomlin,*

Victoria Tennant

This comedy is kept alive only by Steve Martin's incredible talent as a performer—he will blow you away to such an extent that you won't care about the film's other shortcomings (namely, a bad script and stolid direction). The movie tells the tale of an up-and-coming lawyer who is handling the estate of an eccentric millionairess. The old woman believes that she can channel her soul into a beautiful young body and thereby live forever, clinging on to her fortune for all eternity. But things go wrong when her soul accidentally enters Martin's body, and the two spirits must cohabitate. You will fall out of your chair with side-splitting laughter during some of the scenes in which Martin tries to keep the two opposing souls under control.

ALL THAT JAZZ (1979)
*** R 2:03

DIR: *Bob Fosse* **CAST:** *Roy Scheider, Jessica Lange, Ann Reinking, Leland Palmer, Ben Vereen, John Lithgow, Keith Gordon, Wallace Shawn, Cliff Gorman* Director/choreographer Fosse's take on Fellini's *8 1/2*, set on the Broadway stage. It balances spectacular musical and dance numbers with a blow-by-blow chronicle of egotistical director Joe Gideon's (Scheider) descent into the pits of a near-fatal heart ailment. Both grittily realistic (the dancers' blood, sweat and tears) and oddly mystical (as Gideon meets and comes to terms with "Death"), this is a creative and striking modern movie musical.

ALL THE PRESIDENT'S MEN (1976)
**** PG 2:18
DIR: *Alan J Pakula* CAST: *Robert Redford, Dustin Hoffman, Jason Robards, Jack Warden, Martin Balsam, Hal Holbrook, Meredith Baxter, Ned Beatty, Jane Alexander*
Tightly-wound, spellbinding political thriller based on the book of the same name by *Washington Post* reporters Bob Woodward (Redford) and Carl Bernstein (Hoffman), who broke open the Nixon administration Watergate break-in cover-up scandal. Combines the best elements of political intrigue, detective yarns and action thrillers into an exciting whole. Robards and screenwriter William Goldman both earned Oscars, but all of the cast is remarkable.

ALTERED STATES (1980)
*** R 1:42
DIR: *Ken Russell* CAST: *William Hurt, Blair Brown, Charles Haid, Bob Balaban, Thaao Penghilis*
Hurt stars as a daring Harvard psychologist who experiments with a South American drug which causes not only strange memories but startling physical transformations. Although a bit heavy-handed, this is an interesting exploration of our

primeval past, and the lengths to which man will go to obtain knowledge. From a screenplay by Paddy Chayefsky (Network).

ALWAYS (1989)
** PG 2:01
DIR: *Steven Spielberg* CAST: *Richard Dreyfuss, Holly Hunter, John Goodman, Audrey Hepburn, Brad Johnson*
There's something overcooked about Spielberg's remake of *A Guy Named Joe*, a 1943 drama about the ghost of a fighter pilot (Spencer Tracy) who offers aid and comfort to the living. Dreyfuss takes on the supernatural role, this time as a firefighter pilot whose girlfriend (Hunter) cannot move on with her life after he dies. He's given the mission of helping a rookie pilot get his wings, but also helps Hunter find her way past grief. Goodman is likeable as Dreyfuss' best buddy, and Spielberg is never less than superior in the directing. But the story isn't really strong enough to warrant all the care and attention he gives it.

AMADEUS (1984)
*** PG 2:38
DIR: *Milos Forman* CAST: *Tom Hulce, F Murray Abraham, Elizabeth Berridge, Simon Callow, Christine Ebersole, Jeffrey Jones, Roy Dotrice*
This Oscar-winner for Best Picture brings all the drama, beauty, comedy and spectacle of Mozart's

music into a compelling, gorgeously filmed biography of the great composer. Hulce plays Mozart as a giddy, offhandedly brilliant child prodigy, while F. Murray Abrahams (in an Oscar-winning role) gives a *tour de force* performance as the tortured composer Salieri, who watches helplessly as his fame and talents are eclipsed by the young genius.

AMAZON WOMEN ON THE MOON (1987)
** R 1:24

DIR: *John Landis, Peter Horton, Joe Dante, Robert Weiss, Carl Gottlieb* **CAST:** *Steve Guttenberg, Rosanna Arquette, Ralph Bellamy, Carrie Fisher, Sybil Danning, Robert Loggia*

In the style of *Groove Tube*, this film follows the adventures of a man sucked into his own television and into a series of parodies of junk television. For satire to work, however, it has to be consistently superior to the thing it's poking fun at. Unlike both *Groove Tube* and *Kentucky Fried Movie*, this film sometimes falls flat. We don't always know if we're watching a send-up of bad TV or the real thing.

AMERICAN GRAFFITI (1973)
*** PG 1:50

DIR: *George Lucas* **CAST:** *Richard Dreyfuss, Ron Howard, Paul LeMat, Charles Martin Smith, Cindy Williams, Candy Clark, Mackenzie Phillips, Wolfman*

Jack, Harrison Ford, Kathy Quinlan, Suzanne Somers
The film that birthed the '70s nostalgia boom (it's
directly responsible for "Happy Days," "Laverne
and Shirley" and others), this is a loving ode to
coming of age in Middle America, circa 1962. It
paints a bittersweet, yet not at all condescending
portrait of that fabled time when cars, drive-ins
and the omnipresent howl of rock and roll were
the essence of small-town teenage existence. Remarkable soundtrack that went a long way to
defining the term "classic rock."

THE ANDERSON TAPES (1972)
*** PG 1:38
DIR: *Sidney Lumet* **CAST:** *Sean Connery, Dyan
Cannon, Martin Balsam, Ralph Meeker, Alan King,
Christopher Walker*
An exciting, ambitious film about a group of first-
class burglars led by Connery who execute a heist
of an entire ritzy Manhattan apartment building.
It's fascinating to watch Connery and his boys
plan the complex job, only to have things go afoul.
Like Francis Coppola's *The Conversation*, the film
casts a wary eye on the growing use of sophisti-
cated surveillance equipment. The stylish editing
and Lumet's directing pack a punch.

ANDREI RUBLEV (1966)
**** NR 3:05
DIR: *Andrei Tarkovsky* **CAST:** *Anatoli Solonitzine,*

Ivan Lapikov, Nikolai Grinko, Nikolai Sergueiev
Deliberately paced, visually challenging, but ultimately rewarding epic of the beatific 15th century Russian icon painter/monk Rublev, caught between the pull of religious traditions, the immediacy of political turmoil and the overwhelming drive of the creative spirit. Shelved by Soviet authorities until 1971, this is one of the best from Tarkovsky, a brilliant, innovative and intensely spiritual poet of the silver screen whose works demand to be seen.

THE ANDROMEDA STRAIN (1971)
*** G 2:10
DIR: *Robert Wise* **CAST:** *Arthur Hill, David Wayne, Kate Reid, James Olson, Paula Kelly*
A deadly virus is brought to earth by an errant satellite, sending government scientists scrambling to find a way to kill it before it spreads around the world. Based on the book by Michael Crichton (*Jurassic Park*), this is a highly suspenseful look at what happens when man tries to exploit nature. The ending is a heart-stopper.

AND THE SHIP SAILS ON (1984)
*** PG 2:10
DIR: *Federico Fellini* **CAST:** *Freddie Jones, Victor Poletti, Barbara Jefford, Elisa Mainardi, Norma West*
An ocean liner full of oddball characters heads into the Mediterranean with the mission of scat-

tering the ashes of a famous opera singer. When the ship is forced to rescue a band of refugees, comedic conflicts arise. Fellini is somehow gentler here than in films like *Amarcord* and *Satyricon*, but his unique vision (including a man and a rhinoceros in a lifeboat) is intact.

THE ANDY GRIFFITH SHOW (1960-65)
*** NR
Dir: *Various* **CAST:** *Andy Griffith, Don Knotts, Ron Howard, Jim Nabors, Frances Bavier, George Lindsay*
More and more of these classic shows are being released on video, which is good news. The doings of small-town Mayberry may seem dated, but closer inspection reveals wonderful writing, quirky characters and fine comic acting. Each video contains four episodes of the hit show, and includes volumes on *The Best of Barney*, and *The Best of Gomer*. All the folks are here—including Opie and Aunt Bea—which makes this collection something like the video equivalent of comfort food.

ANGEL HEART (1987)
*** R 1:53
DIR: *Alan Parker* **CAST:** *Mickey Rourke, Robert DeNiro, Charlotte Rampling, Lisa Bonet*
A nightmarish psycho-thriller about a seedy private detective (Rourke) enlisted by an odd character (De Niro) to track down an aging band

singer. Rourke's search becomes more and more frightening as he closes in on his prey. De Niro is excellent as the hard-boiled egg-eating Lou Cypher, and Rourke is a bit mumbly but good as the confused detective. The movie generated controversy because of a strange sex scene between Rourke and Bonet. Removing a few seconds of footage saved the film from receiving an X-rating.

ANGELO MY LOVE (1983)
*** NR 1:55
DIR: *Robert Duvall* **CAST:** *Angelo Evans*
Duvall was so impressed with a tough-talking gypsy kid he encountered on the streets of New York that he decided to build a movie around him. He went behind the camera to direct, and also enlisted the help of real New York gypsies to tell the story of this ten-year-old who's going on 35. Although the work may seem rough, and the storyline a bit jagged, watching this old soul is enough to make the film worthwhile.

ANGELS WITH DIRTY FACES (1938)
*** NR 1:37
Dir: *Michael Curtiz* **Cast:** *James Cagney, Humphrey Bogart, The Dead End Kids, Pat O'Brien, George Bancroft, Ann Sheridan*
Cagney is the tough-talking gangster and O'Brien is the priest in this classic tale of two friends from the Lower East side who take different paths in

life. The Dead End Kids idolize the wealthy gangster who made it out of the slums. They're headed
straight downhill until O'Brien steps in and gets
Cagney to teach them the error of their ways. As
predictable as it is, the ending's still a tearjerker.

ANIMAL CRACKERS (1930)
*** G 1:38
DIR: *Victor Heerman* **CAST:** *Groucho, Harpo, Chico
and Zeppo Marx, Margaret Dumont, Lillian Roth,
Hal Thompson, Robert Greig*
The second film from the funniest comedy team
in the history of motion pictures is not their best,
but is well worth seeing nonetheless. The rather
thin plot concerning a stolen painting is just an
excuse to get Groucho, Harpo, Chico and the
hapless Zeppo together for their howlingly hilarious wordplay and sublime pranxs. Includes the
famous "Hooray for Captain Spaulding" routine
and a maniacal bridge game between Chico and
Harpo.

ANNIE HALL (1977)
**** PG 1:34
DIR: *Woody Allen* **CAST:** *Woody Allen, Diane
Keaton, Tony Roberts, Paul Simon, Shelly Duvall,
Carol Kane, Colleen Dewhurst, Christopher Walken,
Janet Margolin*
This charming and hilarious autobiographical
love story may be Allen's best. Allen plays the

nebbish Alvy Singer, a veteran/victim of 15 years of therapy who falls hard for WASP-ish Keaton. Allen's rapid-fire witticisms on relationships, friendship, romance and New York play like Cupid with a tommy gun. One of the landmark films of the seventies. Oscars for Best Picture, Actress (Keaton), Direction and Screenplay (Allen and Marshall Brickman).

THE APARTMENT (1960)
*** NR 2:05
DIR: *Billy Wilder* CAST: *Jack Lemmon, Shirley MacLaine, Fred MacMurray, Ray Walston, Jack Kruschen, Edie Adams*
Excellent comedy/drama in which Lemmon plays a ladder-climbing corporate executive who attempts to gain favor with his superiors by loaning out his apartment for their extra-curricular romantic activities, only to find himself falling for his boss' latest girlfriend. Oscars for Best Picture, Director, Screenplay (by Wilder and I.A.L. Diamond), Editing (Daniel Mandell) and Art Direction/Set Decoration (Alexander Trauner, Edward G. Boyle).

APOCALYPSE NOW (1979)
**** R 2:33
DIR: *Francis Ford Coppola* CAST: *Marlon Brando, Robert Duvall, Martin Sheen, Frederic Forrest, Sam Bottoms, Dennis Hopper, Harrison Ford, Scott Glenn*

One of the most infamous films of the '70s, Coppola's Vietnam War allegory, based *very* loosely on Joseph Conrad's short novel *Heart of Darkness*, is also one of the keystone films of the decade. It is also a brutal, unrelentingly caustic and violent film, with brilliant performances by Sheen (who suffered a nervous breakdown during the film's grueling production), Duvall, Hopper and, of course, the inimitable Brando.

THE APPRENTICESHIP OF DUDDY KRAVITZ (1974)
*** PG 2:01
DIR: *Ted Kotcheff* **CAST:** *Richard Dreyfuss, Micheline Lanctot, Jack Warden, Randy Quaid, Denholm Elliott*
A bittersweet coming-of-age story starring Dreyfuss as an overly ambitious youngster from Montreal whose big plans sometimes run roughshod over the people around him. "A man is nothing without a piece of land," his Jewish grandfather tells him, and to that end Duddy seems to stop at nothing. Dreyfuss is excellent as the frenetic go-getter who always seems about ready to burst a vein. Oscar nomination for Best Screenplay From Another Source for Mordecai Richler and Lionel Chetwynd.

ARSENIC AND OLD LACE (1944)
*** NR 1:58
DIR: *Frank Capra* **CAST:** *Cary Grant, Pricilla Lane,*

Raymond Massey, Peter Lorre, James Gleason, Josephine Hull, Jean Adair, Edward Everett Horton
Side-splitting black comedy, adapted from Joseph Kesserling's smash play, about two sweet old spinsters from Brooklyn who murder their lonely gentlemen callers. A classic of frantic, madcap movie humor anchored by hilarious performances from Grant, Massey, Lorre and an overall excellent cast. Directed by Frank Capra, one of the American cinema's true comic geniuses.

ARTHUR (1981)
** PG 1:37
DIR: *Steve Gordon* **CAST:** *Dudley Moore, Liza Minnelli, John Gielgud, Geraldine Fitzgerald*
Enjoyable, if terminally lightweight, 1930s-style comedy about the time-worn confrontation between wealth and true love in the persons of a boozy millionaire playboy (Moore, in a career-making role) and a spunky working-class waitress (Minnelli). Charming, Oscar-winning performance by Gielgud as Moore's loyal, long-suffering butler. The film's theme song, "Best That You Can Do (Arthur's Theme)," also took home an Oscar.

ATLANTIC CITY (1981)
*** R 1:44
DIR: *Louis Malle* **CAST:** *Burt Lancaster, Susan Sarandon, Kate Reid, Michel Piccoli, Hollis McLaren,*

Robert Joy, Al Waxman
Sarandon makes a remarkable major film debut in this winning character study of a city teetering on the cusp between its storied past and its uncertain future. The film zeroes in on the hustlers and losers that stalk the resort city's boardwalk and casinos, creating a touching panorama of glittering dreams and dashed hopes. Lancaster gives one of his finest performances as a washed-up, penny-ante hood who talks the talk, but can't walk the walk.

THE ATOMIC CAFE (1982)
*** NR 1:32
DIR: *Kevin Rafferty, Pierce Rafferty, Jayne Loader*
A funny, frightening documentary about the height of the Cold War (remember that?) full of amazing old footage of films and government folderol. School kids are told repeatedly to "Duck and Cover," as if jumping under a skimpy school desk will shield them from a hydrogen bomb. Even though the topic is the Apocalypse, there's almost a sweet naiveté about all of this. And the further we get away from the cold war, the more anachronistic it becomes.

AUTHOR! AUTHOR! (1982)
*** PG 1:50
DIR: *Arthur Hiller* **CAST:** *Al Pacino, Dyan Cannon, Tuesday Weld, Eric Gurry*

27

This predictable comedy is a charmingly entertaining movie to watch. A loose autobiography of its screenwriter, Israel Horovitz, it is the tale of a successful playwright who is abandoned by his wife. She leaves him to deal with her many children, all of whom she had with other husbands. Needless to say, he is unhappy about the situation; at the very least, he feels that they are not even his kids, and at the most, they interfere with his burgeoning career. But after a while (you guessed it) father and step-children grow closer, and father realizes he can become an even better playwright now. There is certainly nothing new about this movie, but it works. Much of the credit for this deserves to go to Pacino and his young co-stars, who create an endearing family for us to sympathize with.

THE AUTOBIOGRAPHY OF MISS JANE PITTMAN (1974)
**** NR 1:50
DIR: *John Korty* CAST: *Cicely Tyson, Richard Dysart, Thalmus Rasulala, Michael Murphy, Katherine Helmond, Barbara Chaney*
This is one of the finest films ever made for television. Tyson is remarkable as a former slave whose 110-year life mirrors the civil rights struggle, from the Civil War to the battles for freedom in the south of the 1960s. Tyson won an Emmy for her outstanding performance, as did Korty, screen-

writer Tracy Wynn, and make-up artist Stan Wilson.

━━━━━━━━━━━━━ **B** ━━━━━━━━━━━━━

BABETTE'S FEAST (1988)
**** G 1:42
DIR: *Gabriel Axel* **CAST:** *Stephane Audran, Bodil Kjer, Birgitte Federspiel*
A splendid, unique film about an isolated Danish fishing village and the profound effect of one woman on the town's happiness. Audran stars as Babette, an expatriated French woman employed by two kindly aging sisters who head a small religious community. The town is set in its ways, down to the cod-and-bread mush Babette must prepare for them day after day. When Babette wins a lottery, she prepares a stunning French meal for the community. At first frightened by the ungodly excess, the people of the town soon succumb to the food and wine, and warm memories of love and close friendship begin to surface. Don't be put off if the film seems a bit slow at first. This is a cinematic treasure to be savored.

BABY BOOM (1987)
*** PG 1:43
DIR: *Charles Shyer* **CAST:** *Diane Keaton, Sam Shepard, James Spader, Harold Ramis, Sam Wannamaker*

Keaton is a fast-tracker in a Manhattan money firm who ignores a thumping biological clock to pursue a career. When a distant relative dies, she must take charge of a beautiful baby girl. Her latent maternal instincts wreak havoc at the office, and Keaton flees to a dilapidated Vermont farmhouse where she discovers she really *can* have it all. Shepard plays the sexy town Vet in this diverting film about the clash of career and family.

BABY: SECRET OF THE LOST LEGEND (1985)
* PG 1:35
DIR: *B W L Norton* **CAST:** *Sean Young, William Katt, Patrick McGoohan, Julian Fellowes*
This poorly conceived Disney dinosaur movie is unsuccessful in just about every way. First, the dinosaurs look fake, as the technology used in *Jurassic Park* had not been perfected yet. Second, the direction is horrible and the performances misguided. And third, what should have been a kid's movie is inappropriate for children due to its excessive violence.

BACK TO THE FUTURE (1985)
** PG 1:56
DIR: *Robert Zemeckis* **CAST:** *Michael J Fox, Christopher Lloyd, Crispin Glover, Lea Thompson, Wendie Jo Sperber, Thomas F Wilson, Marc McClure*

As the first installment of one of the most successful film series of all time, this is a wonderful
marriage of teen comedy and lightweight science
fiction starring the eminently likeable Fox sup-
ported by a solid team of Hollywood character
actors. Lloyd and Thompson, as the not-so-mad
scientist and the girlfriend, respectively, are especially endearing and the special effects are a lot of
fun. Followed by two sequels.

BADLANDS (1973)
*** PG 1:35
DIR: *Terrence Malick* **CAST:** *Martin Sheen, Sissy
Spacek, Warren Oates, Ramon Bieri, Alan Vint*
Beautifully shot, flawlessly acted, gritty drama
based on the story of the infamous real-life Charlie
Starkweather killing spree of the 1950s. Sheen has
all the presence of James Dean at his most iconic
and Spacek gives a performance exquisitely bal-
anced between plain stupidity and Homecoming
Queen grace. The visuals are stark and beautiful
in their desolation and the casual amorality of
these two murderers will haunt you for years to
come.

BAGDAD CAFE (1988)
*** PG 1:31
Dir: *Percy Adlon* **Cast:** *Marianne Sagebrecht, Jack
Palance, George Aguilar, Monica Calhoun, C C H
Pounder*

An offbeat cult comedy set in a scraggly motel/ cafe/gas station in the middle of the California desert. A gruff German tourist abandons his wife (Sagebrecht); she then wanders aimlessly into the cafe seeking help and quickly becomes a waitress. Her presence has a profound effect on the cafe's odd group of characters, including Palance as an artist who convinces her to pose in the nude, and Pounder as the abrasive owner. This is a sweet little comedy with a nice, light touch.

BAMBI (1942)
**** G 1:09
DIR: *David Hand* **CAST:** *Voices of Bobby Stewart, Peter Behn, Stan Alezander*
Disney's gorgeously detailed story of a young buck deer's life in the forest is one of the most emotionally compelling animated films ever made, ranging from the lovable Thumper's goofy shenanigans to the truly chilling scene of the death of Bambi's mother. Famous for its lush, colorful backgrounds and the work of the best team of animators in the business, this film is a classic for both children and adults.

BANANAS (1971)
*** PG 1:22
DIR: *Woody Allen* **CAST:** *Woody Allen, Louise Lasser, Carlos Montalban, Howard Cosell, Rene Enriquez, Charlotte Rae, Conrad Bain*

One of Allen's best early comedies, this film is built on the unlikely plot idea of Allen as a nebbish New Yorker who flees to South America and becomes a nebbish revolutionary leader. Allen pours on the jokes, puns, gags and literary allusions to create a film essentially composed of a string of hilarious individual bits (especially the honeymoon scene with Allen, Lasser and Howard Cosell, which may be the funniest bedroom sequence Allen ever filmed).

THE BAND WAGON (1953)
**** NR 1:51
DIR: *Vincente Minnelli* **CAST:** *Fred Astaire, Cyd Charisse, Oscar Levant, Nanette Fabray, Jack Buchanan*
Stunning, sophisticated backstage musical that is one of the finest of all the great Hollywood musicals. Astaire plays a has-been movie star who decides to take a chance on the Broadway stage. Musical numbers include "Dancing in the Dark," "Shine on Your Shoes," "That's Entertainment" (all by Howard Dietz and Arthur Schwartz) and the Mickey Spillane parody "The Girl Hunt." Astaire is at his debonair best and Charisse is simply gorgeous.

THE BANK DICK (1940)
*** NR 1:14
DIR: *Eddie Cline* **CAST:** *W C Fields, Cora Witherspoon, Una Merkel, Jessie Ralph, Grady Sutton*

Fields, one of the true pioneers of movie comedy, cuts loose in this insanely wacky film based on the misadventures of a three-time loser, Egbert Sousé (Fields), who is made a bank guard after accidentally apprehending a would-be robber. Sutton as the witless prospective son-in-law and Pangborn as the blowhard bank examiner hold their own against Fields' tomfoolery. Screenplay by "Mahatma Kane Jeeves."

BARBARELLA (1968)
** PG 1:38
DIR: *Roger Vadim* **CAST:** *Jane Fonda, Anita Pallenberg, Milo O'Shea, David Hemmings*
Internationally acclaimed filmmaker Roger Vadim directed this endearingly hammy sci-fi spoof starring Jane Fonda as the "Queen of the Galaxy." Taking place in the 41st century, Fonda encounters a gaggle of strange men and creatures, including a flying-man named Duran Duran (from which the famous rock group took its name). The film opens with a now legendary zero-gravity strip-tease by Fonda, in which she kicks off her clothes inside a space ship! Although the movie isn't great, it is a lot of fun, thanks mostly to the talents of its performers.

BARFLY (1987)
*** R 1:40
DIR: *Barbet Schroeder* **CAST:** *Mickey Rourke, Faye Dunaway, Alice Krige*

A dark comedy starring Rourke as a skid row poet who has serious troubles with both women and booze. This is a faithful recreation of the works of L.A. writer Charles Bukowski, who himself spent much of his life drinking cheap wine in downtown gin joints. Bukowski thought that Rourke's portrayal was a bit "weird," but it's still great fun to watch him brawl his way through life. Dunaway is wonderful as his drinking partner and lover whose position is threatened with the entrance of a beautiful young publisher. The film's sordidness may not be to everyone's taste, but Bukowski fans won't be disappointed.

BATMAN (1966)
** NR 1:45
DIR: *Leslie H Martinson* **CAST:** *Adam West, Burt Ward, Burgess Meredith, Cesar Romero, Lee Meriwether, Frank Gorshin*
Long before Michael Keaton ever put on a cape and turned Batman into a neurotic sour-puss, the popular A.B.C. series was made into a feature film about the caped crusader of Gotham. The gang's all here—West and Ward as Batman and the Boy Wonder, Romero and Meredith as the Joker and the Penguin. Meriwether as Cat Woman (purists might prefer Julie Newmar) and Gorshin as the Riddler. Just like its sequel, the movie's short on plot and long on BANG!, BOFFF! and SPPLAAATT!, but still plenty of silly fun.

BATMAN (1989)
*** PG-13 2:06
DIR: *Tim Burton* **CAST:** *Jack Nicholson, Michael Keaton, Kim Basinger, Robert Wuhl, Pat Hingle, Jack Palance, Billy Dee Williams*
This dark, gothic, nightmarish reworking of the classic comics saga is a technical and visual masterpiece that has less story line than your average fairy tale. Nonetheless, Nicholson's maniacal, over-the-top romp as the Joker and Keaton's cold-as-ice portrayal of Batman make this a fascinating study in contrasting personalities. Plus, director Burton's uniquely twisted eye for detail will take you for a captivating ride.

THE BEAR (1989)
**** PG 1:33
dir: *Jean-Jacques Annaud* **Cast:** *Bart the Bear, Douce the Bear, Andre Lacombe, Tcheky Karyo, Jack Wallace*
This is the magnificent story of two bears struggling for survival in the mountains of the Pacific Northwest. The adult bear (Bart) grudgingly takes a cub under his wing after its mother is killed in a landslide, and must then fight off both hunters and other animals. Annaud and the animal trainers are uncanny in their ability to get moving, emotional performances from wild animals (better acting, in fact, than most of their human counterparts). The action sequences are stunning, as are the mountains of Italy and Austria where the film was shot.

BEAUTY AND THE BEAST (1946)
**** NR 1:30
DIR: *Jean Cocteau* **CAST:** *Jean Marais, Josette Day, Marcel André*

The most perfectly realized fantasy film ever made. Cocteau's vision of this classic fairy tale is so beautifully written and filmed that even more than 45 years after its release, it will still take your breath away. Both Jean Marais' performance as the Beast and Josette Day's portrayal of Beauty are definitive and the film's art direction includes some of the most remarkable sets and costumes ever captured on film. *Beauty and the Beast* is pure magic.

BEETLEJUICE (1988)
*** PG 1:32
DIR: *Tim Burton* **CAST:** *Michael Keaton, Geena Davis, Alec Baldwin, Winona Ryder, Dick Cavett, Catherine O'Hara, Jeffrey Jones, Sylvia Sydney*

A cute young couple (Davis and Baldwin) love their old Connecticut home so much that they return there after they die in a car crash. Things are fine until an obnoxious New York family (O'Hara, Jones, Ryder) buys the place and turns it into a high-tech nightmare. The friendly ghosts turn to a 'bio-exorciser' named Beetlejuice (Keaton) to rid them of the living. A clever script, energetic direction and Keaton's wonderfully over-the-top performance make for a great time. Kids invariably love this film.

BEING THERE (1979)
*** PG 2:07
DIR: *Hal Ashby* **CAST:** *Peter Sellers, Shirley MacLaine, Melvyn Douglas, Jack Warden, Richard Basehart, Richard Dysart*

Marvelous black humor based on Jerzy Kosinski's wise and witty novel of a simple man named Chance (Sellers, in a brilliantly understated performance), whose entire existence consists of gardening and watching television. When his rich caretaker dies, Chance is thrust into the real world, and through a string of funny and touching happenstances, ends up a candidate for President of the United States. Douglas won an Oscar as the political kingmaker.

BELIZAIRE THE CAJUN (1986)
*** PG 1:41
DIR: *Glen Pitre* **CAST:** *Armand Assante, Michael Schoeffling, Gail Youngs*

Assante stars as a Cajun medicine man from the last century in this charming, low-budget piece about a little-known American subculture. The story revolves around conflicts with local bigots after Belizaire's cousin is accused of murder. Writer/director Pitre is himself a Cajun, which probably accounts for the fine eye for detail, including Assante's sometimes-impenetrable Cajun brogue.

BEN-HUR (1959)
*** NR 3:32

DIR: *William Wyler* **CAST:** *Charlton Heston, Jack Hawkins, Stephen Boyd, Haya Harareet, Hugh Griffith, Martha Scott, Sam Jaffe*

More than a mere epic, this is Hollywood movie making at its most gargantuan. The film chronicles the story of Judah Ben-Hur (Heston) and Massala (Griffith), and through them, the whole historical conflict between the Romans and the Jews in ancient Palestine. The famous sea battle and chariot race (directed by Andrew Martin) scenes are among the most gripping action spectaculars in cinematic history. The film won 11 Oscars, including Best Picture.

BEVERLY HILLS COP (1984)
** R 1:45

DIR: *Martin Brest* **CAST:** *Eddie Murphy, Judge Reinhold, John Ashton, Lisa Eilbacher, Ronny Cox, Steven Berkoff, Bronson Pinchot*

A fish-out-of-water storywwith a twist: the fish in question is a fast-talking, street-smart Detroit cop (Murphy) who makes the trek to Beverly Hills to hunt down his ex-partner's murderers. Murphy is at his brassy best here, and the supporting cast (particularly Reinhold and Pinchot) can be fall-on-the-floor funny, but the script is fatally weak, the attempted mixture of comedy and drama never gels and the shoot-em-up finale is inappropriately violent.

BEST SELLER (1987)
** R 1:50
DIR: *John Flynn* CAST: *James Woods, Brian Dennehy, Victoria Tennant*

James Woods plays a retired assassin who has worked his whole life "eliminating" enemies to big business. Dennehy plays a cop who has taken up the pen, chronicling his adventures in pulp fiction. Together, the two decide to make a best-seller out of James Woods' life. But soon Dennehy realizes that his partner is not entirely trustworthy. What secrets is he hiding, and how can the author find out? This movie features a great deal of tension, and the two leading actors are perfect, but things never click. Nonetheless, if you're in the mood for a thriller and cannot find anything else more appealing, then you might want to try this one on for size.

THE BICYCLE THIEF (1949)
**** NR 1:30
DIR: *Vittorio De Sica* CAST: *Lamberto Maggiorani, Enzo Staiola, Lianella Carell, Elena Altieri*

A classic film about a poor man and his son as they search for his stolen bicycle. This is a favorite of cinephiles because of its remarkable cinematography and poignant, simple script. Maggiorani is moving as the desperate man who must retrieve his bicycle in order to work.

BIG (1988)
*** PG 1:42

DIR: *Penny Marshall* **CAST:** *Tom Hanks, Elizabeth Perkins, John Heard, Jared Rushton, Robert Loggia, Jon Lovitz, Mercedes Ruehl*

Charming fantasy about a frustrated boy who, while at a mysterious carnival fortune-telling booth, wishes he were "big" and wakes up the next morning in the body of Tom Hanks! Hanks is perfect as the 12-year-old in a 30-year-old's skin, all goofy innocence and pre-adolecent awkwardness, who stumbles into a job as a designer for a toy company. Perkins and Loggia are the ideal adult foils as his bewildered co-worker and boss, respectively.

THE BIG CHILL (1983)
*** R 1:43

DIR: *Lawrence Kasdan* **CAST:** *Tom Berenger, Glenn Close, Jeff Goldblum, William Hurt, Kevin Kline, Mary Kay Place, Meg Tilly, JoBeth Williams*

Yuppie drama concerning seven former college buddies who are reunited years later at the funeral of a friend who has committed suicide. The collection of performances is extraordinary, the Motown-hits soundtrack fits the film like a glove, and the well-constructed script keeps things moving along at a brisk pace.

THE BIG EASY(1987)
*** R 1:48

DIR: *Jim McBride* **CAST:** *Dennis Quaid, Ellen Barkin, John Goodman, Ned Beatty, Charles Ludlam*

A stylish film-noir mystery set amidst the back streets and bayous of Louisiana. The film revolves around the highly-charged affair between an uptight D.A. investigating police corruption (Barkin) and a sexy, semi-corrupt New Orleans detective (Quaid). As the odd couple investigate gangland killings, their antagonism for each other turns quickly to lust (there's a bedroom scene in here that made Quaid an overnight heartthrob). Needless to say, Barkin loosens up a bit.

THE BIG PICTURE (1988)
*** PG-13 1:40

DIR: *Christopher Guest* **CAST:** *Kevin Bacon, Martin Short, Terri Hatcher, Michael McKean, J T Walsh*

A star film school grad (Bacon) wins a big award and is swooped down on by an agent (played hysterically by Short) and a movie exec (Walsh) in this rags-to-riches-to-rags-to riches comedy. Seduced by Hollywood glitz, the young auteur leases a Porsche, dumps his girlfriend, and alienates his best friend. When his movie deal disintegrates, he scrambles to pick up the pieces. Guest, a *Saturday Night Live* alum, is at his best when taking aim at the Hollywood machine. Bacon is just right as a young director way over his head in show biz hype.

THE BIG SLEEP (1946)
**** NR 1:54
DIR: *Howard Hawks* **CAST:** *Humphrey Bogart, Lauren Bacall, John Ridgely, Martha Vickers, Loius Jean Heydt, Regis Toomey*
This classic screen version of Raymond Chandler's first Philip Marlowe novel is a true landmark in the hard-boiled detective genre. Bogart is perfect as the unflappable gumshoe who stumbles into the hornet's nest of racketeers, hopheads and murderers surrounding a burned-out socialite (Bacall) and her out-of-control little sister (Vickers). With gorgeously atmospheric direction by Hawks and a razor-sharp script by William Faulkner and Leigh Brackett.

THE BIG TOWN (1987)
*** R 1:50
DIR: *Ben Bolt* **CAST:** *Matt Dillon, Diane Lane, Bruce Dern, Tommy Lee Jones, Lee Grant, Tom Skerritt*
Dillon plays a young man with a good head for gambling who heads to Chicago, but is soon overwhelmed by life in the underworld. Enlisted by a semi-sleazy pair of hustlers (Dern, Grant), he goes up against a violent gangster (Jones) while sleeping with his wife (Lane). Although the plot is over-ripe, this is still a stylish period piece with fine performances from all the players.

BILLIONAIRE BOYS CLUB (1987)
*** NR 3:20
DIR: *Marvin J Chomsky* **CAST:** *Judd Nelson, Fredric Lehne, Brian McNamara, Raphael Sbarge, John Stockwell, Barry Tubb, Stan Shaw, Ron Silver*
Based on the unbelievable true story of a bunch of rich kids from L.A. whose svengali-like leader, Joe Hunt, turned some of them into murderers. Nelson is good as the bright, amoral Hunt, whose promise of wealth without work entrapped a number of young men from the best families in Southern California. The film was rushed into production during Hunt's trial. For legal reasons, the script had to be based mostly on courtroom proceedings, which gives the T.V. mini-series a tense, effective documentary feel. In other words, they didn't have time to mess it up.

BILL & TED'S EXCELLENT ADVENTURE (1989)
*** PG 1:30
DIR: *Stephen Herek* **CAST:** *Keanu Reeves, Alex Winter, George Carlin, Bernie Casey, Terry Camilleri, Jane Wiedlin*
A kind-hearted romp with Reeves and Winter as they travel through time (with the help of a futuristic Carlin) in order to pass their high school history test. The two teenagers have their own unique take on Valley Talk, like the two beautiful princesses who they refer to as "savory." They

hook up with Honest Abe, Napoleon, and Joan of Arc as their strange phone booth propels them through the ages. The gentle humor and fine performances make for a most totally excellent movie.

BILLY BUDD (1962)
*** NR 1:43
DIR: *Peter Ustinov* CAST: *Terence Stamp, Robert Ryan, Peter Ustinov, Melvyn Douglas, David McCallum, John Neville, Paul Rogers*
Stamp received a best supporting actor nomination in this moving adaptation of Herman Melville's tale of youthful innocence confronting injustice. A young sailor (Stamp) joins the crew of an 18th-century British fighting ship. Budd is tormented by an angry, evil officer (Ryan), who drives him to a desperate act. Ustinov gives a fine performance as the kindly captain who must choose between naval law and his own conscience.

BILLY JACK(1971)
*** PG 1:54
DIR: *Tom Laughlin* CAST: *Tom Laughlin, Delores Taylor, Clark Howat, Julie Webb, Kenneth Tobey*
One of the surprise hits of the '70s, the Billy Jack films pitted a quasi-mystical, half-Indian marital arts expert (Laughlin) against, well, the rest of the world. In this first of the trilogy, Laughlin goes up against a town bent on destroying a school for

disadvantaged kids. When a local millionaire's son rapes the school's headmistress (Taylor), Laughlin goes on a rampage—with predictable results. The film retains a healthy anti-establishment wallop.

BILOXI BLUES (1988)
*** PG-13 1:45
DIR: *Mike Nichols* **CAST:** *Matthew Broderick, Christopher Walken, Penelope Ann Miller, Matt Mulhern, Corey Parker*
Broderick is the innocent aspiring writer suffering the humiliations of Army basic training in this adaptation of Neil Simon's autobiographical play. The plot is regulation army-issued stuff, but it's handled with great skill and humor by Nichols and the fine cast. Broderick has trouble with his gruff, cerebral sergeant (Walken), he loses his virginity to a prostitute with a heart of gold, and then meets the girl of his dreams (Miller). This is a diverting film that doesn't try to break new ground.

BIRDMAN OF ALCATRAZ (1962)
*** NR 2:23
DIR: *John Frankenheimer* **CAST:** *Burt Lancaster, Karl Malden, Thelma Ritter, Neville Brand, Edmund O'Brien*
Lancaster was nominated for an Oscar for his portrayal of hardened convict Robert Stroud,

whose life term left him plenty of time to become an expert on birds. His fascination with winged creatures began when an ill bird flew into his cell. With a compassion Stroud rarely showed for his murder victims, he nursed the animal back to health. It was admirable that Stroud was able to make a few significant breakthroughs in the study of birds, but the film ignores the real-life Stroud's utter viciousness (some of his crimes are too grotesque to mention either here or in the film).

THE BIRDS (1963)
**** NR 2:00
DIR: *Alfred Hitchcock* CAST: *Rod Taylor, Tippi Hedren, Suzanne Pleshette, Jessica Tandy, Veronica Cartwright, Ethel Griffies, Charles McGraw*
A frightening look at what happens when Mother Nature gets mad. Hedren and Taylor star in this taut thriller about a small coastal California town that is invaded by tens of thousands of irate birds. The couple must barricade themselves inside their homes, but even this doesn't quite stop an angry flock of seagulls. As far-fetched as this sounds, in Hitchcock's hands it becomes very scary indeed. The last shot of the film is a masterpiece of understated tension.

BIRDY (1984)
*** R 2:00
DIR: *Alan Parker* CAST: *Matthew Modine, Nicholas*

GUIDE TO TV MOVIES

Cage, John Harkins, Sandy Baron, Karen Young
This fine adaptation from the novel by William
Wharton stars Modine as a Vietnam Vet whose
war-time experiences bring on a nervous col-
lapse. Cage stars as the life-long buddy who sup-
ports his friend through his institutionalization.
Modine's hallucinations revolve around his obsession with birds and his belief in his own ability
to fly. This is a powerful, quirky drama with fine
performances throughout.

BITE THE BULLET (1975)
**** PG 2:11
DIR: *Richard Brooks* **CAST:** *James Coburn, Gene
Hackman, Candice Bergen, Jan-Michael Vincent*
This beautiful film gives the legend of the Old
West a new spin by showing how modernization
changed the area. Set at the beginning of the 20th
Century, traditionalists are trying to retain their
heritage by going on a horse race that will take
them through some of the most difficult terrain in
the country. They are fierce and proud, and they
hope to show the world that the pioneering spirit
will not die without a fight. They fight their
competition as if their very lives depended upon
it, none of the entrants wanting to lose the race to
any of the others. Touching and thought provok-
ing, with exceptional performances and direction, this film is a must-see!

THE BLACK STALLION (1979)
*** G 1:56
DIR: *Carroll Ballard* **CAST:** *Kelly Reno, Mickey Rooney, Teri Garr, Clarence Muse, Hoyt Axton, Michael Higgins*
Wonderful family adventure based on Walter Farley's 1941 children's novel about a young boy (Reno) and a black Arabian thoroughbred who are marooned on a desert island after a shipwreck. From the boy's touching reunion with his mother (Garr) to his adventures with a wise old horse-trainer (Rooney) to the film's rousing climax at a racing championship, this is one of the finest children's movies of all time. Stunningly photographed by Caleb Deschanel.

BLACK WIDOW (1987)
** R 1:43
DIR: *Bob Rafelson* **CAST:** *Debra Winger, Theresa Russell, Nicol Williamson, Sami Frey, Dennis Hopper*
No matter how many times the plot jumps, this story of an obsessed Justice Department investigator (Winger) tracking a killer never gets off the ground. Russell plays a femme fatale who leaves a string of rich dead husbands behind her. Winger catches on, and befriends Russell in order to entrap her. Russell and Winger seem to be walking through their roles, and all the script's huffing and puffing doesn't seem to amount to much more than mediocrity.

BLADE RUNNER (1982)
**** R 2:02

DIR: *Ridley Scott* **CAST:** *Harrison Ford, Rutger Hauer, Sean Young, Edward James Olmos, William Sanderson, Daryl Hannah, Joanna Cassidy*

Striking science fiction classic starring Ford as a bounty hunter ("blade runner") who is forced out of retirement to hunt down a team of murderous, renegade androids (including Hauer and Hannah). While the cast and script are uniformly excellent, the real star of the film is Director Scott's *noir*-ish vision of 21st century Los Angeles, a smog-blanketed, multicultural war zone where the machines are often more human than their creators.

BLAZING SADDLES (1974)
*** R 1:33

DIR: *Mel Brooks* **CAST:** *Cleavon Little, Gene Wilder, Harvey Korman, Madeline Kahn, Slim Pickens, Mel Brooks, Alex Karras, Dom DeLuise*

Hilarious parody of movie Westerns starring Little as the unlikely new sheriff in town, Wilder as an over-the-hill gunslinger, Korman as a villainous railroad magnate, Kahn as a Marlene Dietrich clone and Brooks as the brain-dead governor. It's charmingly obnoxious, proudly sophomoric, and packed with cheap laughs, broad physical comedy and a string of jokes about bodily functions.

THE BLOB (1958)
*** NR 1:23

DIR: *Irwin S Yeaworth, Jr* **CAST:** *Steve McQueen, Aneta Corsequt, Olin Howlin, Earl Rowe*

McQueen stars as a James Dean-type teenage rebel who must put aside his drag racing to help save his small town from a horrible space creature. The alien in question looks like a massive jello mold turned evil. After nourishing itself on locals, it gets big enough to cover the high school. McQueen gives this average '50s horror film more class than it deserves. Most films of this genre were allegories about communism, but the monster here is more likely a symbol for the onset of adulthood. Remade unsuccessfully in 1988.

BLOOD SIMPLE (1984)
**** R 1:36

DIR: *Joel and Ethan Coen* **CAST:** *Frances McDormand, John Getz, M. Emmet Walsh, Dan Hedaya*

A stylish, complex murder thriller that marks one of the most accomplished debuts in film history. A sleazy Texas bar owner (Hedaya) conspires with a low-rent private eye (Walsh) to put his philandering wife and boyfriend (McDormand, Getz) on ice. What follows is a spider web of murder and double-cross. Walsh is great as the terrifying, buffoonish detective who plots the murder from a V.W. bug. The Coen brothers have a limitless bag of cinematic tricks, and the result is a remarkable piece of film making. Don't miss this one.

BLUE VELVET (1986)
*** R 2:00

DIR: *David Lynch* **CAST:** *Kyle MacLachlan, Isabella Rossellini, Dennis Hopper, Laura Dern, Hope Lange, Dean Stockwell*

A grippingly original film that, because of its terminal weirdness and graphic violence, is definitely not for the faint of heart. Director Lynch (who went on to make the TV series *Twin Peaks*) peels back the flaking linoleum of a seemingly idyllic middle-class American neighborhood to expose a bizarre, sadistic and disturbing underbelly populated by psychos, drug-dealers and murderers. A beautifully shot, memorably acted cinematic nightmare.

BODY DOUBLE (1984)
*** R 1:50

DIR: *Brian De Palma* **CAST:** *Craig Wasson, Melanie Griffith, Deborah Shelton, Guy Boyd, Gregg Henry*

An engaging murder mystery about a down-and-out L.A. actor who thinks he witnesses a murder. When he realizes he's been set up, he teams up with a porno star (Griffith) to track down the murderer himself. Although some of the violence and sex seem gratuitous, this is still a slick, accomplished bit of filmmaking.

BODY HEAT (1981)
*** R 1:53
DIR: *Lawrence Kasdan* **CAST:** *William Hurt, Kathleen Turner, Richard Crenna, Ted Danson, Mickey Rourke*
Steamy, 1940s-style thriller set in 1980s Florida starring Turner (in her first major role) as the scheming socialite who convinces a dim-witted, down-on-his-luck attorney (Hurt) to kill her husband for the inheritance. Turner's sensual performance will fog up your glasses and the movie's intricate plot will keep you guessing until the final reel. Features a host of talented co-stars (Rourke, Danson, Crenna) and a chillingly effective musical score.

BONNIE AND CLYDE (1967)
*** NR 1:51
DIR: *Arthur Penn* **CAST:** *Warren Beatty, Faye Dunaway, Michael J Pollard, Gene Hackman, Estelle Parsons, Denver Pyle, Gene Wilder*
Dunaway and Beatty (who also produced) lead an impressive cast in this exciting, stylish and well-written saga of Bonnie Parker and Clyde Barrow, the fabled bank robbing couple of the 1930s. This is a film of magnificent scope, ranging from the screwball antics of Bonnie and Clyde's first robberies to their brutal demise in a hail of bullets. Parsons (as Barrow's sister-in-law) and cinematographer Burnett Guffey both won Oscars.

BOOM TOWN (1940)
*** NR 1:56

DIR: *Jack Conway* **CAST:** *Spencer Tracy, Clark Gable, Claudette Colbert, Hedy Lamarr, Chill Wills, Frank Morgan*

A two-fisted, big-shouldered movie about a time when men were men and exploiting Mother Nature was still considered a good thing. Tracy and Gable star as competitive wildcat oil drillers who travel the world in search of black gold. They get rich, go broke, fall for the same girl, and get rich again. A well-made film with a few laughs and plenty of action. Harold Rosson earned an Oscar nomination for his Cinematography.

THE BOOST (1988)
*** R 1:35

DIR: *Harold Becker* **CAST:** *James Woods, Sean Young, John Kapelos, Kelle Kerr, Steven Hill*

Woods stars as a rising business star whose addiction to cocaine leads to ruin in this morality play of Eighties excess. Life seems rosy for Woods and his beautiful wife (Young) when they move to L.A. and make a fortune in the real estate boom. But a few lines of cocaine at a party so entrance Woods that he begins a deadly downward spiral into addiction and abuse of his wife. Although his fall comes too quickly (and melodramatically), Woods' edgy performance gives this film a gritty realism.

THE BORDER (1982)
*** R 1:47
DIR: *Tony Richardson* **CAST:** *Jack Nicholson, Valerie Perrine, Elpidia Carrillo, Harvey Keitel, Warren Oates*
Nicholson stars in one of his best roles as a cynical Border agent who does battle with fellow officers and an unscrupulous adoption ring to help a young Mexican woman (Carrillo) get her child back. The film seems as topical now as it did when first made. Perrine is excellent as Nicholson's dumb, greedy wife. Ry Cooder's score provides a moody backdrop for this fine effort.

BORN FREE (1966)
*** NR 1:35
DIR: *James Hill* **CAST:** *Virginia McKenna, Bill Travers, Peter Lukoye, Geoffrey Keen*
This is the moving true story of an African game warden and his wife (Travers, McKenna) who raise a lion cub from infancy. Based on Joy Adamson's book, the film chronicles the couple's attempt to re-introduce the beautiful animal into the wilderness, and their mixed feelings when the task is accomplished. This is a touching and educational film for everyone in the family.

BORN ON THE FOURTH OF JULY (1989)
** R 2:25
DIR: *Oliver Stone* **CAST:** *Tom Cruise, Willem Dafoe, Raymond J Barry, Caroline Kava, Tom Berenger, Abbie Hoffman*

Based on the true story of Ron Kovic (Cruise), an ex-Marine paralyzed while fighting in Vietnam. Kovic comes home to the cruel realities of physical and mental rehabilitation and in the process emerges as a prominent anti-war activist. Director Stone shows an impressive technical mastery, but no emotional depth, pounding home his message of peace and justice with all the deftness and subtlety of a sledgehammer. Won Oscars for Director and Film Editing.

THE BOSTON STRANGLER (1968)
*** R 2:00
DIR: *Richard Fleischer* **CAST:** *Tony Curtis, Henry Fonda, George Kennedy, Mike Kellin, Hurd Hatfield, Murray Hamilton*
A terrifying account of the life and crimes of Albert De Salvo (Curtis), an average plumber and father convicted of a string of grisly Boston-area murders in the early 1960's. Director Fleischer adopts a near-documentary style (including a fascinating use of split screen) to chronicle the events. Fonda is excellent as the criminologist who tries to get inside the head of an illusive killer.

BOUND FOR GLORY (1976)
*** PG 2:27
DIR: *Hal Ashby* **CAST:** *David Carradine, Melinda Dillon, Ronny Cox, Randy Quaid, Gail Strickland*

Carradine does his finest work in this superb biography of folk singer Woody Guthrie. With never a false moment, he and director Ashby present a vivid picture of Guthrie's rise during the Depression, and the unjust social conditions that led to some of his most memorable songs. Haskell Wexler won an Oscar for his outstanding cinematography, including a harrowing re-creation of the kind of Oklahoma dust storm that sent thousands of poor farmers fleeing. Another Oscar went to Leonard Rosenman for his film arrangements of Guthrie's simple, powerful music.

A BOY AND HIS DOG (1975)
*** R 1:27
DIR: *L Q Jones* **CAST:** *Don Johnson, Jason Robards, Charles McGraw, voice of Tim McIntire, Alvy Moore*
A quirky post-holocaust tale of a young drifter (Johnson) who wanders the ruined landscape with Blood, a telepathic dog who sniffs out both women and danger. When Johnson's imprisoned by a strange underground community which seems like a twisted version of small-town America, he and Blood make a daring escape. This is a funky little film that has garnered cult status for its biting humor and satire.

THE BOYS FROM BRAZIL (1978)
*** R 2:03
DIR: *Franklin Schaffner* **CAST:** *Gregory Peck,*

Laurence Olivier, James Mason, Uta Hagen, Lilli Palmer

Peck seems to relish this rare opportunity to play a bad guy. One of the baddest ever, in fact. He portrays an aging, hair-dyed Joseph Mengele, the sadistic death camp doctor who plots the comeback of Hitler through genetic engineering. Seems Peck has produced dozens of little Fuhrers from cloning, and it's up to a Nazi hunter (Olivier) to track them down. As far-fetched as it sounds, this is still a compelling thriller.

BRAZIL (1985)
** R 2:11

Dir: *Terry Gilliam* **Cast:** *Jonathan Pryce, Robert De Niro, Kim Greist, Michael Palin, Ian Richardson*

This bleak-but-funny look at the future stars Pryce as a low-level bureaucrat mistakenly caught up in a rebel conspiracy. The film's strength comes from former *Monty Python* member Gilliam's unique vision of a future with bad plumbing and worse plastic surgery. Its weakness is that it's way too derivative of George Orwell's *1984*. Still, it's an engrossing film experience, with a funny cameo by De Niro as a futuristic garbage man. Oscar nominations for Screenwriting (Gilliam, Tom Stoppard and Charles McKeown) and Art Direction.

BREAKER MORANT (1980)
*** PG 1:47
DIR: *Bruce Beresford* **CAST:** *Edward Woodward, Jack Thompson, Bryan Brown, John Waters*

A riveting drama based on the true story of three Australian soldiers who were framed for war crimes by British officers who wanted to cover up their own culpability. Set in the Boer War at the turn-of-the-century, this is a superbly-styled court-room drama with a timeless theme. Thompson is excellent as the idealistic attorney who defends the men against overwhelming odds.

BREAKFAST AT TIFFANY'S (1961)
*** NR 1:55
DIR: *Blake Edwards* **CAST:** *Audrey Hepburn, George Peppard, Patricia Neal, Buddy Ebsen, Mickey Rooney, Martin Balsam*

Sweet, endearing comic romance featuring Hepburn in the unforgettable role of Holly Golightly, the small-town girl turned woman-about-town, and Peppard as the young man drawn into her orbit. Witty screenplay by George Axelrod (from a story by Truman Capote) keeps it light and breezy, but never fluffy or overly sentimental. Oscars for Henry Mancini's Score and for Mancini and Johnny Mercer's "Moon River."

BREAKING IN (1989)
*** R 1:31

DIR: *Bill Forsyth* CAST: *Burt Reynolds, Casey Siemaszko, Harry Carey, Sheila Kelley, Lorraine Toussant, Albert Salmi*

A charming, (but little-seen) comedy from the director of *Local Hero*. Reynolds stars as an aging cat burglar who takes a bumbling young thief (Siemaszko) on as his protege. The younger man has the odd habit of breaking into houses just for a beer and a sandwich. The wiser Reynolds puts his habits to better use. Siemaszko is funny as the newly-rich kid who can't resist buying a loud Cadillac to impress his girlfriend. Reynolds is just right as the patient, grumpy professional. It makes one wish Reynolds would take on challenging roles more often.

BRIAN'S SONG (1970)
*** G 1:13

DIR: *Buzz Kulik* CAST: *James Caan, Billy Dee Williams, Jack Warden, Shelley Fabares*

One of the saddest T.V. movies ever made tells the true-life story of Brian Piccolo (Caan) and Gayle Sayers (Williams). The two stars of the Chicago Bears became best friends before Piccolo's death from cancer. The film is so well-made (including a lush score from Michel Legrand), that we don't mind being manipulated into tears. Caan is touching as the dying ball player, and Williams excels as his supportive teammate.

BRINGING UP BABY (1938)
**** NR 1:42

DIR: *Howard Hawks* **CAST:** *Cary Grant, Katherine Hepburn, Charlie Ruggles, May Robson, Barry Fitzgerald, Walter Catlett, Ward Bond*

In this quintessential screwball comedy, an absent-minded zoologist (Grant) has his life turned topsy-turvy by a daffy heiress (Hepburn), her mischievous dog (played by Asta, of *The Thin Man* movies) and "Baby," her pet leopard. Both stars are wonderfully funny—Hepburn tears across the screen with the manic energy of a human tornado, and Grant is at his befuddled best. Hawks' breathless direction is a marvel of comic timing and staging.

BROADCAST NEWS (1987)
*** R 2:11

DIR: *James Brooks* **CAST:** *Holly Hunter, William Hurt, Albert Brooks, Joan Cusak, Jack Nicholson, Robert Prosky, Lois Chiles*

Director Brooks takes on television journalism in this "dramedy" about life behind the cameras at a Washington news bureau. Hunter steals the movie with her portrayal of a hyper kinetic producer who schedules a good cry every morning before work. Albert Brooks is the top-rate reporter who doesn't have the kind of looks that will get him an anchor spot. Hurt is the not-so-bright pin up boy whose fine features let him leapfrog over more-

61

talented colleagues. This is a biting look at what happens when journalism meets entertainment. The film's sub-plot love story is not anywhere near as interesting as the main theme of the film. Nominations for Best Picture, Best Actor (Hunter and Hurt), Best Supporting Actor (Albert Brooks), and Screenplay (James Brooks).

BROKEN ARROW (1950)
*** NR 1:32
DIR: *Delmer Daves* **CAST:** *James Stewart, Jeff Chandler, Debra Paget, Will Geer, Jay Silverheels*
Long before Kevin Costner made *Dances with Wolves*, this film gave the first sympathetic film depiction of the plight of Native Americans. Stewart stars as a Civil War vet who marries an Apache woman (Paget) and proceeds to try to patch up bad blood between white ranchers and the Indians whose land they stole. Whatever flaws the film may contain should be overlooked because of this courageous, against-the-grain stance.

BULL DURHAM (1988)
*** R 1:48
DIR: *Ron Shelton* **CAST:** *Kevin Costner, Susan Sarandon, Tim Robbins, Trey Wilson, Robert Wuhl, Jenny Robertson, Max Patkin*
A modern romantic comedy that is both erotic and hilarious. Susan Sarandon stars as a smart, obsessed fan and groupie of a minor-league base-

ball team. She believes it is her duty in life to move in with one promising player (a talented but cocky pitcher played by Robbins) and give him the benefit of her . . . uh . . . *experience*. Costner plays a hardened vet who decides to break up this relationship and ends up fielding some sexy double-plays with Sarandon.

BULLITT (1968)
*** PG 1:53
DIR: *Peter Yates* **CAST:** *Steve McQueen, Robert Vaughn, Jacqueline Bisset, Robert Duvall*
McQueen stars as a tightly-wound San Francisco cop in pursuit of the killers of a star witness. Most memorable, however, is a chase scene featuring Bullitt's Ford Mustang flying pell mell over the hills of San Francisco. Despite 25 years of high-tech filmmaking, this chase scene has yet to be surpassed.

THE BURNING BED (1984)
*** PG-13 1:36
DIR: *Robert Greenwald* **CAST:** *Farrah Fawcett, Paul LeMat, Richard Masur, Penelope Milford, Grace Zabriske*
Fawcett re-invented her career with her fine portrayal of an abused woman who eventually kills her violent husband (LeMat) by burning his bed as he sleeps. This is powerful stuff for a TV movie, and it earned Fawcett an Emmy nomination for

Best Actress. Although the story now sounds familiar, this was considered a breakthrough film.

BUTCH CASSIDY AND THE SUNDANCE KID (1969)
**** PG 1:52
DIR: *George Roy Hill* **CAST:** *Paul Newman, Robert Redford, Katherine Ross, Strother Martin, Cloris Leachman, Ted Cassidy, Kenneth Mars*
Cassidy (Newman) and Sundance (Redford) scamper across North America robbing trains and breaking hearts in this thoroughly enjoyable, semi-serious western that strikes a seemingly effortless balance between slam-bang action and clownish humor. Oscars for William Goldman's Screenplay, Conrad Hall's Cinematography, Burt Bacharach's Original Score and the Bacharach/Hal David song "Raindrops Keep Fallin' on My Head."

BY DAWN'S EARLY LIGHT (1990)
*** NR 1:43
DIR: *Jack Sholder* **CAST:** *Powers Boothe, Rebecca De Mornay, James Earl Jones, Martin Landau, Rip Torn, Darren McGavin, Peter MacNicol, Nicholas Coster, Jeffrey DeMunn*
One of the last gripping adventures to come out of the Cold War. Boothe and De Mornay star as bomber pilots who must grapple with both strategy and their own consciences on their way to

bomb the Soviet Union. The action in this fast-paced thriller shifts between the cockpit of the plane and Air Force One, where a befuddled Secretary of Agriculture (McGavin) finds himself with his finger on the nuclear button. A hawkish general (Torn) coerces him into a potentially Apocalyptic decision. An intelligent and high-minded look at the human factor in a technological age of war. Originally produced by HBO as a film for cable TV.

C

CABARET (1972)
*** PG 2:03
DIR: *Bob Fosse* **CAST:** *Liza Minnelli, Michael York, Helmut Griem, Joel Grey, Fritz Wepper, Marisa Berenson*
An energetic, visually arresting musical that won eight Oscars, including Best Actress for Minnelli as Sally Bowles, an American singer/dancer at the heart of the much-celebrated artistic/creative mecca that was pre-World War II Berlin. Songs include "Tomorrow Belongs to Me" and "The Money Song," the latter a duet between Minnelli and Best Supporting Actor-winner Grey. Also won Oscars for Best Director, Cinematography and Score Adaptation.

CADDYSHACK (1980)
** R 1:38
DIR: *Harold Ramis* **CAST:** *Chevy Chase, Rodney Dangerfield, Ted Knight, Michael O'Keefe, Bill Murray, Brian Doyle-Murray*
Amusing, and occasionally sublime, star-packed comedy about the goofy shenanigans at a tony country club. Murray fights an ongoing battle with a cat-sized gopher (credited as "Chuck E. Rodent"); Chase does his schtick as a charmingly incompetent golf pro; and Dangerfield, as an obnoxiously rich new club member, charges through his scenes like a bull in a golf pro shop. Not a hole-in-one by any means, but an above-par comedy.

THE CAINE MUTINY (1954)
**** NR 2:05
DIR: *Edward Dmytryk* **CAST:** *Humphrey Bogart, Van Johnson, Jose Ferrer, Tom Tully, Lee Marvin, Fred MacMurray, E G Marshall*
The riveting story of the crew of a World War II escort ship who must mutiny against their mentally imbalanced captain. Bogart gives one of the best performances of his career as the neurotic officer who drives his men to risk court martial and jail rather than submit to his tyranny. The courtroom scene, in which Bogart jangles a pair of steel balls in his hand and rants about stolen strawberries, is one of the classic film trials. Bogart

earned an Oscar nomination for his work, as did Tully for Best Supporting Actor. Stanley Roberts' screenplay, an adaptation of Herman Wouk's play, was also singled-out for nomination.

CAMELOT (1967)
*** G 2:58
DIR: *Josh Logan* **CAST:** *Richard Harris, Vanessa Redgrave, Franco Nero, David Hemmings, Lionel Jeffries*
A lovely film version of the musical based on "Le Morte D'Atur." The classic tale of the love triangle between King Arthur, Guenevere and Lancelot. Harris plays the kind of King who bursts into song at the drop of a crown. Redgrave is entrancing as the Queen who gets herself to a nunnery because of the doomed affair with the virgin Lancelot. The famous Lerner and Lowe score won an Oscar, as did the set direction and costumes.

THE CANDIDATE (1972)
*** PG 1:50
DIR: *Michael Ritchie* **CAST:** *Robert Redford, Peter Boyle, Don Perter, Allen Garfield, Melvyn Douglas, Michael Lerner*
Gripping political drama starring Redford as a somewhat dim-witted attorney who runs for the Senate. It's a sharply observed and finely detailed look behind the scenes of a big-time political campaign that finds real drama in the give-and-

take between the ideals and the realities of power politics. Excellent performances by Redford, Boyle as the campaign manager and Douglas as Redford's father. Jeremy Larner's screenplay won an Oscar.

THE CANNONBALL RUN (1981)
* PG 1:35

DIR: *Hal Needham* CAST: *Burt Reynolds, Dom Deluise, Roger Moore, Dean Martin, Sammy Davis, Jr*
Featuring one of the finest all-star casts ever assembled and a great action director who started his career as a stunt man, this wacky car chase movie tends to fall flat. It tells the story of a group of rich and eccentric people who are participating in a car race from Connecticut to California. When watching this movie, you can't help but feel that most of it must have been improvised. This film also has the dubious distinction of popularizing the trend of showing bloopers during the final credits.

CARNAL KNOWLEDGE (1971)
** R 1:38

DIR: *Mike Nichols* CAST: *Jack Nicholson, Art Garfunkle, Ann Margaret, Rita Moreno, Carol Kane*
Everyone tries hard in this thick, droopy tale of two friends (Garfunkle, Nicholson) as they move from college to middle-age, and through various levels of sexual awareness and moral attitudes.

All their neuroses seem a bit dated (especially in the light of AIDS), but Ann-Margaret turns in an Oscar-winning performance as Nicholson's depressed girlfriend who cajoles him into marriage.

CARRIE (1976)
*** R 1:37
DIR: *Brian De Palma* **CAST:** *Sissy Spacek, Piper Laurie, William Katt, John Travolta, Amy Irving, Nancy Allen, P J Soles*
Spine-chilling horror classic, based on the Stephen King novel, about a shy, tormented high school student (Spacek) who discovers that she has telekinetic powers. When some students decide to play a viscious joke on her at the prom, she causes the kind of bloody havoc that would make Freddy Krueger cringe. Spacek is perfect as the introverted, but powerful young woman, and Laurie really sinks her teeth into the part of Spacek's religious zealot of a mother.

CASABLANCA (1943)
**** NR 1:42
DIR: *Michael Curtiz* **CAST:** *Humphrey Bogart, Ingrid Bergman, Paul Henreid, Claude Rains, Conrad Veidt, Peter Lorre, Sydney Greenstreet*
One of the most celebrated films of all time. The heart-rending love story between nightclub owner Rick (Bogart) and his former flame (Bergman), set against the war-torn backdrop of Casablanca, is

one of the most memorable ever put on film. Add to this the phenomenal cast of supporting characters (particularly Rains as the opportunistic police chief) and Curtiz's atmospheric direction, and it equals Hollywood moviemaking at its best.

CASINO ROYALE(1967)
* NR 2:10
DIR: *John Huston, Ken Hughes, Val Guest, Joseph McGrath, Robert Parrish* CAST: *Peter Sellers, David Niven, Orson Welles, Ursula Andress, William Holden, John Huston, Woody Allen, George Raft, Jean-Paul Belmondo, Jacqueline Bisset*
An unsuccessful satire of a James Bond film, the movie collapses under the weight of a ponderous script and a huge cast. An aging, abstinent Bond (here played suavely by Niven) is brought reluctantly back into service to smash SMERSH, an organization bent on the usual world domination. Niven fights off women and evil spies with equal energy. Allen has a so-so role as Bond's hiccuping nephew, little Jimmy Bond.

CAT BALLOU (1965)
*** NR 1:36
DIR: *Elliot Silverstein* CAST: *Jane Fonda, Lee Marvin, Dwayne Hickman, Michael Callan, Nat King Cole, Stubby Kaye*
Fonda becomes an outlaw after a nasty cattle baron kills her father and steals her land. She

enlists the help of a drunken has-been gunfighter
(Marvin) to do battle with the tycoon's hench-
men, the scariest of whom (also Marvin) wears a
silver nose and black hat. Cole and Kaye appear
intermittently as singer-narrators. This is a send-
up of the classic western, and it has a refreshingly
light touch. Marvin won an Oscar for his dual role
as twin brothers. The title song, sung by Cole and
Kaye, received an Academy nomination.

CHARIOTS OF FIRE (1981)
*** PG 2:03
DIR: *Hugh Hudson* **CAST:** *Ben Cross, Ian Charleson,
Nigel Havers, Nick Farrell, Ian Holm, John Gielgud,
Patrick Magee, Brad Davis*
Part sports film, part character study, part histori-
cal drama, this is the tale of two young British
runners who compete against each other in the
1924 Olympic Games. Based on the true story of
Eric Liddell, the deeply religious Scottish mis-
sionary, and Harold Abrahams, the combative
Jewish Cambridge student. Poignantly acted,
beautifully designed and costumed, the film is
emotionally absorbing and impeccably detailed.
Oscar winner for Best Picture.

A CHARLIE BROWN CHRISTMAS (1973)
**** NR :25
DIR: *Bill Melendez,*
This is the Prime Time debut of the Peanuts kids,

now available on video. Poor Charlie Brown, rebelling against the tawdry commercialization of Christmas, buys a spindly little tree rather than a glitzy, aluminum version. Although his chums (including Snoopy, Lucy and Linus) laugh at first, they eventually come around. A great reminder of the true meaning of Christmas. The late Vince Giraldi wrote what has become a classic score.

CHARLY (1968)
*** PG 1:43
DIR: *Ralph Nelson* CAST: *Cliff Robertson,Claire Bloom, Lilia Skala, Dick Van Patten, Leon Janney*
Robertson won an Oscar for his moving portrayal of a mildly retarded man who is made brilliant by experimental surgery. Bloom plays the teacher who helps him adjust to a new world of high intelligence, but also treats him like something of a guinea pig. When the process begins to reverse, Robertson struggles to find a solution as his mind slips away.

THE CHINA SYNDROME (1979)
*** PG 2:03
DIR: *James Bridges* CAST: *Jane Fonda, Jack Lemmon, Michael Douglas, Scott Brady, James Hampton, Wilford Brimley*
Top-drawer political thriller about an accident at a California nuclear power plant and the attempted

cover-up that followed. Focuses on a relentless television reporter (Fonda) and her radical cameraman (Douglas) who break the story with the reluctant assistant of a plant executive (Lemmon). The film is tense, suspenseful and, oddly enough, very even-handed; it takes as many potshots at the media as it does at the nuclear power industry.

CHINATOWN (1974)
**** R 2:11

DIR: *Roman Polanski* **CAST:** *Jack Nicholson, Faye Dunaway, John Huston, John Hillerman, Diane Ladd, Burt Young, Bruce Glover*

Sly, knowledgeable 1930s-style mystery set in Los Angeles. Nicholson is private eye J.J. Gittes, who finds himself in over his head on a case involving murder, incest and political intrigue (in the form of valuable land and water rights). Polanski's direction paints it all in a harsh, dramatic tones that highlight the twists and turns of Robert Towne's Oscar-winning screenplay. Nicholson, Dunaway and Huston all give performances of the highest caliber.

CINDERELLA (1950)
** G 1:14

DIR: *Wilfred Jackson, Hamilton Luske, Clyde Geronimi* **CAST:** *Vocies of Ilene Woods, William Phillips, Eleanor Audley, Rhoda Williams, Lucille Bliss, Verna Felton*

Enjoyable, but a bit shallow, animated fairy tale

from the talented artists at Disney. In order to stretch out the story's bare-bones plotline of a poor servant girl that captures the heart of the lonely prince, Disney has tacked on a pair of talking mice named Gus-Gus and Jacques and an assortment of small animals that seem like leftovers from *Snow White and the Seven Dwarves*. It doesn't quite hold together, although the animation is top quality.

CINEMA PARADISO (1989)
*** NR 2:03
DIR: *Giuseppe Tornatore* **CAST:** *Phillipe Noiret, Jacques Perrin, Salvatore Cascio, Mario Leonardi, Agnese Nano, Leopoldo Trieste*
Sweet, sentimental story about the artistic and emotional power of motion pictures. Follows the life of a young boy (Cascio) who becomes enraptured by the cinema in his small Italian village. He strikes up a friendship with the blustery but wise projectionist (Noiret), and the two experience the magic of classic Italian, French and American films. Oscar winner for Best Foreign Film.

CITIZEN KANE (1941)
**** NR 1:59
DIR: *Orson Welles* **CAST:** *Orson Welles, Joseph Cotten, Everett Sloane, Agnes Moorehead, Dorothy Comingore, Ray Collins, Erskine Sanford*
Often cited as the best American film ever made,

this is the saga (loosely based on the true story of William Randolph Hearst) of the rise and fall of publishing magnate Charles Foster Kane (Welles). Welles (only 25 years old when he made this, his debut) not only stars and directs, but also co-wrote the Oscar-winning screenplay. Gorgeously filmed, impeccably acted, with production values that set new standards for excellence. *Citizen Kane* is a work of genius.

CITY LIGHTS (1931)
**** G 1:26
DIR: *Charles Chaplin* **CAST:** *Charlie Chaplin, Virginia Cherrill, Harry Myers, Hank Mann*
One of the last masterpieces of the Silent Era, this is Chaplin's funniest comedy and one of the true classics of any era. Stars Chaplin as the beloved "Little Tramp," who falls in love with a blind flower girl, then scrapes up the money to pay for an operation to restore her sight. Along the way, the Tramp meets a boozy millionaire who acts like his best friend when he's drunk, but a stranger when he's sober. Chaplin also wrote the film's musical score.

CITY SLICKERS (1991)
*** PG-13 1:52
DIR: *Ron Underwood* **CAST:** *Billy Crystal, Daniel Stern, Bruno Kirby, Helen Slater, Patricia Wettig, Jack Palance, Josh Mostel, Jeffrey Tambor*

Palance made a memorable acceptance speech when he took home the Best Supporting Actor Oscar for his portrayal of a leathery cowboy who takes three friends on a dude-ranch cattle drive. When Palance dies, and the other cowboys jump ship, it's up to Crystal, Kirby and Stern to bring in the herd. Cast and script are both first rate. A very funny take on the old trail song, "Roll Em, Roll Em, Roll Em . . . "

CLASH OF THE TITANS (1981)
*** PG 1:58
DIR: *Desmond Davis* **CAST:** *Laurence Olivier, Harry Hamlin, Claire Bloom, Burgess Meredith, Maggie Smith, Judi Bowker*
A classy retelling of Greek mythology in the best tradition of the Saturday afternoon Technicolor extravaganza. Hamlin plays Perseus, a heroic mortal who does battle with a collection of imaginative monsters (including a spooky Medusa) in order to save a beautiful woman (Bowker). His quest is observed with great interest by competing Gods (Olivier, Bloom). The special effects from Ray Harryhausen will remind you of the object animation in the old Hercules and Sinbad films. It was great in the 1960s, and it's great here.

A CLOCKWORK ORANGE (1971)
*** R 2:15
DIR: *Stanley Kubrick* **CAST:** *Malcolm McDowell,*

Patrick Magee, Adrienne Corri, Aubrey Morris, James Marcus, David Prowse
Disturbing, violent and visionary tale of a society out of control that focuses on the story of a sadistic young punk (McDowell) who, in the name of rehabilitation, is forced to undergo an equally disturbing and violent "cure." Filmed with cold, clinical distance by Kubrick, the film, even more than 20 years after it was made, remains a potently graphic satire on both violence and society's response to violence. Adapted from Anthony Burgess' novel.

CLOSE ENCOUNTERS OF THE THIRD KIND
(1977)
*** PG 2:15
DIR: *Steven Spielberg* **CAST:** *Richard Dreyfuss, Francois Truffaut, Teri Garr, Melinda Dillon, Cary Guffey, Bob Balaban*
Endlessly enjoyable science fiction film about man's first contact with extraterrestrials. Stars Dreyfuss and Dillon as UFO contactees who are mysteriously compelled by a vision of Devil's Tower, Wyoming, and Garr as Dreyfuss' bewildered wife. The film's state-of-the-art special effects make for a glorious finale awash in wonder and hope. Re-released in 1980 in a 2-hour, 12-minute version that adds footage inside the alien spaceship.

77

COAL MINER'S DAUGHTER (1980)
*** PG 2:05
DIR: *Michael Apted* **CAST:** *Sissy Spacek, Tommy Lee Jones, Beverly D'Angelo, Levon Helm, Phyllis Boyens, Ernest Tubb*
Stellar film biography of Loretta Lynn (Spacek), who sang her way out of the Appalachian coal town where she was born to become one of country music's living legends. Spacek (who did all of her own singing) gives a performance of astonishing depth and focus that won her the Oscar for Best Actress. The supporting cast (especially Jones, as Lynn's husband, and Helm, as her father) are also excellent.

COCOON (1985)
*** PG-13 1:58
DIR: *Ron Howard* **CAST:** *Don Ameche, Hume Cronyn, Wilford Brimley, Brian Dennehy, Jack Gilford, Steve Guttenberg, Maureen Stapleton, Jessica Tandy, Tahnee Welch, Tyrone Power, Jr*
Heartwarming fantasy film in which three Florida senior citizens (Ameche, Cronyn, Brimley) stumble onto an actual fountain of youth: a swimming pool with mysterious, cocoon-like pods at the bottom. The pods turn out to be friendly, hibernating aliens left on the ocean floor ages ago. This film is magical fun, anchored by a talented ensemble of veteran actors that are an absolute joy to watch. Ameche won the Academy Award for Best Supporting Actor.

THE COLOR OF MONEY (1986)
*** R 1:57

DIR: *Martin Scorsese* **CAST:** *Paul Newman, Tom Cruise, Mary Elizabeth Mastrantonio, Helen Shaver, John Turturro, Forest Whitaker*

Newman won an Oscar for this reprise of his 1961 portrayal of Fast Eddie Felson, an edgy pool shark who takes on Minnesota Fats in *The Hustler*. It's 25 years later and Felson, now a liquor salesman, discovers a talented-but-naive protege (Cruise) who reminds him of himself as a much younger man. Felson tries to teach him the finer points of hustling, but the kid is too hot-headed to listen. The climax has the two of them facing off. This is a skilled, energetic production with top-rate performances, including Mastrantonio as Cruise's street-wise girlfriend.

THE COLOR PURPLE (1985)
*** PG-13 2:32

DIR: *Steven Spielberg* **CAST:** *Whoopi Goldberg, Danny Glover, Margaret Avery, Oprah Winfrey, Willard E. Pugh, Adolph Caesar, Akosua Busia, Rae Dawn Chong*

Goldberg stars in a fine portrayal of an abused black woman in the south during the first part of the century. Glover is her uncaring, brutal husband who torments her both physically and emotionally. Based on Alice Walker's splendid book, this is the story of a woman who triumphs over betrayal and poverty. Winfrey is accomplished as Goldberg's step-daughter who is put in prison unjustly. The film received 11 nominations, including Best Picture.

COME BACK TO THE FIVE AND DIME, JIMMY DEAN, JIMMY DEAN (1982)
** PG 1:50
DIR: *Robert Altman* CAST: *Cher, Sandy Dennis, Karen Black, Kathy Bates*
Internationally acclaimed director Robert Altman leads a cast of talented women in this powerful drama about encountering the inner pain of growing old. The film, which is based on the play of the same title, centers on the reunion of the members of a James Dean fan club. In reminiscing about Dean's death 20 years earlier, the women cannot help but succumb to their emotions, revealing all of their lost dreams and desires. Featuring brilliant performances and direction, this movie suffers a great deal from its poor script.

CONRACK (1974)
*** PG 1:46
DIR: *Martin Ritt* CAST: *Jon Voight, Hune Cronyn, Paul Winfield, Tina Andrews, Madge Sinclair*
Voight stars as an idealistic schoolteacher who moves to a small island off South Carolina to work with disadvantaged black students. Based on Pat Conroy's (*Prince of Tides*) semi-autobio-

graphical story of the challenge of education in a poor school system. Cronyn plays the superintendent who refuses to let Conrack's kids go trick-or-treating in a white neighborhood. A lovely, small film with fine performances.

THE CONVERSATION (1974)
**** PG 1:53
DIR: *Francis Ford Coppola* **CAST:** *Gene Hackman, John Cazale, Allen Garfield, Frederic Forrest, Cindy Williams, Teri Garr, Harrison Ford, Robert Duvall*
Disturbingly brilliant film about a professional wire-tapper whose eavesdropping uncovers the plans for a murder. Hackman makes all the right connections as the guilt-wracked devout Catholic bugging expert torn between his professional pride and his religious ethics. Produced, written and directed by Coppola, who would go on to create the *Godfather* trilogy, this film is one of the tautest, most chilling thrillers of the 1970s.

COOL HAND LUKE (1967)
*** PG 2:06
DIR: *Stuart Rosenberg* **CAST:** *Paul Newman, George Kennedy, J D Cannon, Lou Antonio, Strother Martin, Wayne Rogers, Ralph Waite, Harry Dean Stanton, Joe Don Baker*
One of the best and most popular of all Hollywood prison dramas. Stars Newman in one of his most memorable performances as the irreverent

and gutsy new addition to a Southern chain gang. Although the film can be brutal in its portrait of life behind bars, it can also be very funny and unexpectedly touching. Kennedy, playing a hard-as-nails gang foreman, won an Oscar for Best Supporting Actor.

THE COURT JESTER (1956)
**** NR 1:41
DIR: *Norman Panama, Melvin Frank* **CAST:** *Danny Kaye, Glynis Johns, Basil Rathbone, Mildred Natwick, Angela Lansbury*
Many adults remember this as one of their favorite films from childhood. Kaye stars as a bumbling English minstrel turned outlaw in this medieval Technicolor adventure. The plot involves an attempt to restore the rightful King, an infant with a unique birthmark, to his throne. You may remember the famous "vessel with the pestle has the pellet with the poison" routine. If not, you're in for a pleasant film experience.

THE COWBOYS (1972)
*** PG 2:08
DIR: *Mark Rydell* **CAST:** *John Wayne, Bruce Dern, Roscoe Lee Brown, Colleen Dewhurst, Slim Pickens*
Wayne plays a rancher who's desperate for hands after his help runs off to mine gold. He turns to a bunch of local kids to help him on a cattle drive. Dern plays a psycho bent on killing Wayne for

refusing him work. This is a fine coming-of-age story in which the boys learn what it means to be men. Wayne is great as a hard-as-rock cowboy who must be both mentor and mother to his wet-behind-the-ears charges.

CRIMES AND MISDEMEANORS (1989)
*** PG-13 1:44
DIR: *Woody Allen* **CAST:** *Woody Allen, Mia Farrow, Alan Alda, Anjelica Huston, Martin Landau, Sam Waterson, Caroline Aaron*
A complicated tapestry of a movie, weaving together two separate stories, one crime (murder) and one misdemeanor (love). In the former, an unhappily married ophthalmologist (Landau) goes to extremes to stop his mistress (Huston) from exposing him. In the latter, a nebbish film-maker (Allen) falls for an attractive producer (Farrow) while making a documentary on her annoying boss (Alda). One of Allen's most ambitious and most rewarding late films.

THE CRYING GAME (1992)
**** R 1:52
DIR: *Neil Jordan* **CAST:** *Stephen Rea, Jaye Davidson, Miranda Richardson, Forrest Whitakker*
This Oscar-winning film contains one of the best kept secret plot twists ever to escape Hollywood, and if you don't already know the secret, then you're not going to find it out here! Rea plays a

member of the Irish Republican Army who realizes the error of his ways after kidnapping a British soldier (Whitakker). He grows very close to the soldier, and the two share some of their innermost secrets. When the soldier is killed by some of the other captors, Rea flees to England to start a new life. He meets the soldier's girlfriend and instantly falls in love with her. They pursue a relationship, but Rea soon realizes that some of his ex-colleagues might be coming after them. Featuring extraordinary performances, a great script, and perfect direction, this is one of the best movies of recent years. A must-see.

CYRANO DE BERGERAC (1950)
*** NR 1:52

DIR: *Michael Gordon* **CAST:** *Jose Ferrer, Mala Powers, William Prince, Morris Carnovsky, Elena Verdugo*

Jose Ferrer steals this film with his force-of-nature portrayal of the great Cyrano De Bergerac, a soldier, hero, swordsman, poet, bon vivant and lover beyond equal, with a nose long enough for a bird to perch on. Based on the classic 17th century play by Edmond Rostand, this film version suffers from an unimpressive supporting cast. But Ferrer (who won the Oscar for Best Actor) is simply marvelous. Gorgeously remade in 1990 with Gerard Depardieu in the lead role.

D

DAMN YANKEES (1958)
*** NR 1:50
DIR: *George Abbott, Stanley Donen* **CAST:** *Tab Hunter, Gwen Verdon, Ray Walston, Nathaniel Frey*
A depressed middle-aged man (Hunter) enters into a pact with Satan (Walston) so that he can return to his youth and live out his life-long unfulfilled dream of playing major league baseball. He falls for Verdon, who's made her own deal with the devil. Based on the hit play, the movie has a number of memorable songs, including "You Gotta Have Heart'" and "Whatever Lola Wants." The score earned an Oscar nomination.

DANCES WITH WOLVES (1990)
*** PG 3:10
DIR: *Kevin Costner* **CAST:** *Kevin Costner, Mary McDonnell, Graham Greene*
Costner walked off with both of the Academy Awards for Best Picture and Best Director for this remarkably moving film, his directorial debut. Costner also stars as a Civil War lieutenant who befriends a tribe of Plains Indians. This is the old-time Hollywood Western at it most expansive, filled with sweeping vistas of the American plains and highlighted by McDonnell's performance (as a white woman adopted by the Indians) and a breathtaking buffalo stampede sequence.

DANGEROUS LIASONS (1988)
**** R 2:00
DIR: *Stephen Frears* **CAST:** *Glenn Close, John Malkovich, Michelle Pfeiffer, Keanu Reeves, Swoosie Kurtz, Uma Thurman, Mildred Natwick, Peter Capaldi*
Malkovich and Close play two unconscionable 18th-century French aristocrats who conspire to seduce a young virgin (Thurman) as an act of revenge against her fiance. The tables are turned when Malkovich finds his calloused heart melting in the face of Pfeiffer. Close, meanwhile, has taken Reeves into her budoir for a tutorial in the art of love. This is an elegant, beautifully-realized adaptation of *Les Liaisons Dangereuses*. Christophe Hampton won an Oscar for his screenplay adaptation of his play. The detailed costumes also earned an Academy Award.

DAS BOOT (THE BOAT) (1981)
*** R 2:30
DIR: *Wolfgang Petersen* **CAST:** *Jurgen Prochnow, Herbert Gronemeyer, Klaus Wennemann, Hubertus Bengsch, Martin Semmelrogge, Bernd Tauber*
Tightly-wound German-made drama that chronicles the lives of a Nazi U-boat captain (Prochnow, in a career-making performance) and his crew on a harrowing undersea mission during World War II. Most of the action takes place inside the grimy, clanking confines of the submarine as it dodges depth charges and enemy ships. The

film's final scene is one of the most emotionally chilling anti-war statements ever put on film. Dubbed in English as *The Boat*.

A DAY AT THE RACES (1937)
*** NR 1:51
DIR: *Sam Wood* **CAST:** *Groucho, Harpo and Chico Marx, Allan Jones, Maureen O'Sullivan, Margaret Dumont, Douglass Drimble, Sig Ruman*

One of the Marx Brothers' funniest films. Like all of their movies, this one doesn't bother much with plot, and is bogged down by several completely useless musical numbers, but it does include the classic sketch with Chico (as a wily sanitarium employee) selling racing tips to the hapless Groucho (as horse doctor Dr. Hackenbush) and some madcap romantic shenanigans between Groucho and the ever-droll-and-befuddled Dumont (as a hypochondriac patient).

THE DAY OF THE LOCUST (1975)
*** R 2:24
DIR: *John Schlesinger* **CAST:** *Donald Sutherland, Karen Black, Burgess Meredith, William Atherton, Geraldine Page*

A powerful adaptation of Nathaniel West's tale of the dark underbelly of depression-era Hollywood. Sutherland stars as a milquetoast-ish accountant who begins a destructive relationship with a floozy (Black) who cheats on him. The climax, in which a glitzy premiere ends in a riot, is apocalyptic.

DAYS OF HEAVEN (1978)
*** PG 1:35

DIR: *Terrence Malick* **CAST:** *Richard Gere, Brooke Adams, Linda Manz, Sam Shepard, Robert Wilke*
The simple, although deeply felt plot takes second billing to the masterful photography of Nestor Almendros (assisted by Haskell Wexler) in this film set in early 20th century Texas. Gere, Adams, and Manz start out as workers on Shepard's farm, but when Shepard falls in love with Adams, they begin living the life of luxury. While the breathtaking visuals will be diminished on television (the film was originally shown in 70mm), they are still well worth viewing on the small screen. A heartbreaking, haunting, beautiful work of art.

DEAD CALM (1989)
*** R 1:35

DIR: *Phillip Noyce* **CAST:** *Nicole Kidman, Sam Neill, Billy Zane*
This overlooked, brilliant film features Neill and Kidman as a couple mourning the loss of their young child. They go on a long sailing trip to recover, but are interrupted when they must take aboard a young American whose boat has sunk. Trapped on the high seas, it becomes apparent that Zane is a dangerous loon. Director Noyce (*Patriot Games*) wrings every bit of claustrophobic tension (including a remarkable scene with Neill struggling to get out of a sinking ship) from the

fine script. This is one of the best thrillers of the last ten years.

DEADLY FRIEND (1986)
** R 1:32
DIR: *Wes Craven* CAST: *Matthew Lamborteaux, Kristy Swanson, Michael Sharrett*

A slight departure from Wes Craven's usual gore-laden fright films, this romantic little thriller is similar to *Frankenstein*. It is the story of a brilliant teenager who falls in love with the girl next door, only to discover that she is being abused by her father. One day the father goes so far that she dies from his beating, and the teenager decides to bring her back to life using high tech computer technology. The movie is romantic, in a twisted sort of way, but its script could use a lot of work. Moreover, the young actors are never all that convincing, and Craven seems out of his league. Overall, an average film.

DEAD RINGERS (1988)
*** R 1:55
DIR: *David Cronenberg* CAST: *Jeremy Irons, Genevieve Bujold, Shirley Douglas*

Based loosely on the true story of two identical twins who shared each other's lives so much that they could actually feel each other's emotions, this haunting movie is not for the faint of heart. Irons plays twin gynecologists, both of whom are in love with the same woman, but express their passion in very different ways. They decide to play a trick on her and switch roles, but they soon have trouble switching back, and eventually fall into the depths of dimentia. Cronenberg's direction is thought-provoking and brilliant, verging at once on the profound and the distasteful. Irons is amazing as the two brothers, and it is very easy to forget that he is just one actor. If you enjoy films that are slightly "different," then this one is a must-see!

DEAR AMERICA: LETTERS HOME FROM VIETNAM (1987)
**** PG-13 1:27
DIR: *Bill Couturie* **CAST:** *The voices of Robert De Niro, Kathleen Turner, Tom Berenger, Sean Penn, Randy Quaid, Martin Sheen, Ellen Burstyn*
An emotional documentary about the struggles and sorrows of the Vietnam war. An all-star cast reads actual letters from U.S. soldiers on duty in Vietnam and their families, over rarely seen archival footage from the war. Produced for broadcast on H.B.O., this fine, moving film has moments of humor, heroism, and overwhelming sadness. The final letter, from a mother whose son has died, placed on the Vietnam Memorial in Washington, is extraordinary. The film was later released theatrically because of the praise it received.

DEMON SEED (1977)
*** R 1:34
DIR: *Donald Cammell* **CAST:** *Julie Christie, Fritz Weaver, Gerrit Graham, Barry Kroeger*
A strange film about a brilliant inventor (Weaver) who designs a super-computer. The computer (with Robert Vaughn's voice) ensnares the inventor's wife (Christie) and manages to impregnate her with the first computer/human hybrid. Some of the images are rather disturbing, but the film as a whole is oddly compelling.

DEATH OF A SALESMAN (1985)
**** NR 2:14
DIR: *Voker Schlondorff* **CAST:** *Dustin Hoffman, John Malkovich, Stephen Lang, Charles Durning*
Hoffman is excellent as the tragic Willy Loman in this made-for-T.V. version of Arthur Miller's classic tale of family strife and alienation. Malkovich and Lang are both superior as Loman's sons, whose relationship with their salesman father is strained to breaking. The gut-wrenching portrayal of a desperate, aging man won Hoffman both an Emmy and a Golden Globe.

DEEP COVER (1992)
** R 1:52
DIR: *Bill Duke* **CAST:** *Lawrence Fishburne, Jeff Goldblum, Charles Martin Smith*
Fishburne and Goldblum are two of the best

actors working in Hollywood today, and they certainly bring a great deal of energy to this production, but not even their talents can save it entirely from its predictable script. Goldblum is a lawyer who goes out on the streets with undercover narcotics agents in order to help bring justice to the world. Fishburne is such an agent, but he has a huge chip on his shoulder as he is trying to live up to the legacy of his father, who was killed during a drug bust. The film certainly tries its best to be a new brand of buddy-picture for the '90s, not afraid to be emotional and controversial, but it never quite succeeds.

THE DEER HUNTER (1978)
**** R 3:03
DIR: *Michael Cimino* **CAST:** *Robert De Niro, John Cazale, John Savage, Meryl Streep, Christopher Walken, George Dzundza, Chuck Aspergren*
Intense, gripping drama that follows a group of Pennsylvania steelworkers as they go to fight in Vietnam. Divided into three segments (before, during and after the war) the film is a beautifully shot, and at times unflinchingly brutal portrayal of the horrors of war and the physical and emotional shrapnel wounds that remain long after the shooting stops. The picture won five Oscars, including Best Picture, Director, Supporting Actor (Walken) and Editing.

DELIVERANCE (1972)
*** R 1:49

DIR: *John Boorman* **CAST:** *John Voight, Burt Reynolds, Ned Beatty, Ronnie Cox, Billy McKinney, Herbert Coward, James Dickey*

Riveting thriller from the James Dickey novel tells the chilling tale of three Atlanta businessmen (Voight, Beatty and Cox) and their macho guide (Reynolds) whose weekend canoe trip down a Georgia river turns into a fatal nightmare when they find themselves hunted by a pair of murderous backwoods yokels. Includes the famous "Dueling Banjos" scene, lots of exciting white-water action and excellent performances by the entire cast.

DIAL M FOR MURDER (1954)
*** PG 1:45

DIR: *Alfred Hitchcock* **CAST:** *Ray Milland, Grace Kelly, Robert Cummings, John Williams, Anthony Dawson*

Enjoyable thriller in which a cheating husband (Milland) plots to kill his wife (Kelly), but is thwarted when she kills the killer (Dawson) instead. Hitchcock, in his adaptation of Frederick Knott's play (which took place entirely on a single set), has broadened the story's scope while at the same time tightening the suspense. Includes the classic scene in which Kelly and Dawson struggle to the death over a pair of scissors. Originally released in 3-D.

DICK TRACY (1990)

** PG 1:50

DIR: *Warren Beatty* **CAST:** *Warren Beatty, Madonna, Al Pacino, Mandy Patinkin, Charles Durning, William Forsythe, Dustin Hoffman, Dick Van Dyke, Catherine O'Hara, James Caan*

Beatty's blockbuster brings the style, but little of the panache, of Chester Gould's classic comic strip to the big screen. The film's vivid color schemes, in homage to the garish tones of the Sunday comics of the '30s and '40s, are as much characters in the film as the actors themselves. Lots of big-name stars (hidden under several tons of make-up) ham it up nicely. Madonna, in her most cartoonish (and best) performance yet, steals the show.

DIE HARD (1988)

** R 2:11

DIR: *John McTiernan* **CAST:** *Bruce Willis, Alan Rickman, Bonnie Bedelia, Alexander Gudunov, Paul Gleason, William Atherton*

A wholly one-dimensional movie that soars during the action scenes but snores when the shooting stops. Willis (as a New York cop caught in an L.A. high-rise that is commandeered by terrorists) spews out one-liners like tracer bullets, but never amounts to more than an annoyingly smug chatterbox. In truth, Willis plays a co-starring role to the film's real draw: the seemingly endless (although beautifully filmed) array of shoot-ups, stunts and explosions.

DINER (1982)
*** R 1:50
DIR: *Barry Levinson* CAST: *Steve Guttenberg, Mickey Rourke, Kevin Bacon, Ellen Barkin, Paul Reiser, Daniel Stern, Timothy Daly*
Sweet, nostalgic film set in 1959 Baltimore about a group of just-out-of-high school buddies facing up to adulthood from the Naugahyde seats of their local diner. Well-acted ensemble cast includes screen debuts of Barkin and Reiser and great performances by Rourke as a sleazy self-styled playboy and Guttenberg as an uptight baseball fanatic. Writer-director Levinson's first film (he went on to make *Tin Man* and *Avalon*).

THE DIRTY DOZEN (1967)
*** NR 2:30
DIR: *Robert Aldrich* CAST: *Lee Marvin, Ernest Borgnine, Jim Brown, John Cassavetes, George Kennedy, Telly Savalas, Donald Sutherland, Charles Bronson, Trini Lopez*
One of the most entertaining war movies of all time. A bullet-headed Major (Marvin) recruits a dozen convicts (including a near-psycho Cassavetes) for a suicide mission against the Nazis. The action is well done, but the movie really shines when it focuses on the interaction of this very motley crew of soldiers.

DIRTY HARRY (1971)
*** R 1:42

DIR: *Don Siegel* **CAST:** *Clint Eastwood, Harry Guardino, Reni Santoni, John Vernon, John Larch, Andy Robinson*

This is the film that set the standards for all action films that followed. San Francisco detective Harry Callahan (Eastwood) throws the penal code out the window as he tracks down a psychotic murderer (Robinson) who is demanding a $200,000 ransom for his young hostage. Fast-paced, witty and numbingly violent, the film spawned several successful sequels (*Magnum Force, The Enforcer, Sudden Impact* and *The Dead Pool*).

DIRTY ROTTEN SCOUNDRELS (1988)
*** PG 1:50

DIR: *Frank Oz* **Cast:** *Steve Martin, Michael Caine, Barbara Harris, Glenne Headly, Anton Rodgers*

Martin stars as a two-bit con man who hooks up with Caine, a four-bit con man who trolls the French Riviera for rich widows. Caine teaches the younger man a few tricks before they enter into a bet to see who's first to access the bank account of a young heiress (Headly). This remake of the 1964 *Bedtime Story* is one of the funniest films in recent memory, especially the scene in which Martin portrays Caine's loony brother.

DIVA (1982)
*** R 1:58
DIR: *Jean-Jacques Beineix* **CAST:** *Wilhelminia Wiggins Fernandez, Frederic Andrei, Richard Bohringer, Jacques Fabbri*

An intriguing thriller about opera, punk and an obsessive fan. Fernandez, herself an opera star, plays a Diva with a young fan who secretly tapes her never-before recorded voice. When the young messenger's tapes are mixed up with an incriminating recording of criminals, the film veers off into a stylish, tense chase. Listen for Fernandez' rendition of the aria from La Wally; it's the highlight of this fine film.

THE DOCTOR (1991)
*** PG-13 2:05
DIR: *Rand Haines* **CAST:** *William Hurt, Christine Lahti, Elizabeth Perkins, Mandy Patinkin, Adam Arkin, Bill Macy, Charlie Korsmo, Wendy Crewson*

An arrogant, successful doctor (Hurt) confronts both his own methods and mortality in this moving drama of a physician facing disease. Based on the true story of Dr. Ed Rosenbaum, Hurt sees the workings of medicine from the vantage point of patient when he contracts throat cancer. He realizes his cold, scientific approach is woefully inadequate. Perkins gives a fine performance as a brain tumor patient who teaches Hurt the value of life.

DOCTOR DOOLITTLE (1967)
** NR 2:32
DIR: *Richard Fleischer* **CAST:** *Rex Harrison, Samantha Eggar, Anthony Newley, Richard Attenborough, Peter Bull, Geoffrey Holder*
Lightweight but enjoyable musical adaptation of Hugh Lofting's classic children's stories about a man (Harrison) who can talk to the animals, his beautiful, long-suffering fiancée (Eggar) and their endearing, big-mouthed neighbor (Newley) who tags along. Leslie Bricusse won an Oscar for the song "Talk to the Animals," as did the film's special visual effects of the strange and wonderful creatures the good doctor meets on his voyage around the globe.

DOCTOR ZHIVAGO (1965)
*** PG 3:17
DIR: *David Lean* **CAST:** *Omar Sharif, Julie Christie, Geraldine Chaplin, Rod Steiger, Ralph Richardson, Alec Guinness*
Long, sprawling historical epic based on Nobel Laureate Boris Pasternak's novel of the 1917 Russian Revolution. The film is highlighted by its gorgeously filmed vistas of winter scenery (shot on location in Spain and Finland) and the two lead performances by Sharif as the doctor and Christie as his beautiful lover. Winner of five Oscars, including Robert Bolt's screenplay, Maurice Jarre's musical score and Freddie Young's cinematography.

DOG DAY AFTERNOON (1975)

**** R 2:04

DIR: *Sidney Lumet* **CAST:** *Al Pacino, John Cazale, Charles Durning, James Broderick, Chris Sarandon, Carol Kane*

The true story of a bungled bank robbery which transfixed New Yorkers one hot summer afternoon. Pacino stars as the inept thief who holds up a bank to raise cash for his gay lover's (Sarandon) sex change operation. When the robbery goes bad, Pacino must negotiate with police for the release of the hostages and his own escape. The film's blend of dark humor, rich characters and suspense earned it a Best-Picture nomination. Lumet, Pacino and Sarandon were all nominated. The fine screenplay by Frank Pierson took home an Oscar.

DONA FLORA AND HER TWO HUSBANDS (1978)

*** R 1:46

DIR: *Bruno Barreto* **CAST:** *Sonia Braga, Jose Wilker, Mauro Mendonca, Dinorah Brillanti*

Braga is delightful as the woman who wants it all. Widowed from a lusty, unreliable husband, she marries a good, boring pharmacist who comes home every night, but does nothing to quench her passion. When the ghost of her first husband arrives on the scene, she manages to work out a *menage a trois* that's beneficial for all parties. An

American version, *Kiss Me Goodbye*, with James Caan and Sally Field wasn't as racy, nor as good.

DO THE RIGHT THING (1989)
**** R 2:00
DIR: *Spike Lee* **CAST:** *Danny Aiello, Ossie Davis, Ruby Dee, Richard Edson, Giancarlo Esposito, John Turturro, Spike Lee, John Savage*

Excellent, and highly controversial, drama starring Aiello as the owner of a pizzeria in the black Bedford-Stuyvesant neighborhood of Brooklyn. Actor/writer/director/producer Lee has created an explosive, stunningly filmed and confrontational exploration of the racial tension between the white-owned restaurant and its mostly black customers during one tense, swelteringly hot summer day. One of the finest, and bravest, films of the 1980s.

DOUBLE INDEMNITY (1944)
**** NR 1:46
DIR: *Billy Wilder* **CAST:** *Barbara Stanwyck, Fred MacMurray, Edward G Robinson, Porter Hall, Fortunio Bonanova, Jean Heather*

An acknowledged classic of the 1940s *film noir* genre, this film stars perennial Disney father-figure MacMurray as a devious insurance salesman caught up in a murder plot hatched by housewife Stanwyck to kill her husband and collect on the insurance policy. Based on a classic hard-boiled detective thriller by James M. Cain, and with an airtight script by Raymond Chandler and Billy Wilder, this is a shining example of the mystery movie at its best.

DOWN BY LAW (1986)
*** R 1:47
DIR: *Jim Jarmusch* **CAST:** *Tom Waits, John Lurie, Ellen Barkin, Roberto Benigni, Billie Neal*
Director Jarmusch's quirky take on the classic chain-gang genre. This black-and-white-film follows three deadbeats (Lurie, Waits, Benigni) as they escape from a small southern jail. Benigni, a well-known comedian in Italy, steals the show as a foreigner whose knowledge of America comes exclusively from old movies. As in *Stranger than Paradise*, Jarmusch has a thick, slow-moving sense of humor that you'll either love or despise.

DRACULA (1931)
**** NR 1:15
DIR: *Tod Browning* **CAST:** *Bela Lugosi, David Manners, Helen Chandler, Dwight Frye, Edward Van Sloan, Herbert Bunston, Frances Dade*
With his eerie, hypnotic portrayal, Bela Lugosi defined the role of the blood-sucking Transylvania Count who preys on a hapless group of Londoners in this, the best of the classic 1930s Hollywood monster movies. Browning's direction is appropriately Gothic and moody, seeped in shadow

101

and fog, and the supporting cast is great, especially Frye as the crazy Renfield and Van Sloan as the down-to-Earth Professor Van Helsing. Often remade, but never equaled.

THE DRESSER (1983)
*** PG 1:58
DIR: *Peter Yates* **CAST:** *Albert Finney, Tom Courtenay, Edward Fox, Zena Walker, Eileen Atkins, Michael Gough*
Finney earned an Academy nomination for his portrayal of a bombastic English stage actor on the verge of nervous exhaustion during the German Blitzkrieg. Courtenay, reviving his stage performance, is magnificent as his personal dresser who night after night must make sure that his boss is ready for the stage. The odd attachment between the two desperate men is at the heart of this fine film.

DRIVING MISS DAISY (1989)
*** PG 1:39
DIR: *Bruce Beresford* **CAST:** *Morgan Freeman, Jessica Tandy, Dan Aykroyd, Patti LuPone, Esther Rolle*
Well-acted drama set in post-World War II Atlanta traces the 25-year friendship between a black man (Freeman) and the cranky, old-world Southern lady (Tandy) he is hired to chauffeur. The film gets heavy-handed and preachy at times, but the understated performances by Tandy (who won

the Academy Award for Best Actress) and Freeman pull it through the rough spots. Based on Alfred Uhry's stage play. Also won Oscars for Best Picture, Screenplay and Makeup.

DR. NO (1962)
*** PG 1:51
DIR: *Terence Young* **CAST:** *Sean Connery, Ursula Andress, Joseph Wiseman, Jack Lord, Bernard Lee, Lois Maxwell, Anthony Dawson*
The first, and still the best, James Bond movie in which the famous 007 (Connery, who couldn't be more debonair, or more deadly) is sent off to Jamaica to investigate the mysterious murder of a fellow agent. He eventually meets up with the voluptuous Andress and the villainous Wiseman as the evil Dr. No, whose plans to sabotage Cape Canaveral must be stopped with all the wile and wisecracks that Bond can muster.

DR. STRANGELOVE OR: HOW I LEARNED TO STOP WORRYING AND LOVE THE BOMB (1964)
**** PG 1:35
DIR: *Stanley Kubrick* **CAST:** *Peter Sellers, George C Scott, Sterling Hayden, Slim Pickens, Keenan Wynn, Peter Bull, James Earl Jones*
Uproarious black comedy about nuclear holocaust, starring Sellers in the triple roles of the President of the United States, a goofy British

Group Captain and the nefarious Dr. Strangelove; and Hayden as Air Force General Jack D. Ripper, who launches a nuclear strike on the Soviet Union. The entire cast is hilarious, particularly Sellers, who careens across the screen like a pinball loose in an arcade. Hands-down, the best thing to ever come out of the Cold War.

DRUGSTORE COWBOY (1989)
**** R 1:40
DIR: *Gus Van Sant* **CAST:** *Matt Dillon, Kelly Lynch, James Remar, James le Gros, Heather Graham, Grace Zabriskie, William S Burroughs*
A challenging and extremely rewarding film set in Portland, Oregon in the early '70s that gets under the collective skin of a quartet of charismatic junkies who fuel their habits by knocking off pharmacies for prescription drugs. Van Sant's direction, ranging from horrific to mundane to hallucinatory, and Dillon's sublime, laconic performance as the group's leader, mark this as one of the most uniquely disturbing, visually arresting films of the 1980s.

DUCK SOUP (1933)
**** NR 1:10
DIR: *Leo McCarey* **CAST:** *Groucho, Harpo, Chico and Zeppo Marx, Margaret Dumont, Louis Calhern, Raquel Torres, Edgar Kennedy, Charles Middleton*
The Marx Brothers' best, and one of the funniest

films of all time. Groucho plays Prime Minister Rufus T. Firefly of the imaginary kingdom of Freedonia, who starts a war on neighboring Sylvania for no reason other than to set up some side-splitting scenes with Chico and Harpo who play inept enemy spies out to steal Groucho's secret battle plans. Standout routines include the classic mirror sequence and Harpo's destructive meeting with a lemonade vendor (Kennedy).

DUEL (1971)
**** PG 1:30
DIR: *Steven Spielberg* **CAST:** *Dennis Weaver, Eddie Firestone, Gene Dynarksi, Tim Herbert*
This early made-for-TV-movie directed by a young Spielberg is still one of his best. Weaver stars as an average salesman who is inexplicably stalked by an unseen villain and his huge truck. Weaver's fear builds as he races through the Southwest trying to understand why he's being pursued. Spielberg's fine direction keeps the suspense at peak levels. The film received such good notices that it was released theatrically. Emmy nomination for Jack Marta's cinematography.

DUMBO (1940)
*** G 1:04
DIR: *Ben Sharpsteen* **CAST:** *Voices of Sterling Holloway, Edward Brophy, Verna Felton, Herman Bing, Cliff Edwards*

One of the funniest of Disney's animated classics, this tells the heartwarming tale of Dumbo, the little elephant with big ears who discovers that he can fly. The supporting cast of characters that befriend Dumbo (his pal Timothy the Mouse and a murder of sarcastic crows) are among the most memorable in Disney lore. Includes a great musical score (which won an Oscar), with the songs "Baby Mine," "Look Out For Mr. Stork" and "Pink Elephants on Parade."

DUNE (1984)
** PG-13 2:20
DIR: *David Lynch* **CAST:** *Kyle MacLachlan, Jose Ferrer, Francesca Annis, Brad Dourif, Linda Hunt, Freddie Jones, Virginia Madsen, Richard Jordan, Sting* A nearly-impenetrable rendition of Frank Herbert's wildly popular sci-fi book. MacLachlan plays a young prince of a distant future who visits a desert planet and becomes its savior. It might take several viewings to get the plot, but the visual energy of the film is enough to make it worthwhile. Lynch also gave us *Blue Velvet*, and some of his same strange tastes come through in this bizarre, rewarding film.

E

EAST OF EDEN (1955)
*** NR 1:55
DIR: *Elia Kazan* **CAST:** *James Dean, Julie Harris, Raymond Massey, Jo Van Fleet, Burl Ives, Richard Davalos, Albert Dekker*
An emotionally draining drama based on the Biblical story of Cain and Abel with Dean in top form as Cal, the rebellious bad boy whose confusion and curiosity nearly tear his family apart. Kazan directs like a master chef, perfectly balancing all of the film's intense, yet eloquent performances, particularly Harris' portrayal as the radiant girlfriend of Cal's good brother, Aaron (Davalos). Van Fleet won the Oscar for Best Supporting Actress as the brothers' cold-hearted mother, Kate.

EASY RIDER (1969)
*** R 1:35
DIR: *Dennis Hopper* **CAST:** *Peter Fonda, Dennis Hopper, Jack Nicholson, Karen Black, Luke Askew, Luana Anders, Phil Spector*
Hopper's directorial debut, made on a shoestring budget of less than $400,000, not only re-defined the American road movie, for many people it also defined the entire '60s generation. Two dropouts (Fonda and Hopper) deal some dope in sunny Southern California, stash the cash in the gas tank

107

of a motorcycle and hit the road in search of America, in the general direction of New Orleans. Nicholson plays a boozy, wisecracking lawyer along for the ride

8 1/2 (1963)
**** NR 2:18
DIR: *Federico Fellini* **CAST:** *Marcello Mastroianni, Claudia Cardinale, Anouk Aimee, Sandra Milo, Barbara Steele*
A semi-autobiographical account of a famous film maker (Mastroianni) and his struggle to complete his latest project. Fellini's cinematic vision is complex and highly challenging, but everything comes together (both literally and figuratively) in the film's spectacular final scenes. A gorgeous, intensely personal ode to art, love, life and film making. Winner of Oscars for Costume Design and as Best Foreign Language Film.

THE ELEPHANT MAN (1980)
*** PG 2:05
DIR: *David Lynch* **CAST:** *Anthony Hopkins, John Hurt, Anne Bancroft, John Gielgud, Wendy Hiller, Freddie Jones.*
Based on the Victorian-era true story of the hideously deformed John Merrick (played by Hurt under several pounds of extraordinary make-up), who is rescued from a circus freak show by a curious, compassionate doctor (Hopkins). Lynch's

richly detailed direction (together with Freddie Francis' beautiful black-and-white camera work) create a vividly believable portrait of turn-of-the-century London, and the performances are all top-notch.

ELMER GANTRY (1960)
*** NR 2:26
DIR: *Richard Brooks* **CAST:** *Burt Lancaster, Jean Simmons, Dean Jagger, Arthur Kennedy, Shirley Jones, Patti Page, Hugh Marlowe*
Powerful drama starring Lancaster as a charismatic con man in the 1920s Midwest who convinces a barnstorming evangelist (Simmons) to let him join her troupe. Jones stars as a small-town girl scorned by Lancaster who turns to prostitution. Grand drama in the best Hollywood style, with memorable performances from Lancaster and Jones, who both won Oscars, as did director Brooks for his screenplay (based on the Sinclair Lewis novel).

EL NORTE (1984)
*** R 2:19
DIR: *Gregory Nava* **CAST:** *Zaide Silva Guitierrez, David Villalpando, Ernesto Gomez Cruz, Alicia Del Lago, Lupe Ontiveros, Trinidad Silva*
The harrowing story of a brother and sister who flee their home in Guatemala after their father is killed by the army. After a brutal journey north,

they cross the border and settle in Los Angeles, but their struggles are not over. Nava's fine direction make this a moving, topical story about the plight of political refugees. The screenplay earned an Oscar nomination.

THE EMPIRE STRIKES BACK (1980)
*** PG 2:08
DIR: *Irvin Kershner* **CAST:** *Mark Hamill, Harrison Ford, Carrie Fisher, Billy Dee Williams, Anthony Daniels, David Prowse, Peter Mayhew, Frank Oz, Kenny Baker, Alec Guinness*
The second, and best, of the *Star Wars* trilogy, *Empire* picks up where the first film left off, as the heroic rebel forces, led by Luke Skywalker (Hamill), Princess Leia (Fisher) and Han Solo (Harrison), battle the evil Empire and the mighty Darth Vader (Prowse, with James Earl Jones' voice). A masterpiece of special-effects wizardry, this is the best-looking science fiction film since *2001*. Won the Oscar for Sound and a special award for its special effects.

ENDLESS SUMMER (1966)
*** NR 1:35
DIR: *Bruce Brown* **CAST:** *Mike Hynson, Robert August*
A classic sports documentary which follows two American surfers as they travel from Malibu to Australia to South Africa in search of the perfect

wave. The idea was to cross and re-cross the equator to be in a perpetual summer, but the film was actually shot over two years because of budget trouble. Still, the warm, tropical sands and spectacular surfing are beautifully shot. Brown's own narration, which moves from sarcasm to social analysis, helps turn this into a fine piece of filmmaking

ENEMIES, A LOVE STORY (1989)
**** R 1:59
DIR: *Paul Mazursky* CAST: *Anjelica Huston, Ron Silver, Lena Olin, Alan King*
One of the finest films of the 1980s, this is the story of a widowed Jewish man who managed to escape from the Holocaust thanks to the help of a woman in America. The two get married, but the man does not really love her, and his eyes quickly begin to wander. He soon embarks on an affair, and to make things even worse, the wife that he thought had died in a concentration camp shows up on his doorstep. Featuring brilliant performances all around and solid direction by Mazursky, this intelligent, funny and sad movie will remind you of the beauty of a great film. A must-see!

ESCAPE FROM NEW YORK (1981)
*** R 1:39
DIR: *John Carpenter* CAST: *Kurt Russell, Harry*

Dean Stanton, Ernest Borgnine, Lee Van Cleef, Donald Pleasance

If you can get over the central implausibility of Manhattan Island, which features some of the most coveted real estate in the world, being turned into one huge jail in the near future, then you will actually enjoy this exciting adventure yarn. A terrorist hijacks Air Force One and crash lands it into the center of Manhattan. The President survives, but how long will he be able to stay alive within this prison? Kurt Russell, a newly arrived inmate, is "volunteered" to get him out in exchange for his freedom. Will he be able to find the President? Gripping from beginning to end, this is one of director John Carpenter's best movies.

E.T.—THE EXTRATERRESTRIAL (1982)
*** PG 1:55
DIR: *Steven Spielberg* **CAST:** *Dee Wallace, Henry Thomas, Peter Coyote, Robert MacNaughton, Drew Barrymore, C. Thomas Howell, Sean Frye*

A young boy named Elliot (Thomas) gives shelter and friendship to an adorable, child-like alien who was accidentally stranded on Earth by his fellow space travelers. This is the highest-grossing movie of all time, and it's easy to see why. Spielberg has created a sweet, heartwarming movie that never once talks down to its audience. Won Oscars for Sound and Visual Effects, as well as for John Williams' rousing score.

EVERYTHING YOU ALWAYS WANTED TO KNOW ABOUT SEX (BUT WERE AFRAID TO ASK) (1972)
*** R 1:27

DIR: *Woody Allen* **CAST:** *Woody Allen, Gene Wilder, Burt Reynolds, Lynn Redgrave, John Carradine, Tony Randall, Louise Lasser, Lou Jacobi*

Allen is hysterical in this send-up of the best-selling book with the long title. In a series of vignettes, Allen illustrates various aspects of our intimate habits. Wilder plays a dignified doctor who risks everything for a fling with a cuddly sheep. Randall plays the captain in the brain control room of a man who's had some, ahh, *difficulty*, as of late. Carradine is a mad doctor who unleashes a massive breast into the countryside. Everything you need to know to make you laugh like a hyena.

EXCALIBUR (1981)
*** PG 2:20

DIR: *John Boorman* **CAST:** *Nicol Williamson, Nigel Terry, Helen Mirren, Nicholas Clay, Corin Redgrave, Gabriel Byrne, Liam Neeson*

Breathtaking version of the King Arthur legends sports a crack cast who all really sink their teeth into the roles (especially Williamson as the crafty, cackling warlock Merlin). The film traces the legend from Arthur's birth to his discovery of the sword Excalibur to Camelot to the Holy Grail, all

113

in just over two exciting hours. Features a number
of spectacular (and very bloody) battle scenes and
the most gorgeous armor ever designed for the
silver screen.

THE EXECUTIONER'S SONG (1982)
*** NR 3:20
DIR: *Lawrence Schiller* CAST: *Tommy Lee Jones,
Rosanna Arquette, Christine Lahti, Eli Wallach*
A gripping adaptation of Norman Mailer's account of the story of Gary Gillmore, a Utah killer
who demanded that the state put him to death for
his crimes, unleashing an avalanche of media
attention and film offers. Jones won an Emmy for
his portrayal of the uneducated, temperamental
murderer who only becomes somebody after he
asks to die. Arquette is first-rate as his spacey
girlfriend. Originally broadcast as a television
mini-series.

THE EXORCIST (1973)
**** R 2:02
DIR: *William Friedkin* CAST: *Ellen Burstyn, Max
von Sydow, Linda Blair, Jason Miller, Lee J. Cobb,
Kitty Winn, Jack MacGowan*
One of the most intense and frightening horror
films of all time. The movie is based on William
Peter Blatty's best-selling occult novel about a 12-
year-old Georgetown girl (Blair) whose body is
possessed by the Devil. Her mother, a famous

film star (Burstyn), a self-doubting young priest (Miller) and the crusty old exorcist Father Merrin (Von Sydow) each try to confront the horror, with varying degrees of success. Blatty won an Oscar for his screenplay.

———————— **F** ————————

THE FABULOUS BAKER BOYS (1989)
*** R 1:53
DIR: *Steve Kloves* **CAST:** *Jeff Bridges, Beau Bridges, Michelle Pfeiffer, Elie Raab, Jennifer Tilly*
Beautifully acted drama about the Baker Boys (Jeff and Beau Bridges), a piano-playing lounge act who, after a mind-numbing 15 years on the Holiday Inn circuit, decide to spice up their routine by hiring a sexy, but aloof, ex-hooker (Pfeiffer) as a vocalist. At the film's heart is the mature, richly drawn relationship between the three leads. Pfeiffer's sizzling performance could melt asbestos, especially during her sultry piano-top version of "Makin' Whoopee."

FAHRENHEIT 451 (1967)
*** NR 1:52
DIR: *Francois Truffaut* **CAST:** *Julie Christie, Oskar Werner, Anton Diffring, Cyril Cusack, Jeremy Spenser*
Werner stars as a futuristic fireman whose job is to burn books, not save houses, in Truffaut's stylish rendition of the famous Ray Bradbury novel.

When Werner encounters the literate Christie, he rebels against the totalitarian government that has banned books for fear of subversion. An interesting, thought-provoking film.

FAIL SAFE (1964)
**** NR 1:51
DIR: *Sidney Lumet* CAST: *Henry Fonda, Walter Matthau, Fritz Weaver, Larry Hagman, Dan O'Herlihy*
A remarkably tense story of a glitch in the "fail safe" system that launches nuclear bombers against Moscow. The President (Fonda) scrambles to retrieve the errant planes, while trying to convince the Kremlin that it's all a horrible mistake. As the seconds tick by, the tension grows until Fonda is forced to make a terrible decision. One of the best anti-war films to come out of the Cold War.

THE FALCON AND THE SNOWMAN (1985)
**** R 2:11
DIR: *John Schlesinger* CAST: *Tim Hutton, Sean Penn, Lori Singer, Pat Hingle, Dorian Harewood*
The wild true story of two middle-class kids from Southern California who transform themselves into Russian spies. Hutton plays Christopher Boyce, the son of a military technocrat who finds work in a super-secret division of a defense contractor, and then turns to espionage. Penn is remarkable as Boyce's manic partner, Daulton Lee,

116

who crumbles under the tension. You may re-member that the real-life Boyce escaped from jail and became the subject of a massive man-hunt that took several years to track him down.

FANNY AND ALEXANDER (1983)
**** R 3:17
DIR: *Ingmar Bergman* **CAST:** *Pernilla Allwin, Bertil Guve, Gunn Wallgren, Allan Edwall, Ewa Froling, Jan Malmsjo, Erland Josephson, Harriet Andersson*
This is actually the *edited* version of Bergman's masterful seven-hour epic (shown in Europe and occasionally on cable) that traces two years in the life of siblings Fanny and Alexander Ekdahl and their loving, if somewhat eccentric, extended family. Gorgeously filmed, deliberately paced and overflowing with exquisite turn-of-the-century period details, the film won Oscars for Best For-eign Film, Costumes, Art Direction and Sven Nykvist's cinematography.

FANTASIA (1940)
*** G 2:00
DIR: *Joe Grant, Dick Huemer* **CAST:** *Leopold Stokowski, Deems Taylor*
Although *Fantasia* is not, as it is often billed, Walt Disney's masterpiece (that honor goes to *Pinocchio*), it is nonetheless a fine, if occasionally self-possessed, example of state-of-the-art 1940's animation from a studio at its creative peak. After

117

the aimless, somewhat experimental opening sequences, the film hits its stride, from the justly famous "The Sorcerer's Apprentice" (starring Mickey Mouse), right up to the dramatic finale, "Night on Bald Mountain."

FANTASTIC VOYAGE (1966)
*** NR 1:40
DIR: *Richard Fleischer* CAST: *Stephen Boyd, Raquel Welch, Donald Pleasence, Arthur O'Connell, Edmond O'Brien*

A wonderfully far-fetched story about a team of scientists who are shrunk down to the size of pinpoint, put into a like-sized sub, and injected into the body of an important scientist who needs detailed brain surgery. As wacko as this sounds, the special effects and drama (provided by a bad guy on board the sub) make for a diverting story. They don't make 'em like this anymore. Oscars for Art Direction, Set Decoration and Special Visual Effects.

FATAL ATTRACTION (1987)
* R 2:00
DIR: *Adrian Lyne* CAST: *Michael Douglas, Glenn Close, Anne Archer, Ellen Hamilton Latzen, Stuart Pankin, Ellen Foley, Fred Gwynne*

A predictable, paint-by-the-numbers thriller starring Douglas as a hapless married man who gets drawn into a terrifying weekend affair with a sexy, but psychotic book editor (Close). The film, although sporting an excellent cast (Douglas, Close and Archer were all nominated for Oscars), is merely an up-scale pastiche of slasher-film clichés that adds nothing new to the genre. Accordingly, the original ending was cut after negative audience previews.

FAT CITY (1972)
*** PG 1:35
DIR: *John Huston* CAST: *Stacy Keach, Jeff Bridges, Susan Tyrell, Candy Clark*
A gritty look at a drunken has-been boxer (Keach) as he makes a futile attempt at a comeback on the hardscrabble back streets of Stockton, Ca. Bridges is a naive, aimless young man who thinks he can make it as a boxer, but instead gets the tar whomped out of him. Tyrell is memorable as Keach's barfly girlfriend. This is a poetic look at losers.

FERRIS BUELLER'S DAY OFF (1986)
*** PG-13 1:43
DIR: *John Hughes* CAST: *Matthew Broderick, Jeffrey Jones, Jennifer Grey, Mia Sara, Alan Ruck*
Broderick stars as a gifted high school underachiever who fakes out parents and vice-principals so he can have a day off from classes. He cajoles his best friend (Ruck) into borrowing his dad's classic Ferrari, gets his girlfriend out of

119

class, and then heads to Chicago for the perfect day. He's pursued by a jerky school official (Jones) who's obsessed with catching the errant student. A stylish, funny romp.

FIDDLER ON THE ROOF (1971)
**** G 3:01

DIR: *Norman Jewison* CAST: *Topol, Norma Crane, Leonard Frey, Michele Marsh*

If you enjoy musicals, then this one is for you! Featuring some great musical numbers and a score by famed composer John Williams, *Fiddler on the Roof* will make you want to get up and dance! Topol plays Teyve, an old-fashioned thinking Jewish man who is shocked to see his daughters turn their back on tradition. The characters in this musical are rich and complex, and above all likeable. This allows it to rise above the usual mere escapism of such movies.

FIELD OF DREAMS (1989)
** PG 1:46

DIR: *Phil Alden Robinson* CAST: *Kevin Costner, Amy Madigan, Gaby Hoffman, Ray Liotta, James Earl Jones, Burt Lancaster*

New Age fable about an Iowa farmer who hears a mysterious voice telling him to build a baseball diamond in the middle of his cornfield. When Shoeless Joe Jackson (Liotta) returns from the dead to play ball, and a reclusive novelist (Jones)—

J.D. Salinger in the original W.P. Kinsella novel, *Shoeless Joe*—comes to watch him, the film builds to a touching climax. Overly sentimental, *Field of Dreams* will either move you to tears or make you wince.

FINAL ANALYSIS (1992)
** R 2:05
DIR: *Phil Joanou* CAST: *Richard Gere, Kim Basinger, Uma Thurman, Eric Roberts*
If you can withstand a slight slump in the middle of the film, then you might just find this to be one of the better thrillers of recent years. Gere plays a psychologist who has grown tired of his stagnant life, so he decides to have an affair with his beautiful sister-in-law. The tension mounts as he realizes that he may have been played for a fool, and he believes that he has been set up to take a murder rap. Featuring an intelligent, albeit sluggish script and solid direction, this is at times a riveting movie. The performances are exceptional all around.

A FISH CALLED WANDA (1988)
*** R 1:47
DIR: *Charles Crichton* CAST: *John Cleese, Jamie Lee Curtis, Kevin Kline, Michael Palin*
The entire cast (including several Monty Python veterans) shines in this wild comedy of sex and crime amidst London's upper crust. Cleese stars

as a proper British lawyer who is seduced by a sexy young thief (Curtis) hoping to find the location of jewels hidden by one of Cleese's clients. Kline is hysterical as Curtis' jealous, moronic boyfriend. Palin is side-splitting as another member of this odd gang of jewel thieves. Crichton was nominated for Best Director, Kline for Best Supporting Actor. Cleese and Crichton shared a nomination for their screenplay.

FITZCARRALDO (1982)
*** PG 2:37
DIR: *Werner Herzog* **CAST:** *Klaus Kinski, Claudia Cardinale, Jose Lewgoy, Paul Hittscher, Miguel Angel Fuentes*

Art reflects life in this vexing story of a man whose dream to build an opera house in the middle of the South America jungle turns into a nightmare. Kinski stars as the obsessed opera fan who must transport a huge steamboat over a jungle mountain in order to open up passage to his performing arts center. The scenes involving this Herculean task are both beautiful and frustrating. Kinski's strange passion is mirrored by Herzog's own struggle to finish this film—actors quit in the middle of production, forcing him to start from scratch. It took five years to realize his vision. The ordeal is depicted in *Burden of Dreams*, the fine documentary by Les Blank.

THE FIVE THOUSAND FINGERS OF DR. T
(1952)
*** NR 1:29
DIR: *Roy Rowland* **CAST:** *Hans Conried, Tommy Rettig, Mary Healy, Peter Lind Hayes*

A strange and delightful Technicolor fantasy about a little boy's worst nightmare—a mountain-top camp for would-be musicians run by a dictatorial piano teacher (Conried) whose plans for the young maestro (Rettig) strike a distinctly sour note. With the help of a friendly plumber, Rettig plans his escape from Conried's clutches. The art direction, including a Texas-sized piano, is surreal and sublime. If all the rhyming in the script sounds familiar, it's because it was co-written by Dr. Seuss. A wonderful departure from the average Disney-style kid's movie.

THE FLAMINGO KID (1984)
*** PG-13 1:40
DIR: *Garry Marshall* **CAST:** *Matt Dillon, Richard Crenna, Hector Elizondo, Janet Jones, Fisher Stevens, Jessica Walter*

Dillon is just right as a working-class kid in the early '60's who finds a job at a swanky Long Island beach club. He is entranced by the wealthy lifestyle of a sports car dealer (Crenna) and his beautiful daughter (Jones, now Mrs. Wayne Gretzky). But Crenna's svengali-like behavior alarms Dillon's dad, an honest plumber (Elizondo) who resents Crenna talking his son out of college. This is a first-rate story about growing up.

FLIGHT OF THE NAVIGATOR (1986)
** PG 1:30
DIR; *Randal Kleiser* CAST: *Joey Cramer, Pee-Wee Herman, Sarah Jessica Parker, Howard Hesseman*
This is a wonderful film for the whole family to enjoy! Joey Cramer plays a young boy who goes into the woods one day, and is amazed to find out that he has emerged twelve years later (even though he has not aged a day!). He soon unravels the mystery, learning that he was abducted by a friendly UFO that studied him and accidentally returned him to the wrong time. Now the government wants to get him and use him as a guinea pig, but he'll do anything it takes to return to the correct point in time. Fun and exciting, and featuring the voice of Pee-Wee Herman as the computer in the spaceship, this movie is sure to delight one and all.

THE FLY (1986)
*** R 1:36
DIR: *David Cronenberg* CAST: *Jeff Goldblum, Geena Davis, John Getz, Joy Boushel, Les Carlson*
David Cronenberg's brilliant remake of the 1958 film of the same name is most definitely not for the faint of heart. Goldblum plays a scientist who invents a "teleportation" machine. When he acci-

dentally fuses his own genes with those of a fly, the film takes off in a fusion of high-tech gore and extremely dark humor. Geena Davis is excellent as Goldblum's romantic interest, and as a result the story takes on a surprisingly tender dimension.

48 HRS. (1982)
*** R 1:36
DIR: *Walter Hill* CAST: *Nick Nolte, Eddie Murphy, Annette O'Toole, James Remar, Frank McRae, David Patrick Kelly, Brion James*
Eddie Murphy made his movie debut in this funny, action-packed "buddy-cop" film. Nick Nolte is the tough as nails detective who gets cool con man Murphy out of prison on a two-day furlough in order to help him capture a couple of San Francisco police killers. The film was a huge box office hit, and Murphy's hilarious scene in a redneck bar is a classic.

THE 400 BLOWS (1959)
**** NR 1:44
DIR: *Francois Truffaut* CAST: *Jean-Pierre Leaud, Patrick Auffay, Claire Maurier, Albert Remy*
French director Francois Truffaut's autobiographical directorial debut about the adventures of troubled adolescent Antoine Doinel, played with great sensitivity by Jean-Pierre Leaud. It follows the story of the Parisian youth as he

becomes a small time criminal in reaction to his
selfish, neglectful parents. One of the best of the
French New Wave film movement, *The 400 Blows*
features brilliant photography and inventive editing. Truffaut would follow the story of his alter
ego in four subsequent films.

FRANTIC (1988)
*** R 2:00
DIR: *Roman Polanski* **CAST:** *Harrison Ford, Betty
Buckley, Emmanuelle Seigner, John Mahoney, Jimmie
Ray Weeks, Gerald Klein*
The tension in the beginning of this film shows
Polanski at his very best. Ford is an American
doctor who arrives in Paris with his wife for a
conference. Within a day, she disappears without
a trace from their hotel room. As hours and then
days pass, Ford becomes more and more frantic.
He receives little help from authorities, and must
investigate himself. Ford is great as a man over his
head in intrigue. Unfortunately, the film's early
promise gives way to a conventional semi-thriller
with the usual cast of bad guys who Ford must
track down to save his wife. Even with this flaw,
the first hour is worth the price of the rental.

THE FRENCH CONNECTION (1971)
**** R 1:44
DIR: *William Friedkin* **CAST:** *Gene Hackman,
Fernando Rey, Roy Scheider, Tony LoBianco*

One of the great action pictures of all-time. Gene Hackman plays maverick New York City detective Popeye Doyle, who is trying to break up an international drug ring. The story is based on the real-life experiences of a former cop. The chase scene, featuring Hackman in an automobile trying to catch up with a runaway subway train, is perhaps the most exciting ever filmed. The movie won Oscars for Best Picture, Director, Screenplay, Editing, and Actor.

THE FRESHMAN (1990)
*** PG 1:42
DIR: *Andrew Bergman* CAST: *Matthew Broderick, Marlon Brando, Maximilian Schell, Penelope Ann Miller, Bruno Kirby, Frank Whaley*
Brando lets down his guard and pokes fun at himself in this screwball comedy about the Mafia, film school and extinction. Broderick plays an NYU film student hired by Brando (who satirizes his own Godfather character) for menial chores, including chauffeuring a Komodo dragon. Broderick soon finds himself as heir-apparent to Brando's crime family. When he discovers he's involved in an exclusive dining club that eats animals on the endangered species list, all hell breaks loose. Bergman's energetic style makes this reminiscent of a madcap 1940's comedy.

FROM HERE TO ETERNITY (1953)
**** NR 1:53

DIR: *Fred Zinnemann* **CAST:** *Burt Lancaster, Montgomery Clift, Deborah Kerr, Donna Reed, Frank Sinatra, Philip Ober, Ernest Borgnine, Jack Warden, Claude Akins.*

This adaptation of the James Jones novel features a blockbuster cast. The story is about Army life in Hawaii in the months leading up to Pearl Harbor. The performances alone are worth the price of admission, particularly Sinatra's turn as the pathetic soldier Maggio. Lancaster and Kerr's love scene on the beach sets the screen on fire. The film won Oscars for Best Picture, Director, Screenplay, Cinematography, and Supporting Actor and Actress.

THE FRONT (1976)
*** PG 1:34

DIR: *Martin Ritt* **CAST:** *Zero Motel, Michael Murphy, Woody Allen, Andrea Marcovicci, Herschel Bernardi*

Allen leads this cast of once-blacklisted actors in the tale of a deli cashier who uses his identity to front for writers unable to work because of the communist scare of the '50s. Allen manages to mix in some humor, but this is an unflinching examination of a dark period in American history. Screenwriter Walter Bernstein, himself once blacklisted, earned an Academy nomination.

FULL METAL JACKET (1987)
*** R 1:57
DIR: *Stanley Kubrick* **CAST:** *Matthew Modine, Dorian Harewood, Adam Baldwin, Arliss Howard, Vincent D'Onofrio, Lee Ermey*
Kubrick takes on the military in this powerful anti-war film. The story begins in boot camp, where a dictatorial drill sergeant takes the recruits (including one badly disturbed young man) through the paces. A shattering event at the end of their training sends them spiraling into the violence of Vietnam. Kubrick casts a cynical eye on U.S. involvement. Modine is excellent as a cocky recruit, as is Ermey, a real-life Marine whose performance as a man who must prepare boys for battle is so convincing that he almost has the audience doing jumping jacks. Kubrick, Michael Herr, and Gustav Hasford were nominated for their screenplay, an adaptation of Hasford's *The Short Timers.*

FUNNY FACE (1957)
*** NR 1:43
DIR: *Stanley Donen* **CAST:** *Audrey Hepburn, Fred Astaire, Kay Thompson, Michel Auclair, Suzy Parker, Ruta Lee.*
A thoroughly enjoyable musical featuring a top-notch Gershwin score ("He Loves and She Loves," "How Long Has This Been Going On," "S'Wonderful"). Astaire plays a fashion photog-

rapher who takes a plain bookstore clerk (Hepburn) and turns her into an internationally famous fashion model. The Parisian locations and the Oscar-nominated costumes give the film a sparkling look.

F/X (1986)
*** R 1:48
DIR: *Robert Mandel* **CAST:** *Bryan Brown, Brian Dennehy, Diane Venora, Cliff De Young, Jerry Orbach, Mason Adams*
Adams plays a Hollywood special effects expert enlisted by the government to stage an assassination of a Mafioso (Orbach). When Brown is betrayed by the government agents, he uses his masterful effects to escape. A stylish, fully-realized piece of entertainment.

━━━━━━━━━━ **G** ━━━━━━━━━━

GALLIPOLI (1981)
*** PG 1:51
DIR: *Peter Weir* **CAST:** *Mel Gibson, Mark Lee, Robert Grubb, Bill Kerr, David Argue*
A powerful, disturbing anti-war film based on the true story of a horrific World War I battle. An idealistic group of young Australian soldiers is sent to Gallipoli, where they are used as fodder in an insane attempt to take an enemy position. It would seem like bad drama if it were not the

truth. The excellent cast and direction find humanity and dignity in this terrible piece of Australian history.

GANDHI (1982)
**** PG 3:11
DIR: *Richard Attenborough* **CAST:** *Ben Kingsley, Candice Bergen, Edward Fox, John Gielgud, Trevor Howard, John Mills, Martin Sheen, John Ratzenberger*
Richard Attenborough's sweeping epic about the life of Mohandas K. Gandhi, the nonviolent man who led India to freedom from British occupation. Ben Kingsley gives a magnificent performance which serves to hold the larger-than-life film together. A then little-known Daniel Day-Lewis shows up as a youth who accosts Gandhi in the street. The film won eight Oscars, including Best Picture, Actor, Director, Screenplay, Cinematography, and Costumes.

THE GENERAL (1927)
**** NR 1:18
DIR: *Buster Keaton* **CAST:** *Buster Keaton, Marion Mack, Glen Cavender, Jim Farley, Joseph Keaton*
Buster Keaton's genius is on full display in this marvelous Civil War tale. A Confederate engineer (Keaton) pursues a train hijacked by Union soldiers into Northern territory. Aside from the fantastic sight gags and loads of laughs, there's beautiful Matthew Brady-influenced photogra-

phy to look at. The film was later remade by Disney as *The Great Locomotive Chase*.

GHOST (1990)
** PG 2:07
DIR: *Jerry Zucker* **CAST:** *Patrick Swayze, Demi Moore, Whoopi Goldberg, Tony Goldwyn, Vincent Schiavelli*
This romantic thriller was a hit with audiences, who alternately laughed and cried as a medium (Goldberg, in an Oscar-winning role) used her psychic powers to help the ghost of the murdered Swayze communicate with his long-suffering girl-friend (Moore). Critics found the film absurd and overly sentimental, but who can argue with a box office that was tops for the year, and ranks it among the most popular of all-time?

THE GHOST AND MRS. MUIR (1947)
**** NR 1:44
DIR: *Joseph Mankiewicz* **CAST:** *Rex Harrison, Gene Tierney, George Sanders, Edna Best*
Harrison is the gruff, pipe-smoking ghost of an English seaman who refuses to leave his magnificent home on the British coast. Tierney is a new widow who is the only renter who won't be scared away. When the two strike an agreement on cohabitation, their initial hostility turns to love. This is a charming, beautifully realized romance.

GHOSTBUSTERS (1984)
*** PG 1:45

DIR: *Ivan Reitman* **CAST:** *Bill Murray, Dan Aykroyd, Harold Ramis, Sigourney Weaver, Rick Moranis, Annie Potts, Ernie Hudson*

Bill Murray shines as one of a trio of parapsychologists (the other two are Ramis and fellow "Saturday Night Live" alumnus Aykroyd) who set out to battle ghosts and other assorted spooks in New York City. Weaver's haunted refrigerator and a giant Staypuff Marshmallow are among the spirits they fight. The special effects and the hilarious comedic bits attracted audiences in droves and spawned a sequel and an animated television series.

GIANT (1956)
**** G 3:20

DIR: *George Stevens* **CAST:** *Rock Hudson, James Dean, Elizabeth Taylor, Carroll Baker, Mercedes McCambridge, Dennis Hopper, Sal Mineo, Chill Wills, Jane Withers*

A Texas soap opera as big as all outdoors features Hudson as a mega-rancher who brings home a bride from the East (Taylor). Dean is the angry young oil man in love with Taylor. McCambridge is Hudson's jealous spinster sister. Contains the famous scene where an oil-covered Dean boasts about finally striking it rich. Before there was *Dallas*, there was *Giant*.

GIGI (1958)
*** G 1:55

DIR: *Vincente Minnelli* **CAST:** *Leslie Caron, Maurice Chevalier, Louis Jourdan, Hermoine Gingold, Jacques Bergerac, Eva Gabor*

Lerner and Loewe musical features Caron in the title role of a young Parisian tomboy who resists her family's efforts to groom her to be a courtesan. When she meets and is charmed by Jourdan, she falls in love and becomes a beautiful woman. Chevalier almost steals the film with his performance of "Thank Heaven for Little Girls." Six Academy Awards, including Best Picture, Director, Writing, Cinematography, Song, Scoring, and Costumes.

GLORY (1989)
**** R 2:02

DIR: *Edward Zwick* **CAST:** *Denzel Washington, Morgan Freeman, Matthew Broderick, Cary Elwes, Jane Alexander, Cliff De Young*

This long-overdue epic tells the story of the 54th regiment of Massachusetts, the first black unit to fight in the Civil War. They fought not only the south, but also for the honor of being more than a token force relegated to menial tasks. Broderick plays the idealistic Union officer who leads them through training and into battle. This overlooked piece of American history makes for a fascinating, important film. Zwick used real Civil War enthusiasts to recreate the bloody battle scenes, and the effect is stunning. Academy nominations for Art Direction and Editing.

THE GODFATHER (1972)
**** R 2:55
DIR: *Francis Ford Coppola* CAST: *Marlon Brando, Al Pacino, James Caan, Richard Castellano, John Cazale, Diane Keaton, Talia Shire, Robert Duvall, Sterling Hayden, Abe Vigoda*
Francis Ford Coppola's epic drama about the Corleones, a powerful Mafia family. Marlon Brando heads an outstanding cast as the aging patriarch, Don Vito Corleone. James Caan, as hotheaded Sonny, and Al Pacino, as Brando's sensitive youngest son Michael, are superb. The action takes us from turn-of-the-century Sicily to Long Island in the 1940s and '50s. Oscars for Best Picture, Actor (Brando), and Screenplay Adaptation.

THE GODFATHER, PART II (1974)
**** R 3:23
DIR: *Francis Ford Coppola* CAST: *Al Pacino, Robert De Niro, Robert Duvall, John Cazale, Diane Keaton, Talia Shire, Lee Strasberg, Michael V. Gazzo, G.D. Spradlin, Harry Dean Stanton*
Coppola pulled off what many thought could never be done: he created a follow-up film that may actually be stronger than his brilliant original. *Part II* masterfully weaves together the life of

the current "Don" (Pacino), who sees his marriage destroyed as he tries to expand the family's
empire, with the early years of Don Vito (De
Niro). Six Oscars, including Best Picture, Director, Supporting Actor (De Niro).

THE GODFATHER, PART III (1990)
*** R 2:41
DIR: *Francis Ford Coppola* **CAST:** *Al Pacino, Diane
Keaton, Talia Shire, Andy Garcia, Eli Wallach, Joe
Mantegna, George Hamilton, Bridget Fonda, Sofia
Coppola, Don Novello, John Savage*
Coppola and Puzo pull it off once again! While
not as strong as the first two films, *The Godfather,
Part III* is still packed with searing drama. This
time around, Pacino tries to break free from the
underworld, only to have fate bring him back into
its clutches. While Coppola's daughter, Sofia, almost sinks the film with her amatuerish performance, this is still a worthy successor to the first
two masterpieces. Garcia is particularly good as
Pacino's pistol-packing nephew.

THE GOLD RUSH (1925)
**** NR 1:12
DIR: *Charlie Chaplin* **CAST:** *Charlie Chaplin, Geor-
gia Hale, Makc Swain, Tom Murray*
An extremely moving, yet very funny classic set
against the Klondike Gold Rush. Chaplin plays

the Little Tramp, a prospector who falls in love with Hale, a dance hall girl, and struggles with a burly gold seeker. Memorable scenes: Chaplin eating an old leather shoe, and Chaplin dancing with two bread rolls. Perhaps the best-loved Chaplin comedy of all-time.

GONE WITH THE WIND (1939)
**** G 3:42
DIR: *Victor Fleming* **CAST:** *Clark Gable, Vivien Leigh, Leslie Howard, Olivia de Havilland, Thomas Mitchell, Hattie McDaniel*
One of the greatest stories ever put on the screen, *Gone With the Wind* somehow manages to keep us on the edge of our seats for almost four hours. The film is based on Margaret Mitchell's novel about the trials and tribulations of an aristocratic plantation family during the Civil War. Vivian Leigh is brilliant as Southern belle Scarlett O'Hara, and Clark Gable still makes women's hearts flutter with his performance as Rhett Butler. Winner of eight Oscars.

GOODBYE, COLUMBUS (1969)
*** PG 1:45
DIR: *Larry Peerce* **CAST:** *Richard Benjamin, Jack Klugman, Ali MacGraw*
In the best tradition of such films as *The Graduate*, this is the wonderful tale of two young lovers (Ali MacGraw and Richard Benjamin) and the social

forces that threaten to separate them. Benjamin is a Christian and MacGraw is Jewish, and the families of each do not appreciate their relationship. Featuring many tender moments, including Jack Klugman's wonderful monologue to onscreen daughter MacGraw during a Bar Mitzvah, this movie will touch your heart in a way that few others films ever will.

GOODBYE MR. CHIPS (1939)
*** NR 1:54
DIR: *Sam Wood* **CAST:** *Robert Donat, Greer Garson, Paul von Henreid, Terry Kilburn, John Mills*
Robert Donat beat out Clark Gable for the Oscar with his masterful performance as shy English schoolmaster Mr. Chips. The scene in which Donat insists on teaching his class in spite of the tragedy he has just suffered has moved many to tears. The fairly slow movement of the film works against it's overall effectiveness, but Donat's performance alone is worth the price of admission. Based on James Hilton's novel.

GOODFELLAS (1990)
*** R 2:26
DIR: *Martin Scorsese* **CAST:** *Robert De Niro, Ray Liotta, Joe Pesci*
Martin Scorsese's film adaptation of *Wiseguy*, Nicholas Pileggi's 1985 book about the rise and fall of Mafia hood Henry Hill (Liotta). Not quite

in the same league as Coppola's *Godfather* epics—
the overly long film falters during its final third—
but excellent acting, cinematography, and editing
mark it as a work to be admired. Joe Pesci, chilling
as a psychotic mobster, won an Oscar for his
performance.

THE GOOD, THE BAD, AND THE UGLY
(1966)
**** NR 2:41
DIR: *Sergio Leone* **CAST:** *Clint Eastwood, Lee Van
Cleef, Eli Wallach, Rada Rasasimov, Mario Brega,
Chelo Alonso*
Ranks at the top of Leone's so-called "spaghetti
westerns," and certainly the best of the director's
"Dollars" trilogy. Bounty hunter Eastwood as the
Man with No Name searches for stolen gold that
belongs to the Confederate government. A thor-
oughly evil Van Cleef and a crooked Wallach join
the scramble for the treasure. Memorable score by
Ennio Morricone.

GORKY PARK (1983)
*** R 2:08
DIR: *Michael Apted* **CAST:** *William Hurt, Brian
Dennehy, Lee Marvin, Joanna Pacula*
This tense and terrific thriller is a movie you won't
want to miss! Hurt plays Soviet police inspector
Arkady Renko, a man who has had one too many
run-ins with the KGB in his pursuit of justice.

When two mutilated bodies are found in Gorky Park, Renko decides that he must get to the bottom of the mystery, even if it means the KGB branding him as a dissident. Intelligently written, nerve wracking, and unpredictable to the very end, this is one of the best (and least seen) suspense thrillers of the 1980s. The direction is intense and economical, and the performances are all excellent.

THE GRADUATE (1967)
**** PG 1:45
DIR: *Mike Nichols* CAST: *Anne Bancroft, Dustin Hoffman, Katherine Ross, Murray Hamilton, Norman Fell, Alice Ghostly*
Mike Nichols' 1960's masterpiece about a young college graduate (Hoffman) who is seduced by an older woman (Bancroft), only to fall in love with her daughter (Ross). Hoffman's search for the meaning of life beyond his parent's world of plastics and swimming pools hit the pulse of an entire generation, and still manages to move audiences with a mixture of pathos and laughter. Soundtrack by Simon and Garfunkle worked perfectly, as did Hoffman's performance in his first major role.

GOTHIC (1986)
** R 1:30
DIR: *Ken Russell* CAST: *Julian Sands, Natasha*

140

Richardson, Gabriel Byrne
A must for horror fans, this movie is based on the true experiences of authors Mary Shelley and Dr. Polidori (who wrote *Frankenstein* and *The Vampyre* respectively). An extremely visual and cerebral piece, this movie is certainly not intended for all viewers, as it can be quite confusing in some parts. The performances of the ensemble cast, under the concise direction of Russell, make for a highly enjoyable film.

GRAND ILLUSION (1937)
**** NR 1:57
DIR: *Jean Renoir* **CAST:** *Erich Von Stroheim, Pierre Fresnay, Jean Gabin*
A group of French prisoners in World War I interact with their German captors in this classic anti-war film from Renoir. Stroheim stars as a courteous German officer who at first treats his fellow French officers, themselves aristocrats, more like guests than prisoners. These war victims are thrown together by economic class, not nationality, in this fascinating film. An Oscar nomination for Best Picture.

THE GRAPES OF WRATH (1940)
**** NR 2:09
DIR: *John Ford* **CAST:** *Henry Fonda, Jane Darwell, John Carradine, Charley Grapewin, Dirros Bowden, Russell Simpson, John Qualen*

John Ford's masterful re-telling of John Steinbeck's Pulitzer Prize-winning novel features Henry Fonda in his greatest role. The story of a group of Okies migrating from the Dust Bowl to California during the Depression is the quintessential tale of people struggling to hold onto their dignity against all odds. Fonda, as ex-con Tom Joad, has one of the most moving moments in the history of cinema with his "I'll be there" speech.

THE GREAT DICTATOR (1940)
*** G 2:05
DIR: *Charles Chaplin* CAST: *Charles Chaplin, Paulette Goddard, Jack Oakie, Reginald Gardiner, Maurice Moscovich, Billy Gilbert, Henry Daniell*
Chaplin's first full-length talkie finds him in a dual role: as a poor Jewish barber and as Adenoid Hynkel, the Great Dictator. This brave and effective spoof of Hitler also features Jack Oakie as Benzino Napaloni, the Mussolini-like leader of "Bacteria." Chaplin's scene with a giant globe/balloon is most memorable. A wonderful blend of slapstick, satire, and social commentary.

THE GREAT ESCAPE (1963)
**** NR 2:48
DIR: *John Sturges* CAST: *Steve McQueen, James Garner, Richard Attenborough, Charles Bronson, James Coburn, David McCallum, Donald Pleasence*
Macho adventure story about Allied prisoners

attempting to break out of a German POW camp during World War II. Fantastic ensemble cast, especially McQueen as the "Cooler King," who has an extraordinary scene in which he races to freedom aboard a motorcycle. Beautifully filmed on location in Germany. James Clavell's script is based on a true story.

THE GREAT SANTINI (1979)
*** PG 1:55
DIR: *Lewis John Carlino* **CAST:** *Robert Duvall, Blythe Danner, Michael O'Keefe, Stan Shaw, Lisa Jane Persky* Duvall is memorable as Bull Meechum, a cigar-chewing, bullet-head Marine pilot who serves his country better than his own family. The emotionally-distant father is more drill sergeant than friend to his troubled son (O'Keefe) who must learn to come out from under his father's thumb. Danner is superior as Duvall's warm, strong wife who must balance family life with her husband's demanding career. Based on the book *The Ace* by Pat (*Prince of Tides*) Conroy. O'Keefe earned an Oscar nomination for his fine performance.

GREEN CARD (1990)
** PG-13 1:48
DIR: *Peter Weir* **CAST:** *Gerard Depardieu, Andie McDowell, Bebe Neuwirth, Gregg Edelman* Depardieu is a down-and-out French composer who's desperate for a green card to stay in New

York. MacDowell is a flower nut who needs a husband to get her dream apartment. The couple set up a phony marriage, but soon find they must do battle, first with themselves and then with the Immigration Service Weir and his cast handle the story with such skill and sweetness that the film's predictability (yes, they fall in love) is overlooked.

THE GREY FOX (1983)
*** PG 1:32
DIR: *Phillip Borsos* **CAST:** *Richard Farnsworth, Wayne Robson, Jackie Burroughs*
Based on the true story of Bill Miner, a train robber of the last century whose well-mannered hold-ups earned him the nickname "Gentleman Bandit." Released into the 20th century after 30 years in prison, the aging thief struggles to adjust to demeaning day labor. A fine, bittersweet story with beautiful scenes of the Northwest and a soft, antique style of cinematography. Look for the poignant scene where Miner watches a silent film of a train robbery, and yearns for the old days. The role fits Farnsworth like a well-worn cowboy hat.

THE GRIFTERS (1990)
**** R 1:53
DIR: *Stephen Frears* **CAST:** *John Cusack, Angelica Huston, Annette Bening*
A stylish story of a group of con artists doing battle against each other. Cusack plays a young,

unambitious grifter who plays it safe and saves his money from small con jobs. Bening, in the best tradition of femme fatale, plays a sex-pot who tries to lure him into bigger schemes. Huston is Cusak's young mother, who works as a money runner for the mob. This is a brilliantly realized adaptation of Jim Thompson's (*After Dark, My Sweet*) novella of greed and deception. Martin Scorsese produced the film, which earned nominations for Best Director, Best Adapted Screenplay by Donald Westlake, and Huston for Best Supporting Actress.

GUNGA DIN (1939)
**** NR 1:57
DIR: *George Stevens* **CAST:** *Cary Grant, Victor McLaglen, Douglas Fairbanks, Jr., Joan Fontaine, Sam Jaffe, Eduardo Ciannelli*
Generally regarded as the finest action-adventure movie of all-time. Based on Rudyard Kipling's poem, the story centers around three heroic British soldiers (Grant, McLaglen and Fairbanks) in 19th century India who fight off a native revolt with the help of local water boy Jaffee. An irresistible blend of action, humor and romance.

GUYS AND DOLLS (1955)
**** NR 2:29
DIR: *Joseph L. Mankiewicz* **CAST:** *Marlon Brando, Jean Simmons, Vivian Blaine, Stubby Kaye, Frank Sinatra*

Sinatra and Brando are two cartoonish New York gangsters who bet on whether Brando can woo a sweet, spinsterish Salvation Army officer (Simmons). Damon Runyon created these memorable gangsters who strangulify da' english language. First-rate retelling of the Broadway smash.

H

HAMLET (1948)
**** NR 2:33
DIR: *Laurence Olivier* **CAST:** *Laurence Olivier, Eileen Herlie, Basil Sydney, Felix Aylmer, Jean Simmons, Stanley Holloway, Peter Cushing*
The definitive film version of Shakespeare's classic about the melancholy Dane. Olivier concentrated on the indecisiveness of the Prince, as well as on the haunting atmosphere that surrounds the action. Though much of the play has been discarded in the interest of a more quickly paced storytelling, this is a wonderful adaptation for both those who are familiar with the work and those who've never read it or seen it performed. Oscars for Best Picture and Best Actor (Olivier) among others.

HAMMETT (1982)
** PG 1:37
DIR: *Wim Wenders* **CAST:** *Frederic Forrest, Marilu Henner, Peter Boyle, Roy Kinnear, Elisha Cook, Jr.*

A stylish story which pits real-life writer Dashiel Hammett against the elite and the underworld of San Francisco. Director Wenders (*Wings of Desire*) has a good feel for Hammett's fictional world and real-life struggles, but the story doesn't add up to anything Hammett would write on his worst day. Still, the look and atmosphere of the film are first rate. And in one nice reference, Elisha Cook Jr. has a small part—he also played the punk killer in the *Maltese Falcon*, the finest screen version of Hammett's work.

HANNA AND HER SISTERS (1986)
**** PG-13 1:47
DIR: *Woody Allen* **CAST:** *Woody Allen, Michael Caine, Mia Farrow, Carrie Fisher, Barbara Hershey, Maureen O'Sullivan, Max von Sydow, Sam Waterston, Julie Kavner, John Turturro, Joanna Gleason*
Stands next to *Annie Hall* and *Manhattan* as Allen's most accomplished and satisfying film. Ostensibly about the lives of three sisters over a two year period, Allen masterfully weaves several subplots together to create a humorous and heartwarming portrait of contemporary New Yorkers. The cast is nothing short of fantastic, especially the delicious Barbara Hershey and the crazed Dianne Weist (who won an Oscar for her performance).

A HARD DAY'S NIGHT (1964)
*** G 1:27

DIR: *Richard Lester* **CAST:** *John Lennon, Paul McCartney, George Harrison, Ringo Starr, Wilfred Brambell, Victor Spinetti*

Richard Lester, working in the style of the Marx Brothers comedies, surprised everyone by delivering a musical-comedy classic in the Beatles' first go-around with film. The humor and energy of the young mop tops is conveyed effortlessly, and of course the soundtrack is filled with such gems as "Can't Buy Me Love," "And I Love Her," and "I Should Have Known Better."

HARD TIMES (1975)
*** PG 1:37

DIR: *Walter Hill* **CAST:** *Charles Bronson, James Coburn, Strother Martin, Jill Ireland*

A stylish, gritty tale of a jobless drifter (Bronson) who scratches out a living as a bare-knuckle fighter during the Depression. Coburn is a manager who sees a potential gold mine in Bronson. Together they take on all comers in a series of well-directed back alley fights. The violence, while graphic, is never gratuitous.

HAROLD AND MAUDE (1972)
*** PG 1:32

DIR: *Hal Ashby* **CAST:** *Bud Cort, Ruth Gordon, Vivian Pickles, Cyril Cusack, Charles Tyner, Ellen Geer*

This cult favorite has aged surprisingly well. Harold (Cort), a bored and rich 20 year old obsessed with death falls in love with Maude (Gordon), a lively and wacky 79 year old who turns him on to the joys of life. Black humor abounds, especially in Cort's phony suicide scenes. The music by Cat Stevens somehow manages to ideally suit the overall mood and tone of the film.

HEAD (1968)
*** R 1:26
DIR: *Bob Rafelson* CAST: *Jack Nicholson, The Monkees, Teri Garr, Timothy Carey*
Jack Nicholson wrote this drug-induced screenplay before bursting into fame with his performance as George, the alcoholic lawyer in Dennis Hopper's counter-culture classic *Easy Rider*. Featuring The Monkees (that Fab Four influenced band) in roles unlike any they had ever had on television, this interesting and funny psychedelic movie is to be experienced, rather than followed (as with a conventional plot). Unlike almost any other film you have ever seen, *Head* is a very good movie.

HEARTLAND (1981)
*** PG 1:33
DIR: *Richard Pearce* CAST: *Conchata Ferell, Rip Torn, Lilla Skala, Megan Folsom, Barry Primus, Amy Wright*

A low-budget, big-talent film about a widow (Ferell) and her young daughter who become housekeepers for a Wyoming rancher (Torn). They marry, as much for survival as for love. The film is at its best when defining the hardships of early 20th century ranch life.

HEARTS OF DARKNESS: A FILMMAKER'S APOCALYPSE (1991)
**** R 1:36
DIR: *Fax Bahr, Eleanor Coppola* **CAST:** *Francis Coppola, Martin Sheen, Marlon Brando, Dennis Hopper*
Many people consider this documentary about the making of *Apocalypse Now* to be even better than the movie! Filled with all of the delightful gossip that makes Hollywood so enticing, this film chronicles the problems faced by acclaimed director Francis Ford Coppola in trying to bring his controversial vision of the Vietnam War to the screen. Featuring many frank interviews, in which we see just how charismatic and exciting many filmmakers and actors really are, this documentary is loads of fun to watch. There is even a wonderful blooper in which Marlon Brando winces in pain and announces, "I swallowed a bug!" A must-see.

HEATHERS (1989)
*** R 1:42
DIR: *Michael Lehmann* **CAST:** *Winona Ryder, Chris-*

tian Slater, Shannen Doherty, Lisanne Falk, Penelope Milford

Probably the only comedy ever made about teen suicide. Ryder plays a newly-initiated "Heather," a group of stuck-up, popular high school girls who are so much alike they go by the same name. Slater plays a Jack Nicholson-like newcomer who enlists Ryder in his murderous plans, which include writing hoaky suicide notes for his high school victims. This is a biting satire about popularity, peer pressure and media hype. Both Ryder and Slater are excellent.

HEAVEN CAN WAIT (1978)
*** PG 1:40
DIR: *Warren Beatty, Buck Henry* **CAST:** *Warren Beatty, Julie Christie, Jack Warden, Dyan Cannon, Charles Grodin, James Mason, Buck Henry*

Beatty's remake of 1941's *Here Comes Mr. Jordan*, is a gentle romantic comedy/fantasy that tends to grow on you with repeated watchings. When an inept angel (Henry) takes a star quarterback (Beatty) before his time, the angel's superior (Mason) puts the quarterback back on Earth in the body of a millionaire. Unfortunately, the millionaire's wife (Cannon) and her lover (Grodin) are plotting his murder. Grodin and Cannon provide the laughs, while Beatty and Christie dish out the romance.

HEAVEN HELP US (1985)
*** R 1:44
DIR: *Michael Dinner* CAST: *Andrew McCarthy, Keivn Dillon, Wallace Shawn, Donald Sutherland, Mary Stuart Masterson*
Underappreciated story of teenagers coping with angst and coming of age within a Catholic school, this movie is sure to delight you. Warm and funny, it focuses on Andrew McCarthy, the new kid in town, and his attempts to woo an insular young woman (Mary Stuart Masterson). Featuring brilliant performances which bring life to the variety of characters (Kevin Dillon almost steals the show as a homophobic schoolmate with a bad attitude), and an intelligent and witty script, this movie is not to be missed. Wallace Shawn (*The Princess Bride*) is terrific in his bit part as a priest who oversees a dance at the Catholic school.

HELTER SKELTER (1976)
*** NR 3:14
DIR: *Tom Gries* CAST: *Steve Railsback, George DiCenzo, Nancy Wolfe, Christina Hart, Marilyn Burns*
A compelling television mini-series adapted from the book by Vincent Bugliosi, the L.A. prosecutor who put Charles Manson and his followers behind bars. The film uses a documentary style to tell the story of the Manson family and the gruesome Tate-LaBianca murders. Railsback bears a chilling resemblance to Manson. Remarkably, the

film makers did not sensationalize this horrific story.

HENRY: PORTRAIT OF A SERIAL KILLER
(1989)
*** NR 1:30
DIR: *John McNaughton* **CAST:** *Michael Rooker, Tom Towles, Tracy Arnold*
This is not a film for the faint of heart. Unlike *Silence of the Lambs*, this examination of a psychopath has a raw, documentary feel. Rooker, in a powerful, understated performance, is absolutely chilling as the drifter who kills indiscriminately. His character is based partly on real-life killer Henry Lee Lucas, who wandered the country in search of victims. Don't expect good cops and chase scenes here. The film is all the more frightening because it smacks of real life, not Hollywood.

THE HIDDEN FORTRESS (1958)
**** NR 2:06
DIR: *Akira Kurosawa* **CAST:** *Toshiro Mifune, Misa Uehara, Kamatari Fujiwara, Susumu Fujita, Takashi Shimura*
This is the film that inspired George Lucas to make the epic *Star Wars* trilogy. Mifune stars as a deposed General who enlists two inept samurai to help rescue an ungrateful princess and a considerable treasure. Those not comfortable with

Japanese film may find the acting stilted and the pace slow. But keep an open mind—this is a wonderful, action-packed film. Make sure to get the long version, since another version was cut to 90 minutes for American audiences.

HIGH NOON (1952)
**** NR 1:25
DIR: *Fred Zinnemann* CAST: *Gary Cooper, Grace Kelly, Lloyd Bridges, Thomas Mitchell, Katy Jurado, Otto Kruger, Lon Chaney*
A great Western featuring a stand-out performance from Gary Cooper as the brave sheriff who faces an outlaw gang on his wedding day. Kelly plays Cooper's Quaker wife, a woman who abhors violence and who refuses to support her husband's decision to carry out the gunfight. A great deal of suspense was achieved by the Oscar-winning editors, who allow the story to unfold in real time.

HIGH PLAINS DRIFTER (1973)
*** PG 1:45
DIR: *Clint Eastwood* CAST: *Clint Eastwood, Verna Bloom, Mitchell Ryan, Stefan Gierasch, Marianna Hill*
Eastwood is at his surly best in this moody, supernatural western about a loner who rides into town and then protects the populace from a gang of menacing thugs. The twist here is that Eastwood's

cowboy is a bit of a thug himself who terrorizes the locals before he saves them. Sort of like *Shane* meets *Ghost*. Eastwood has a sure hand in this early outing as director.

HOLLYWOOD SHUFFLE (1987)
*** R 1:22
DIR: *Robert Townsend* CAST: *Robert Townsend, Anne-Marie Johnson, Starletta Dupois, Keenan Ivory Wayans*

Townsend maxed out his VISA card to complete this low-budget comedy about the struggles of a young black actor who faces rejection and stereotyping at every turn. The movie hops back and forth between Townsend's fantasies (we see him as a Super Hero, a street-wise movie reviewer, and an Indiana-Jones type) and the harsh reality of the limits placed upon black actors. When he finally finds work playing a jive-talking pimp, the actor must choose between a paycheck and his pride. This is a funny and thoughtful first-effort by Townsend.

HOME ALONE (1990)
** PG 1:42
DIR: *Chris Columbus* CAST: *Macaulay Culkin, Joe Pesci, Daniel Stern, John Heard, Catherine O'Hara*

One of the biggest box office hits of all time features Culkin as an 8 year old boy who is accidentally left home alone by his parents when they take a vacation to Paris. Two bumbling thieves (Pesci and Stern) try to rob Culkin's home, but the clever boy thwarts their every attempt with ingenious schemes. Director Columbus's cartoonish style helps to take the bite out of the potentially violent situations, and dishes up plenty of healthy laughs as well.

HOMEWARD BOUND: THE INCREDIBLE JOURNEY (1993)
*** G 1:24
DIR: *DuWayne Dunham* **CAST:** *Robert Hays, Kim Greist, Jean Smart, Benj Thall, Kevin Chevalia, the voices of Michael J. Fox, Don Ameche, Sally Field*
Two dogs and a cat are left with family friends for an extended visit. But when a gate is left open, the trio (with the voices of Fox, Ameche and Field) take off into the mountains in an attempt to make their way home. They face separation, hunger and danger on their journey, but also learn the meaning of inter-species friendship. Pet owners will cry their eyes out during this fine Disney film. Non-pet owners probably won't.

HOMICIDE (1991)
*** R 1:42
DIR: *David Mamet* **CAST:** *Joe Mantegna, William Macy, Natalija Nogulich, Ving Rhames, Rebecca Pidgeon, Vincent Guastaferro, Lionel Mark, Jack Wallace*

A hard-boiled detective (Mantegna) investigates the murder of an elderly shopkeeper, which leads to a shadowy conspiracy. As with much of Mamet's work, the distinct rhythm of the dialogue and fine acting mitigates any flaws in the story.

HONEY, I SHRUNK THE KIDS (1989)
** PG 1:33
DIR: *Joe Johnston* **CAST:** *Rick Moranis, Matt Frewer, Marcia Strassman, Keistine Sutherland, Thomas Brown, Jared Rushton*
Rick Moranis invents a shrinking machine only to have it accidentally reduce his children and their next door neighbors to a microscopic size. The four kids must battle everything from bees to a bowl of cereal in order to make it back to their normal size alive. Excellent special effects add to the family fun quality of the comedy / adventure / fantasy.

HOPE AND GLORY (1987)
*** PG-13 1:53
DIR: *John Boorman* **CAST:** *Sarah Miles, David Hayman, Derrick O'Connor, Susan Woolridge, Sammi Davis, Ian Bannen*
John Boorman's perfectly realized memoir of what it was like to be a young boy in London during the early years of World War II. Told through the eyes of ten year old Edwards, the film displays the War

as one big adventure—ducking air raids and
bombings, collecting shrapnel and other war sou-
venirs, searching through bombed-out homes,
etc. Unlike any other War movie you're ever
likely to see, *Hope and Glory* is at once moving,
funny, and dramatic.

THE HOT SPOT (1990)
** R 2:10
DIR: *Dennis Hopper* **CAST:** *Don Johnson, Virginia
Madsen, Jennifer Connelly, Charles Martin Smith*
A stranger (Johnson) wanders into a mean little
Texas town and finds work as a hustling used-car
salesmen. Within a week or two, he's gotten involved with adultery, blackmail, a bank robbery
and murder. Johnson is good as the drifter who
must choose between two beautiful women.
Madsen is sexy, but perhaps a bit too broad, as the
film's femme fatale. The film is a stylish homage
to *film noir*, and the acting is uniformly good, but
the story is not unique enough to keep our attention.

HOT TO TROT (1988)
** PG 1:23
DIR: *Michael Dinner* **CAST:** *Bob Goldthwait, Dabney
Coleman, Gilbert Gottfried, Tim Kazurinsky*
One of the silliest films in recent memory.
Goldthwait, the manic comic of *Police Academy*
fame, stars here as a dumb stockbroker who is

befriended by a talking horse a la Mr. Ed. John Candy did the voice for the brainy thoroughbred who helps Goldthwait outflank a partner (Coleman) plotting to take control of the firm. Although it's no work of film genius, this is a diverting bit of entertainment with a few real belly laughs. Watch for the horse lounging on a sofa.

HOUSE OF GAMES (1987)
*** R 1:42
DIR: *David Mamet* **CAST:** *Lindsay Crouse, Joe Mantegna, J.T. Walsh, Lilia Skala, Ricky Jay*
Playwright David Mamet excels here directing his own script about a group of con artists plying their trade. Crouse plays an esteemed, troubled psychiatrist who is drawn into the underworld by a slick, well-dressed confidence man (Mantegna). She's fascinated by this strange world of manipulation and fraud. But things get ugly as she's seduced deeper and deeper into the game. What follows is a virtual roller coaster of plot twists, brilliantly executed by Mamet and this fine ensemble cast. Although not a big hit, this was one of the finest films of the year.

HOW TO SUCCEED IN BUSINESS WITHOUT REALLY TRYING (1967)
**** NR 2:01
DIR: *David Swift* **CAST:** *Robert Morse, Michele Lee,*

Rudy Vallee, Anthony Teague, Maureen Arthur, Sammy Smith, Robert Q. Lewis

Morse stars in this frolicking musical based on the smash Broadway hit. The ambitious young man starts out as a window washer, but with the help of a dime-store handbook he quickly rises through the ranks of a wicket company. A first-rate score.

THE HUNCHBACK OF NOTRE DAME (1939)
**** NR 1:57

DIR: *William Dieterle* **CAST:** *Charles Laughton, Sir Cedric Hardwicke, Thomas Mitchell, Maureen O'Hara, Edmond O'Brien, Alan Marshall*

The Victor Hugo story brought to the screen once again—Lon Chaney starred in the original 1923 silent version—courtesy of a haunting performance by Charles Laughton, who is magnificent as Quasimodo. Most touching scene: The deformed bell ringer rescues the gypsy girl who had been so kind to him. A beautiful recreation of 15th century Paris.

THE HUNT FOR RED OCTOBER (1990)
*** PG 2:15

DIR: *John McTiernan* **CAST:** *Alec Baldwin, Sean Connery, Sam Neill, Scott Glenn, James Earl Jones, Richard Jordan, Tim Curry, Peter Firth*

The first of writer Tom Clancy's military potboilers to be brought to the screen. The film features Baldwin as a reluctant hero who must try to save a renegade Soviet sub from its own military. Connery is charismatic as the Soviet sub captain making a desperate attempt to defect to America along with his state-of-the-art nuclear submarine. McTiernan (*Die Hard*) keeps the story rolling along at a thrilling pace. It's lucky the film was made when it was, since the American-Soviet conflict seems happily outdated. The film won an Academy Award for Sound Effects Editing, and was nominated for Editing and Sound.

THE HUSTLER (1961)
*** NR 2:15
DIR: *Robert Rossen* **CAST:** *Paul Newman, Jackie Gleason, Piper Laurie, George C. Scott, Jake LaMotta, Vincent Gardenia*
Perhaps Newman's most brilliant performance as Fast Eddie Felson, a pool shark who has an affair with alcoholic Laurie and challenges Minnesota Fats (Gleason) to a big match. A vivid portrait of the world of seedy pool halls and flophouses. Twenty five years later, Martin Scorsese would make its sequel, *The Color of Money*.

INCIDENT AT OGLALA (1992)
*** PG 1:29
DIR: *Michael Apted* **CAST:** *Robert Redford*
This documentary, which features Redford as its

narrator, is so precise that it can get somewhat confusing to watch. It recounts the "incident at Oglala," a Native American reservation in South Dakota, in which several FBI agents were killed. The documentary asserts that Leonard Peltier, the man currently serving time in prison for the murders, is innocent and was framed. An interesting and unusual glimpse into the life and culture of Native Americans.

IN COLD BLOOD (1967)
*** R 2:14
DIR: *Richard Brooks* **CAST:** *Robert Blake, John Forsythe, Scott Wilson, Paul Stewart, Gerald S. O'Loughlin*
A stark, tense rendition of Truman Capote's classic piece of New Journalism. Wilson and Blake play two sociopaths who wipe out a Kansas farm family for no apparent reason. The story follows them through their getaway, to their capture and execution. Brooks wisely kept Capote's remarkable sense of doom throughout this fine film, and received an Oscar nomination for his directorial effort.

THE INCREDIBLE MR. LIMPET (1964)
*** NR 1:42
DIR: Arthur Lubin **CAST:** *Don Knotts, Carole Cook, Jack Weston, Andrew Duggan*
Knotts plays a sad-sack civilian who's been rated

4-F during World War II. His obsession with fish annoys his wife (Cook) and best friend (Weston), but he persists anyway. On an outing to the ocean, he takes a tumble into the water and turns miraculously into a big, intelligent fish who wears glasses. Thus metamorphosized, he gets to help the war effort and meets the girl fish of his dreams. Seems like Knotts was always a fish trapped in the body of a man.

INDECENT PROPOSAL (1993)
* R 1:58

DIR: *Adrien Lyne* **CAST:** *Demi Moore, Woody Harrelson, Robert Redford, Oliver Platt*

Demi Moore and Woody Harrelson are a couple down on their luck, but things seem more promising when Redford offers them *one million dollars* for one night of passionate lovemaking with Moore. Naturally, Harrelson gets jealous and the couple is torn apart, but will they have the strength to make up again? Who really cares? Featuring some of the worst acting of any film in recent years (including Redford, who *obviously* didn't care), this movie nevertheless captured the imagination of a substantial portion of the movie-going public. There is also one scene which is tantamount to movie-going blasphemy, in which Redford describes the one true love of his life . . . in a line copied almost verbatim from Orson Welles' masterpiece *Citizen Kane*!

INDIANA JONES AND THE LAST CRUSADE
(1989)
** PG-13 2:06

DIR: *Steven Spielberg* **CAST:** *Harrison Ford, Sean Connery, Denholm Elliot, Alison Doody, John Thys-Davies, Julian Glover, River Phoenix*

Speilberg regains his touch with his third film in the Indiana Jones saga. This time out, our hero joins his archeologist father (Connery) in a search for the Holy Grail. Lots of suspenseful and fun-filled action and adventure as they fight off Nazis who also want to get their hands on the relic. Still not near the film that *Raiders* was, but much better than *Temple of Doom*.

INDIANA JONES AND THE TEMPLE OF DOOM (1984)
** PG 2:04

DIR: *Steven Spielberg* **CAST:** *Harrison Ford, Kate Capshaw, Ke Huy Quan*

Director Steven Spielberg briefly lost his magic touch with this film, which has none of the charm and wit of the other two in the Indiana Jones series. In this adventure, Indy journeys to Asia to do battle with the slave-driving cult of Thuggee. He finds several magical rocks which are sure to make him famous and rich, but he decides to return them to their rightful owners instead. Dark and frightening, and verging on jingoistic, this movie may be exciting, but it's not fun in the way that *Raiders of the Lost Ark* was. You won't be disappointed, particularly as Harrison Ford is true to form, but you won't be delighted either.

THE INFORMER (1935)
**** NR 1:31
DIR: *John Ford* **Cast:** *Victor McLaglen, Preston Foster, Joseph Sawyer, Una O'Connor, Heather Angel, Margot Grahame, Wallace Ford, Donald Meek*
This is one of those rare films that remains every bit as relevant today as when it was made. McLaglen gives his finest performance as an I.R.A. operative who betrays his fellow members for reward money. The film is built around McLaglen's growing guilt. The hardscrabble world of Ireland's underclass is depicted brilliantly here by legendary director John Ford. This is a gripping, timeless film which should not be missed. Ford and McLaglen both won Oscars for the efforts, as did Dudley Nichols' screenplay and the score by Max Steiner. The film was nominated for Best Picture.

INHERIT THE WIND (1960)
**** NR 2:07
DIR: *Stanley Kramer* **CAST:** *Spencer Tracy, Fredric March, Dick York, Gene Kelly, Florence Eldridge, Harry Morgan*
Tracy shines in this courtroom drama of free speech, evolution and Biblical beliefs. Adapted

from a play about the 1925 Scopes trial, Tracy's character is based on famed trial attorney Clarence Darrow as he defends Scopes for teaching Darwin's theory of evolution to the students of a small, Bible-Belt town. March is excellent as the bible-thumping prosecutor who argues for Creationism. One of the best courtroom dramas ever made. Tracy received an Oscar nomination for his performance. Nathan Douglas and Harold Smith received nominations for their screenplay, as did Ernest Laszlo for his cinematography.

IN THE HEAT OF THE NIGHT (1967)
**** NR 1:49
DIR: *Norman Jewison* **CAST:** *Sidney Poitier, Rod Steiger, Warren Oates, Lee Grant, Scot Wilson, Larry Gates, Quentin Dean*
A superbly made film in every respect. The performances, especially Poitier as the big-city detective and Steiger, who won the Oscar for his portrayal of a Mississippi sheriff. Norman Jewison's direction and Stirling Sylliphant's screenplay have aged well. A thrilling mystery with a powerhouse social conscience. Oscar for Best Movie among others. Later a television series.

INVASION OF THE BODY SNATCHERS (1956)
*** PG 1:56
DIR: *Don Siegel* **CAST:** *Kevin McCarthy, Dana*

GUIDE TO TV MOVIES

Wynter, Larry Gates, King Donovan, Carolyn Jones, Virginia Christine
Science-fiction thriller with McCarthy-era overtones hasn't lost its power to send a chill up the spine. A doctor (McCarthy) and his wife (Wynter) try to put a halt to an invasion of soulless pod people in their small hometown. Based on Jack Finney's novel, *The Body Snatchers*. The climax, with McCarthy running onto the freeway to shout his warning, is memorable.

IRONWEED (1987)
*** R 2:23
DIR: *Hector Babenco* **CAST:** *Jack Nicholson, Meryl Streep, Carroll Baker, Tom Waits, Michael O'Keefe, Fred Gwynne*
Nicholson stars as a homeless drifter in the 1930s who is haunted by the ghosts of men he has killed in barroom brawls or self-defense, and guilt-ridden over the death of his infant son many years before. Streep is his boozy companion who fantasizes about singing again. The film's grim surrealism about lost lives is in keeping with William Kennedy's Pulitzer Prize-winning book. Both Streep and Nicholson were nominated for Oscars.

IT HAPPENED ONE NIGHT (1934)
**** NR 1:45
DIR: *Frank Capra* **CAST:** *Clark Gable, Claudette Colbert, Walter Connolly, Roscoe Karns, Alan Hale*

167

A great screwball comedy with plenty of romance and wit. Spoiled heiress Colbert meets and falls in love with reporter Gable during a cross-country bus trip. At first intending to use each other, the argumentative couple winds up falling in love. The first film to win all five major Academy Awards: Best Picture, Director, Actor, Actress, and Screenplay.

IT'S A WONDERFUL LIFE (1946)
**** NR 2:09
DIR: *Frank Capra* CAST: *James Stewart, Donna Reed, Lionel Barrymore, Thomas Mitchell, Henry Travers, Beulah Bondi, Ward Bond.*
Frank Capra's feel-good Christmas classic. George Bailey (Stewart) thinks he's a failure and is close to suicide when he is rescued by an angel (Travers) who shows him what life in his small town would have been like had he never been born. A warm, sensitive, and sentimental film. Stewart is in top form. Capra called this his personal favorite.

--- **J** ---

JACKKNIFE (1989)
*** R 1:41
Dir: *David Jones* CAST: *Robert De Niro, Ed Harris, Kathy Baker*
One of the better films exploring the psychic harms inflicted by Vietnam. De Niro and Harris

play war buddies who struggle to survive in small-town America, even though their memories torment them. Baker is excellent as Harris' spinsterish sister who falls for De Niro's alcoholic vet. Although both are wounded in one way or another, they manage to connect. This is a small, touching film based on Stephen Mcnally's play, *Strange Snow*.

THE JACKSONS: AN AMERICAN DREAM
(1992)
** NR 3:45
DIR: *Karen Arthur* **CAST:** *Lawrence-Hilton Jacobs, Angela Bassett, Vanessa Williams, Holly Robinson, Billy Dee Williams*
This movie lives up quite well to its title. It chronicles the rise of the Jackson 5, from their origins as a poor family in Indiana to superstar status in Hollywood, California. The cast is quite excellent, featuring such award-winning actors as Angela Bassett and Billy Dee Williams, and the actor who portrays Michael is especially convincing (although his face does not change in the same way that Michael's did!). Lawrence-Hilton Jacobs is particularly memorable as Joe Jackson, the famous singers' abusive and egomaniacal father who almost caused their breakup on more than one occasion. Entertaining for most viewers, this is definitely a must-see for fans of the Jackson family!

JACOB'S LADDER (1990)
*** R 1:55
Dir: *Adrian Lynne* **CAST:** *Tim Robbins, Danny Aiello, Elizabeth Pena, Jason Alexander, Matt Craven*
Robbins stars as a haunted Vietnam vet in this disturbing, nightmarish psycho-thriller. Working as a Manhattan postman, he is suddenly overcome by hallucinations that he suspects are related to events during the war. Or is he having a psychotic breakdown? As the film progresses, it becomes more and more difficult for both the character and the audience to discern fantasy from reality. It's to the credit of the screenplay that it all ends up making sense.

JAILHOUSE ROCK (1957)
** NR 1:36
DIR: *Richard Thorpe* **CAST:** *Elvis Presley, Judy Tyler, Vaughn Taylor, Dean Jones, Mickey Shaughnessy*
Presley's best, and most popular, film. Elvis is accused of manslaughter and sent to prison. Once in the big house, he learns how to play guitar and sing, and he soon becomes a rock and roll star. Tyler plays the record producer who guides his career. Elvis is outstanding, particularly when performing such great tunes as "Treat Me Nice," "Don't Leave Me Now," "Baby I Don't Care," and the title song.

JAWS (1975)
*** PG 2:04

DIR: *Steven Spielberg* **CAST:** *Roy Scheider, Robert Shaw, Richard Dreyfuss, Lorraine Gary, Murray Hamilton, Jeffrey Kramer*

A vacation spot on the Atlantic Ocean is terrorized by a 25 foot great white shark. Oceanographer Dreyfuss, shark hunter Shaw, and local cop Scheider go after the creature in some spine-tingling action. Great score by John Williams. Director Speilberg took Peter Benchley's bestseller and turned it into a highly entertaining, suspenseful film. Don't close your eyes during the breathless finale!

JEAN DE FLORETTE (1986)
**** PG 2:01

DIR: *Claude Berri* **CAST:** *Gerard Depardieu, Yves Montand, Daniel Auteuil*

Depardieu stars as a transplanted urbanite who inherits a small farm in 1920's France. Although the location is foreign, the film is reminiscent of an old-fashioned Western in which greedy ranchers try to run off dirt farmers. As Depardieu struggles to survive by growing flowers, his neighbors (subtly played by Montand and Auteuil) conspire to ruin him. It's excruciating to watch Depardieu's idealism dry up along with his land. The film's sequel, *Manon of the Spring,* continues this classic story.

171

JEREMIAH JOHNSON (1972)
**** PG 1:50
DIR: *Sydney Pollack* **CAST:** *Robert Redford, Will Geer, Stefan Gierasch, Josh Tyner, Allyn Ann McLerie*
A beautiful film about a mountain man (Redford) who hunts and traps his way through the Rockies in the 1800s. He is given an Indian woman as a bride, takes a young boy under his wing, and takes revenge after Indians attack. Geer is excellent as a grizzled old man who teaches Redford the ways of the mountains. The scenery and story are magnificent.

THE JERK (1979)
*** R 1:34
DIR: *Carl Reiner* **CAST:** *Steve Martin, Bernadette Peters, Mabel King, Richard Ward*
One of Steve Martin's most hilarious movies of all times, this is the story of a white man who was "born a poor black child in the South." He is so stupid that he doesn't realize he was adopted until he becomes a man. He then decides to venture off into the great big world in order to find himself, and he eventually arrives in Hollywood, California. There, he marries a beautiful woman and becomes a rich man after inventing a ridiculous pair of sunglasses. But his stupidity threatens him even when he has enough money to burn: he is so gullible that he will give huge sums of money to anyone who comes up to him with a sob

story. Featuring a performance that could only be delivered by Steve Martin, and hilarious direction by veteran comedian Carl Reiner, this is a comedy classic not to be missed.

JEZEBEL (1938)
*** NR 1:44
DIR: *William Wyler* **CAST:** *Bette Davis, Henry Fonda, George Brent, Margaret Lindsay, Donald Crisp, Fay Bainter, Richard Cromwell, Henry O'Neill*
A tour-de-force by Davis as the Southern belle who drives beau Fonda away when she attempts to make him jealous. She later redeems herself when Fonda contracts yellow fever and Davis reenters his life to nurse him. Set in the years preceding the Civil War, the film has the expansive feel of a historical drama. Davis won the Oscar for Best Actress (her second), while Bainter took home the Award for Best Supporting Actress.

JOHNNY HANDSOME (1989)
*** R 1:35
DIR: *Walter Hill* **CAST:** *Mickey Rourke, Ellen Barkin, Elizabeth McGovern, Morgan Freeman, Scott Wilson*
Rourke gives one of his best performances as a disfigured criminal given a second chance. In prison for a violent crime, Rourke's character undergoes lengthy plastic surgery to repair a horrible birth defect. He is both physically and emotionally transformed by the operation, but

must then confront his past by taking revenge against those who put him in jail. McGovern portrays a kind, attractive women who the now-handsome Rourke falls for, but his appetite for vengeance is too great. Ry Cooder delivers a moody, atmospheric score.

JOURNEY TO THE CENTER OF THE EARTH (1959)
*** NR 2:12
DIR: *Henry Levin* **Cast:** *James Mason, Pat Boone, Arlene Dahl, Diane Baker, Thayer David*
A fine adaptation of the far-fetched Jules Verne yarn about a group of explorers—led by an unctuous Scottish professor (Mason)—who find their way past reptilian monsters and lost civilizations to the center of the globe. As outlandish as the plot may be, the film is surprisingly compelling, with enough humor to keep the whole thing in perspective. The special effects, score and acting are all first-rate. A perfect movie for a lazy Sunday afternoon.

JUDGMENT AT NUREMBERG (1961)
*** NR 3:09
DIR: *Stanley Kramer* **CAST:** *Spencer Tracy, Burt Lancaster, Richard Widmark, Marlene Dietrich, Judy Garland, Maximilian Schell, Montgomery Clift, William Shatner*
A collection of excellent performances raises this

film above the typical World War II, moralistic drama. Tracy is memorable as a judge presiding over the Nuremberg war crimes trials, and Garland and Clift turn in absorbing characterizations as Holocaust survivors. But it is Schell as the German defense attorney who is most impressive (he won an Oscar for the role). Intelligent, thoughtful, distinguished film.

JULES AND JIM (1961)
**** NR 1:50
DIR: *Francois Truffaut* **CAST:** *Jeanne Moreau, Oskar Werner, Henri Serre, Marie Dubois, Vanna Urbino*
Truffaut's beautiful story about Jules (Werner) and Jim (Serre), two friends—one Austrian, one French—who fall in love with the same woman (Moreau) in pre-World War I Paris. The menage a trois unfolds into the Postwar years, ultimately ending in tragedy. Moreau is sexy and charming in her best-loved role. A highlight of the French New Wave.

JULIA (1977)
*** PG 1:58
DIR: *Fred Zinnemann* **CAST:** *Jane Fonda, Vanessa Redgrave, Jason Robards, Hal Holbrook, Maximillian Schell*
Fonda and Redgrave are both excellent as two close friends who journey from a peaceful childhood to pre-war Europe. Based on the memoirs of

writer Lillian Hellman, the film works best as a character study, but seems to falter when dealing with the plotty intrigue involving Nazis it tries to impose on the story. Jason Robards is excellent as a declining Dashiel Hammet, with whom Hellman had a long relationship. His performance earned him a Best Supporting Actor award. Redgrave also took home the Best Supporting Actress Oscar. Alvin Sargent won for Best Screenplay From Another Source. The film was also nominated for Best Picture, Best Director, Best Actress (Fonda) and Best Supporting Actor (Schell).

JURASSIC PARK (1993)
*** PG-13 2:06
DIR: *Steven Spielberg* **CAST:** *Sam Neill, Laura Dern, Jeff Goldblum, Richard Attenborough*
Soon to be released on videocassette, this is director Steven Spielberg's masterful return to the action-adventure genre. Featuring some of the best special effects ever put to film, thanks to the miracle of computer animation, this is a dinosaur tale like none before! Neill, Dern, and Goldblum are three scientists who visit Jurassic Park, an island amusement park inhabited by genetically engineered dinosaurs, in order to guarantee the park's safety to insurance underwriters. But while they are there, something goes dreadfully wrong (proving the chaos theory which Goldblum rattles on about incessantly), and the dinosaurs escape.

What follows is some of the most breathtaking and thrilling footage to ever grace the screen. Especially frightening is the scene in which a huge Tyranosaurus Rex stalks our intrepid heroes while they hide inside trucks. Sure to take your breath away, *Jurassic Park* is a must-see. Based on the page-turner by Michael Crichton.

K

THE KARATE KID (1984)
** PG 2:07
DIR: *John G. Avildsen* CAST: *Ralph Macchio, Noriyuki (Pat) Morita, Elisabeth Shue, Randee Heller, Martin Kove, William Zabka, Chad McQueen*
Director John Avildsen applies the same formula to this picture that made his last big film, *Rocky*, such a crowd pleaser. Macchio plays a fatherless, scrawny boy who moves to Los Angeles from New Jersey. Once in Southern California, he runs into a bully who just happens to be a Karate expert. Enter Morita, an elderly karate master turned apartment handyman, who teaches Macchio the ancient Oriental art. Capped off by a show-stopping confrontation between Macchio and his tormentor.

KEY LARGO (1948)
** NR 1:41
DIR: *John Huston* CAST: *Humphrey Bogart, Ed-*

ward G. Robinson, Lauren Bacall, Lionel Barrymore, Claire Trevor, Thomas Gomez, Jay Silverheels
Certainly not the best work any of the well-known actors or director Huston has ever done, but the talent collected here is strong enough to over-come the minor spots of mediocrity; you're bound to be entertained by this film. Based on Maxwell Anderson's play, the story concerns gangster Robinson holding a group of people hostage in a Key West, Florida hotel. Bogart is a tired World War II veteran who is reluctant to fight back until Bacall serves up some inspiration. Oscar for Best Supporting Actress went to Claire Trevor as Robinson's sidekick.

THE KILLING FIELDS (1984)
*** R 2:22
DIR: *Roland Jaffe* **CAST:** *Sam Waterston, Haing S. Ngor, John Malkovich, Julian Sands, Craig T. Nelson, Spaulding Gray*
True story about *New York Times* journalist Sydney Schanberg (Waterston), and his friendship with his Cambodian photographer/assistant Dith Pran (Ngor). When Ngor is captured by the Khmer Rouge after the fall of Cambodia, Waterston tries to find him. The scenes depicting the terror of the reeducation camps are particularly harrowing. Remarkably, Ngor, a doctor who managed to survive the holocaust, won an Oscar for Best Supporting Actor in the first film role of his life.

THE KING AND I (1956)
*** NR 2:13

DIR: *Walter Lang* **CAST:** *Deborah Kerr, Yul Brynner, Rita Moreno, Martin Benson, Terry Saunders, Rex Thompson, Alan Mowbray*

Thoroughly entertaining version of the Rodgers and Hammerstein musical. Kerr is the young, widowed schoolteacher who goes head to head with Brynner, the King of Siam. The two eventually fall in love, surrounded by gorgeous costumes and settings and such classic tunes as "Shall We Dance," "Getting to Know You," and "Hello Young Lovers." Marni Nixon provided Kerr's vocals. Brynner took home the Best Actor award for his commanding performance.

KING KONG (1933)
**** NR 1:40

DIR: *Merian C. Cooper, Ernest B. Schoedsack* **CAST:** *Fay Wray, Robert Armstrong, Bruce Cabot, Frank Reicher, Sam Hardy, Noble Johnson, James Flavin*

One of the great beauty and the beast tales, this classic monster movie has taken its place in the pantheon of American popular culture, with the climactic scene atop the Empire State Building as an indelible image. Willis O'Brien's special effects still hold up after all these years, and Max Steiner's score is very effective. Fay Wray stars as the love of Kong's life.

THE KING OF COMEDY (1983)
*** PG 1:49
DIR: *Martin Scorsese* CAST: *Robert De Niro, Jerry Lewis, Diahanne Abbott, Sandra Bernhard, Shelly Hack, Tony Randall, Ed Herlihy, Fred de Cordova*
Underseen Scorsese film is a most unusual, disturbing picture. De Niro, obsessed with a Johnny Carson-like figure (Lewis), teams up with fellow autograph hound Bernhard to stage an elaborate kidnapping. A piercing look at America's fascination with celebrity that's loaded with plenty of black humor. Scorsese's moralizing ending is the only thing that keeps the movie from receiving a four star ranking. De Niro is brilliant as usual, and Lewis gives his finest dramatic performance ever.

KING OF HEARTS (1966)
*** NR 1:42
DIR: *Phillipe de Broca* CAST: *Alan Bates, Genevieve Bujold, Pierre Brasseur, Jean-Claude Brialy*
This off-beat little film has become something of a cult classic. Bates stars as a World War I Scottish soldier sent into a French village to defuse a bomb. Most everyone in the town has fled, except for the inhabitants of an insane asylum. What ensues is a pointed comedy about the lunacy of war. Bates is excellent as the befuddled solider who doesn't ever quite get a grip on what's happening. Bujold is beguiling as an asylum resident who steals Bates' heart.

KING OF THE GYPSIES (1978)
** R 1:52

DIR: *Frank Pierson* **CAST:** *Eric Roberts, Susan Sarandon, Judd Hirsch, Sterling Hayden*

Clearly trying to catch in on the popularity of *The Godfather* films, this movie examines a subculture within "white America." The subculture in this film is that of the Gypsies, a nomadic group that still follows a great many tribal practices, including that of having a King. Sterling Hayden, the reigning King, is aware of his own imminent death, so he passes on his role to his grandson, Eric Roberts. But Roberts' no-good father, Judd Hirsch, has something to say about this, and the rest of the film focuses on their power struggle. Featuring many brilliant performances, including Eric Roberts' portrayal of a young man on the cusp of two cultures, this movie is destroyed by a lackluster script and unfocused direction.

KING SOLOMON'S MINES (1985)
* PG-13 1:40

DIR: *J. Lee Thompson* **CAST:** *Richard Chamberlain, Sharon Stone, John Rhys-Davies*

Sharing only the same name as an earlier (and much better) film that starred Deborah Kerr and Stewart Granger, this movie is only memorable in any way because it features an early performance by Sharon Stone. The plot is a complete rip off of *Raiders of the Lost Ark*, and the stunts look like copies of the kinds of action-packed situations in which Indiana Jones often finds himself. In fact, Richard Chamberlain even looks and dresses like Indy, and Sharon Stone is highly reminiscent of Willie Scott (Kate Capshaw in *Indiana Jones and the Temple of Doom*).

KISS OF THE SPIDER WOMAN (1985)
**** R 1:59
DIR: *Hector Babenco* **CAST:** *William Hurt, Raul Julia, Sonia Braga*
Hurt plays a sad drag queen incarcerated in a squalid South American prison for seducing a teenage boy. He's joined by a passionate revolutionary (Julia) who at first cannot tolerate his cell mate's wild flights of fancy. A remarkable relationship ensues between the two men, who find they must rely upon each other to survive the horrors of the prison. Hurt, who won an Oscar for his performance, is simply amazing in this courageous portrayal of a weak man who finds great strength to help a friend. The film was also nominated for Best Picture, Best Director and Best Screenplay From Another Medium.

KLUTE (1971)
**** R 1:54
DIR: *Alan J. Pakula* **CAST:** *Jane Fonda, Donald Sutherland, Roy Scheider, Jean Stapleton, Rita Gam, Charles Cioffi*

Fonda won an Oscar for her portrayal as an intelligent New York call girl who is being stalked by a killer. Donald Sutherland plays a square cop from middle America who comes to Manhattan to search for a friend. His quest leads him to Fonda, who at first manipulates him, but the two soon fall in love. Fonda's prostitute is extremely well-drawn, with none of the clichés usually associated with such characters. Screenwriters Andy and Dave Lewis received a nomination from the Academy for their script.

KNIFE IN THE WATER (1962)
**** NR 1:34
DIR: *Roman Polanski* **CAST:** *Leon Niemczyk, Jolanta Umecka, Zygmunt Malanowicz*
Internationally acclaimed filmmaker Roman Polanski was catapulted into fame by his brilliant direction of this thrilling drama. It is the story of a wealthy couple in a Communist country who are having marital problems. One weekend, while on the way to their boat, they pick up a macho hitchhiker and invite him to go sailing with them. While out at sea, the weather turns bad, and they all have to stay in the boat's cabin overnight. The pressure rises when the rich man realizes that the young hitchhiker has eyes for his beautiful wife. One of the finest adult dramas of all-time!

KRAMER VS. KRAMER (1979)
**** PG 1:45
DIR: *Robert Benton* **CAST:** *Dustin Hoffman, Meryl Streep, Jane Alexander, Justin Henry, Howard Duff, George Cole, JoBeth Williams*
Emotional, extremely moving film about an advertising man (Hoffman) who must raise his son (Henry) alone after his wife (Streep) walks out on the two of them. When she returns to get her child back, an impassioned custody battle ensues. The entire cast is brilliant, especially Hoffman, Streep, Henry, and Alexander as the concerned family friend. Academy Awards for Best Picture, Director, Actor (Hoffman), Screenplay, and Supporting Actress (Streep).

L

LADY AND THE TRAMP (1955)
*** G 1:16
DIR: *Hamilton Luske, Clyde Geronimi, Wilfred Jackson* **CAST:** *Voices of Peggy Lee, Barbara Luddy, Bill Thompson*
Disney's first animated feature filmed in Cinemascope is a pure delight. Pedigreed spaniel Lady runs away from home when she feels neglected and meets the stray dog Tramp on the other side of the tracks. Romance and adventure follow, highlighted by a touching spaghetti din-

ner. Peggy Lee, the voice of Peg, Darling, and Si and Am (the Siamese cats) wrote the memorable songs with Sonny Burke, including "We Are Siamese If You Please."

THE LADYKILLERS (1955)
*** NR 1:30
DIR: *Alexander Mackendrick* **CAST:** *Alec Guinness, Katie Johnson, Cecil Parker, Herbert Lom, Peter Sellers.*
Little known comedy about a gang of crooks who, unbeknownst to her, enlist a sweet little old lady (Johnson) in their robbery scheme. The laughs really roll when Johnson catches onto their plan and the thieves decide that she must pay for her knowledge with her death. Only problem is, none of the men can bring themselves to do the job. Side-splitting humor. Particularly funny are Guinness as the leader of the gang, and Sellers in a supporting role. English black humor at its finest.

THE LADY VANISHES (1938)
*** NR 1:37
DIR: *Alfred Hitchcock* **CAST:** *Margaret Lockwood, Michael Redgrave, Paul Lukas, Dame May Whitty, Naunton Wayne, Basil Radford*
Elderly Whitty disappears during a train ride and young Lockwood becomes involved in the search for the missing woman. Redgrave joins the hunt,

while Wayne and Radford provide a great deal of comic relief; they would reprise their roles in future films. A wonderful blend of mystery and comedy from the master of the genre. One of those films that can be watched over and over and over.

LA FEMME NIKITA (1990)
** R 1:57
DIR: *Luc Besson* CAST: *Anne Parillaud, Jean-Hugues Anglade, Jeanne Moreau*
Parillaud plays a street-tough Parisian junkie who is rescued from a life in prison by a super-secret branch of the government who train her to be a world-class assassin. Released back into the real world with a new identity, she goes about her life while waiting for an assignment. She meets and falls in love with a simple man, but cannot tell him who she really is. If the story sounds familiar, it's because it was remade into *Point of No Return* by Hollywood for American audiences. The plot is virtually identical, and both are well-made, but ultimately pointless exercises.

LAST ACTION HERO (1993)
** PG-13 2:10
DIR: *John McTiernan* CAST: *Arnold Schwarzenegger, F. Murray Abraham, Art Carney, Mercedes Ruehl*
This action movie really wasn't as bad as every-

one made it out to be during its brief life in the theatre. Now that it's out on video, it is certainly worth the price of a rental. It is the story of a lonely and idealistic child who magically enters the world of movies that he loves so much. There, he befriends his hero Jack Slater (Schwarzenegger), and the two do battle with some of the baddest villains in town. But the young boy's delight at his new situation comes to a crashing halt when he realizes that if he could get into the film, then these bad guys can get out! Featuring enough one-liners and loud explosions to overcome the mediocre script and direction, this movie is decent.

THE LAST BOYSCOUT (1991)
** R 1:45
DIR: *Tony Scott* CAST: *Bruce Willis, Damon Wayans, Taylor Negron, Halle Berry*
Some corrupt businessmen are ruining the sport of football through their shady dealings, and Bruce Willis and Damon Wayans are out to stop them. Willis is a private investigator with a chip on his shoulder and Wayans is a retired quarterback with an even bigger chip on his shoulder. Both have something to prove, so you better get out of their way if you know what's good for you. Featuring a whole lot of flying bullets, crashing cars, fist fights, and big explosions, this movie has enough action to keep even the most jaded action

fans glued to their seats. Written by Shane Black, of *Lethal Weapon* fame, the script is very predictable.

THE LAST DETAIL (1973)
**** R 1:44
DIR: *Hal Ashby* Cast: *Jack Nicholson, Otis Young, Randy Quaid, Clifton James, Carol Kane, Nancy Allen, Gilda Radner, Luana Anders, Michael Moriarty*
Nicholson stars as a gruff, compassionate Navy Petty officer ordered to transport a young prisoner (Quaid) to the brig. When Nicholson and his partner (Young) realize their prisoner has been unjustly sentenced to a lengthy prison term, they decide to show him a good time along the Eastern seaboard. They also teach him the value of the freedom he's about to lose. Nicholson was nominated by the Academy for his fine performance, as was Quaid. Robert Towne (*Chinatown*) received a nomination for his screenplay.

THE LAST EMPEROR (1987)
*** PG 2:46
DIR: *Bernardo Bertolucci* CAST: *John Lone, Joan Chen, Peter O'Toole*
Impressive epic biography about Pu Yi (Lone), who was crowned emperor of China at the age of three in 1908, only to be deposed during the subsequent revolution when he is in his 20s. The film follows his life from his privileged and shel-

tered childhood to the time of his death in 1967, when he was living as a gardener in the People's Republic. The film is visually arresting; sumptuous costumes, fascinating images from the Forbidden City, and a gorgeous score by Ryuichi Sakamoto add to the splendor. Winner of nine Academy Awards, including Best Picture, Director.

THE LAST METRO (1980)
*** PG 2:13
DIR: *Francois Truffaut* **CAST:** *Gerard Depardieu, Catherine Deneuve, Jean Poiret*
Truffaut's final film is no masterpiece, but it is certainly better than most things you will ever watch. It tells the sad story of the German occupation of France during World War II in a personal and touching way. Deneuve puts all of her heart and soul into keeping her husband's dream, that of running a small playhouse, alive in the face of Nazi pressure and intolerance.

L.A. STORY (1991)
*** PG-13 1:35
DIR: *Mick Jackson* **CAST:** *Steve Martin, Victoria Tennant, Richard Grant, Marilu Henner, Sarah Jessica Parker*
Martin stars as a harried L.A. weatherman who dallies between a ditzy young girl (Parker) and a tuba-playing British journalist (Tennant). But this

GUIDE TO TV MOVIES

is more a movie about L.A. itself then about romance ("Some of these houses are *twenty years old!*" he tells Tennant). Martin pokes fun at the city's kissy-faced Angelenos and snobby restaurants, but there's also a thinly-veiled affection for a place where dreams can come true.

THE LAST PICTURE SHOW (1971)
*** R 1:58
DIR: *Peter Bogdanovich* **CAST:** *Timothy Bottoms, Jeff Bridges, Ben Johnson, Cloris Leachman, Ellen Burstyn, Cybill Shepherd*
Larry McMurtry (with help from director Bogdanovich) adapted his own novel about life in a small Texas town in the 1950s for this poignant, melancholic drama. Filming the bleak landscape in black and white and getting the most out of his stellar cast, Bogdanovich expertly captured the story's theme of loss of innocence. Johnson and Leachman each picked up an Oscar for their respective supporting roles.

LAST TANGO IN PARIS (1973)
**** X 2:09
DIR: *Bernardo Bertolucci* **CAST:** *Marlon Brando, Maria Schneider, Jean-Pierre Leaud*
The most controversial film of its time still packs a wallop. Brando gives the best performance of his distinguished career as an American expatriate living in Paris while trying to rid himself of the

pain he is suffering as a result of his wife's recent suicide. Bertolucci and Brando do a masterful job of exploring the psychology of the character as he enters into an aggressive sexual relationship with a total stranger (Schneider). A deeply passionate film in more ways than one.

THE LAST TEMPTATION OF CHRIST (1986)
*** R 2:40
DIR: *Martin Scorsese* **CAST:** *Willem Dafoe, Harvey Keitel, Barbara Hershey, Harry Dean Stanton*
Director Scorsese and screenwriter Paul Schrader's controversial and powerful film adaptation of Nikos Kazantzakis' novel about the self doubts Jesus has upon realizing that he has been chosen by the Lord to carry His message to the people. Despite the uproar the film created among fundamentalists, this film actually ends on a pious note, with Jesus's courage, faith, and love, shining through. A beautiful, intelligent and challenging work. Peter Gabriel's mesmerizing score helps to drive the film.

THE LAST WALTZ (1978)
*** PG 1:56
DIR: *Martin Scorsese* **CAST:** *The Band, Bob Dylan, Neil Young, Van Morrison, Eric Clapton, Joni Mitchell, Ringo Starr*
Rock and roll fans will not want to miss this documentary about The Band's farewell concert,

which took place in San Francisco on Thanksgiving Day in 1976. Master filmmaker Scorsese cuts back and forth between rollicking performances from the many legendary musicians on hand, and interviews with the members of The Band about their lengthy career. Robbie Robertson is particularly engaging during the interview segments, and Bob Dylan, Neil Young, and Van Morrison provide just a few of the many musical highlights.

LAWRENCE OF ARABIA (1962)
**** G 3:36
DIR: *David Lean* **CAST:** *Peter O'Toole, Alec Guinness, Anthony Quinn, Jack Hawkins, Claude Rains, Omar Sharif, Jose Ferrer*
Stunning epic biography about the exploits of British adventurer T.E. Lawrence, who sought to bring together several Arab factions to revolt against the Turks in the Middle East of World War I. O'Toole, in the role that made him a star, is impeccable, and he receives ample help from the impressive supporting cast. Freddie Young's cinematography and Maurice Jarre's score (both Oscar winners) combine with Lean's direction to create a sweeping, beautiful film. Winner of seven Academy Awards, including Best Picture, Director.

LENNY (1974)
*** R 1:52
DIR: *Bob Fosse* **CAST:** *Dustin Hoffman, Valerie*

Perrine, Jan Miner, Stanley Beck, Gary Morton
Hoffman earned an Academy nomination for his portrayal of the incendiary, self-destructive comic Lenny Bruce, whose outspoken routine shook the world of show business and tested the limits of free speech. The documentary style of the film works well to capture the grittiness of Bruce's life, from his early days performing in dive joints to his untimely death from a drug overdose. Perrine is poignant as Lenny's drug-addicted wife. Nominations for Best Picture, Director, and Screenplay.

LETHAL WEAPON (1987)
** R 1:49
DIR: *Richard Donner* **CAST:** *Mel Gibson, Danny Glover, Gary Busey.*
Entertaining action film with Gibson as an unbalanced cop who teams up with family man Glover to break up a drug ring. Lots of violence, explosions, and shoot-outs hold your attention and keep you from thinking too deeply about the flawed plot. A huge box-office hit, it was followed by two sequels.

LET IT RIDE (1989)
** PG-13 1:30
DIR: *Joe Pytka* **CAST:** *Richard Dreyfuss, Teri Garr, David Johansen, Allen Garfield, Robbie Coltrane, Jennifer Tilly, Mary Woronov, Michelle Phillips*

Dreyfuss plays a habitual gambler whose marriage to Garr is stressed to the breaking point. But he goes to the track anyway, and proceeds to have the kind of day that gamblers dream about. That's pretty much it for the plot, but it's enough for a funny, diverting movie experience. Tilly is engaging as a rich man's girlfriend. Coltrane (*Nuns on the Run*) is also funny as the window man who keeps paying Dreyfuss.

LIFEBOAT (1944)
*** NR 1:36
DIR: *Alfred Hitchcock* **CAST:** *Tallulah Bankhead, Walter Slezak, Henry Hull, Hume Cronyn, Heather Angel, William Bendix, Canada Lee, John Hodiak*
John Steinbeck came up with this tense story about a disparate group of survivors thrown together on a lifeboat in the Atlantic after their ship is torpedoed by a German submarine. Slezak plays the commander of the sunken U-Boat who joins the group of tourists on the cramped vessel. As the group struggles for survival, the best and worst comes out in all of them. Hitchcock wrings every drop of tension from the situation, including a memorable scene in which a wealthy journalist (Bankhead) uses a diamond bracelet as a fishing lure. The cast is excellent. Hitchcock received a Best Director nomination from the Academy, as did Steinbeck for Best Story. Cinematographer Glen MacWilliams was also nominated.

LILIES OF THE FIELD (1963)
** NR 1:34
DIR: *Ralph Nelson* **CAST:** *Sidney Poitier, Lilia Skala, Lisa Mann, Isa Crino*
Poitier became the first black actor to win the Oscar for a lead performance in this film about a handyman (Poitier) who builds a church for a group of nuns who have fled from East Germany. A small film with a huge heart, it was the surprise hit of the year.

THE LION IN WINTER (1968)
*** PG 2:14
DIR: *Anthony Harvey* **CAST:** *Peter O'Toole, Katharine Hepburn, Anthony Hopkins, Timothy Dalton, Jane Merrow*
King Henry II (O'Toole) and his Queen (Hepburn) spend Christmas Eve fighting over which of their three sons will inherit the crown. A witty, feisty historical drama. The Oscar-winning screenplay was written by James Goldman (adapted from his own play). Hepburn, in one of her finest performances, won the Academy Award for Best Actress.

LITTLE BIG MAN (1970)
*** PG 2:30
DIR: *Arthur Penn* **CAST:** *Dustin Hoffman, Faye Dunaway, Martin Balsam, Chief Dan George*
A moving Western epic told through the eyes of

Jack Crabb (Hoffman), a 121 year old man. Crabb reflects on his fascinating life, including his friendship with Wild Bill Hickok, his days as a medicine man, and his experiences as the only white survivor of Custer's Last Stand. Adapted by Calder Willingham from Thomas Berger's novel. The film is also noteworthy for its sympathetic treatment of Indians, and its subtle, metaphorical comparison of America's horrific treatment of Native Americans with the country's involvement in the Vietnam War.

LITTLE CAESAR (1930)
*** NR 1:20
DIR: *Mervyn LeRoy* **CAST:** *Edward G. Robinson, Douglas Fairbanks, Jr. , Glenda Farrel*
Classic gangster picture featuring Robinson as Enrico Bandello, the small-time crook who becomes a big-time killer and gang leader. Robinson's performance set the standard by which all future actors playing criminals would be measured. Watch for his famous line, "Mother of mercy, is this the end of Rico?"

THE LITTLE MERMAID (1989)
*** G 1:22
DIR: *John Musker, Ron Clements* **CAST:** *Voices of Jodi Benson, Pat Carroll, Samuel E. Wright, Kenneth Mars, Buddy Hackett, Christopher Daniel Barnes, Rene Auberjonois*

A loose adaptation of Hans Christian Anderson's story about a young mermaid (Benson) who trades her lovely voice to a witch (Carroll) for a pair of legs so she can experience life on land. In order for her to remain human, the mermaid's beloved prince (Barnes) must kiss her within three days. Wright is memorable as Sebastian the Crab. Features an Oscar-winning score by Alan Menken and the Oscar-winning song "Under the Sea," by Menken and Howard Ashman.

LIVES OF A BENGAL LANCER (1935)
**** NR 1:49
DIR: *Henry Hathaway* **CAST:** *Gary Cooper, Franchot Tone, C. Aubrey Smith, Monte Blue, Sir Guy Standing, Richard Cromwell*
This is a classic adventure set in Northwest India among the legendary Bengal Lancers, a division of the British Army. Cooper and Tone star as experienced, courageous soldiers who take a new recruit (Cromwell), who happens to be their commander's son, under their wings. If made today, the film might mention that the British were an imperialist occupying force, but details like that would simply get in the way of this old-fashioned story of loyalty among comrades. The film was nominated for Best Picture, as was Hathaway for Best Director. Achmed Abdullah, John L. Balderston, William Slavens McNutt, Waldermar Young and Grover Jones were nominated for Best Screenplay.

LOCAL HERO (1983)
**** PG 1:51
DIR: *Bill Forsyth* **CAST:** *Peter Riegert, Burt Lancaster, Fulton MacKay, Jennie Seagrove*

An overlooked little gem of a comedy which has garnered increasing cult status in recent years. A neurotic Houston oil magnate (played beautifully by Lancaster) sends a stiff young exec (Riegert) to negotiate the purchase of a quiet little Scottish town. As with *Gregory's Girl* and *Breaking In*, director Forsyth is able to find warmth and humor in the ensuing culture clash, while avoiding cheap sentimentality. Riegert is just right as the urban dweller who is at first befuddled, then charmed by the business-savvy locals who would be delighted to give up their seaside homes for a few million bucks. A mystery motorcyclist is one of the best sight gags in film.

LOLITA (1962)
*** NR 2:32
DIR: *Stanley Kubrick* **CAST:** *James Mason, Sue Lyon, Shelley Winters, Peter Sellers, Diana Decker, Marianne Stone*

Mason plays Humbert Humbert, the memorable pedophile from Vladimir Nabokov's classic tale of forbidden love. Humbert marries a frumpy widow (Winters) in order to be closer to her teenage daughter, played seductively by Lyon. Although Nabokov's graphic novel has been taken down a notch, there's still a dark humor in this story of a man's sexual obsession played out to its tragic finale. Nabokov received a nomination for the screenplay adapted from his own book.

THE LONGEST YARD (1974)
*** R 2:02
DIR: *Robert Aldrich* **CAST:** *Burt Reynolds, Eddie Albert, Bernadette Peters, Ed Lauter, Michael Conrad, James Hampton*
Reynolds is his laid-back best in this film about a bribe-taking quarterback who ends up in prison. Albert is the football-obsessed Warden who promises an early release if Reynolds will put together a prison team to compete against his guards. Reynolds begrudgingly takes on the task, assembling a band of killers and thieves with little sports experience. On game day, Reynolds must choose between a longer sentence or the newfound dignity of his team. Although the story's a bit predictable, it's a fine piece of entertainment.

LOOK WHO'S TALKING (1989)
* PG-13 1:33
DIR: *Amy Heckerling* **CAST:** *John Travolta, Kirstie Alley, Olympia Dukakis, George Segal, Abe Vigoda, voice of Bruce Willis*
Inexplicable box-office smash featuring Alley as an unmarried woman who gets pregnant and decides to have the baby by herself. Travolta is a

cab driver who falls in love with the new mother and her baby. Audiences apparently found the gimmick which uses Willis as the voice of the baby's inner thoughts irresistible.

LORD OF THE FLIES (1963)
*** NR 1:30
DIR: *Peter Brook* **CAST:** *James Aubrey, Tom Chapin, Hugh Edwards, Roger Elwin, Tom Gaman*
A disturbing story about a group of innocent English schoolboys shipwrecked on a desert island. The boys split up into vying groups, and, as they forget about their proper British manners, eventually devolve into warring savages. This is a powerful allegory about what happens to men when all the trappings of society and class structure are stripped away. Based on the novel by William Golding, the film was remade in 1990, but substituted the English kids with military cadets from America.

LOST IN AMERICA (1985)
*** R 1:31
DIR: *Albert Brooks* **CAST:** *Albert Brooks, Julie Haggerty, Garry Marshall, Art Frankel*
Brooks is hysterical as an ad exec who convinces his wife (Haggerty) to regain their Sixties idealism by quitting their jobs in Los Angeles, buying a Winnebago and heading across country. They make it as far as Las Vegas before Haggerty's

character loses their nest egg in a streak of bad luck at the craps table. From there, they begin a bitingly funny adventure through America.

THE LOST WEEKEND (1945)
**** NR 1:41
DIR: *Billy Wilder* **CAST:** *Ray Milland, Jane Wyman, Philip Terry, Howard da Silva, Frank Faylen*
The best film ever made about alcoholism, and a landmark film in the history of Hollywood because of its treatment of a serious adult subject. Milland's Oscar-winning performance as a writer who spends more time with a bottle than with a typewriter is nothing short of powerful. The supporting cast is also excellent, particularly da Silva as a bartender. Billy Wilder's Academy Award-winning screenplay (with Charles Brackett) and direction pulls no punches in this unrelenting drama. Also the winner of the Best Picture Award.

LOVE AND DEATH (1975)
*** PG 1:25
DIR: *Woody Allen* **CAST:** *Woody Allen, Diane Keaton, Olga Georges-Picot, Frank Adu, Harold Gould*
Allen takes aim at epic literature in this hysterical send-up of *War and Peace*. He stars as a pathetic prisoner who has just a few hours to remember the important events in his life. Like most of Allen's work, the prisoner spends much of his time thinking of death and the meaninglessness

of existence. Only Allen has the talent to turn such subjects into a laugh-riot. Don't miss it.

THE LOVED ONE (1965)
*** NR 1:56
DIR: *Tony Richardson* **CAST:** *Robert Morse, Rod Steiger, John Gielgud, Liberace, Jonathan Winters, Robert Morley, Milton Berle, Tab Hunter, Roddy McDowall, Anjanette Comer*
A stinging, hysterical look at the business of death in America. Morse stars as a young Englishman who comes to Los Angeles to help attend to his uncle's death. He's stunned by both the cost and the obsessiveness of the funeral industry. Steiger gives a funny, over-the-top performance as a cosmetologist for corpses. Based on Evelyn Waugh's novel, the film retains its dark comedy kick.

LUST FOR LIFE (1956)
*** NR 2:02
DIR: *Vincente Minnelli* **CAST:** *Kirk Douglas, Anthony Quinn, James Donald, Lionel Jeffries, Everett Sloane*
Douglas gives a poignant portrayal of Vincent Van Gogh, an emotionally tortured artist who managed to produce works of great beauty despite his profound mental illness. Based on Irving Stone's definitive biography, the film tends to over-romanticize Van Gogh's misery. But Dou-

glas' passion for the part makes this a very moving film. Quinn is superior as Paul Gaugin, the lusty artist who managed to breath some life into Van Gogh's moribund existence.

--------------------------- **M** ---------------------------

M (1931)
**** NR 1:39
DIR: *Fritz Lang* **CAST:** *Peter Lorre, Gustav Grundgens, Ellen Widmann, Inge Landgut*
Lorre made his film debut as the child murderer who is wreaking havoc in Berlin. When the police prove to be incompetent at solving the case, the members of the city's underworld get together to capture the disturbed killer. A thoroughly frightening film that has managed to age extremely well. Lorre's performance is unforgettable.

MAD MAX (1980)
** R 1:33
DIR: *George Miller* **CAST:** *Mel Gibson, Joanne Samuel, Hugh Keays-Byrne, Steve Bisley, Tim Burns*
A terrific action film starring Gibson as an Australian policeman who gets revenge on a biker gang who have killed his wife and child. The desolate, apocalyptic, post-World War III atmosphere adds to the drama, as does the exceptional stunt work. Don't be turned off by the dubbed voices (including Gibson's!)—the distributors apparently

thought that Americans would find the Australian accents disconcerting.

MAD MAX BEYOND THUNDERDOME (1985)
** R 1:46
DIR: *George Miller, George Ogilvie* CAST: *Mel Gibson, Tina Turner, Angelo Rossitto, Frank Thring, Angry Anderson*
This final installment in the Mad Max series ends with a mighty whallop! Featuring a sassy performance by Tina Turner as a town leader (not to mention her terrific theme song ("We Don't Need Another Hero"), this film will push you to the edge of your seat. This time, Max makes a deal with Turner to rid her town of a trouble maker, believing that he's finally found the peaceful oasis of his dreams. He soon realizes that he's been made a patsy, however, and it will take the help of a tribe of savage children to save him.

THE MAGNIFICENT AMBERSONS (1942)
*** NR 1:28
DIR: *Orson Welles* CAST: *Joseph Cotten, Tim Holt, Dolores Costello, Anne Baxter, Agnes Moorehead*
For his follow-up to *Citizen Kane*, Welles chose to film an adaptation of Booth Tarkington's novel about a wealthy, turn-of-the-century Midwestern family who refuse to adapt to the changing times. What could have been an all-time classic was unfortunately taken out of Welles's hands by the

studio. His original 148 minute version was cut down to just 88 minutes, and a phoney, happy ending was tagged on to the film. Still, in a tribute to Welles's genius, enough remains of the work to make it well worth watching.

THE MAGNIFICENT SEVEN (1960)
*** NR 2:06
DIR: *John Sturges* **CAST:** *Steve McQueen, Yul Brynner, Robert Vaughn, James Coburn, Charles Bronson, Brad Dexter, Horst Buchholz*
An American remake of Kurosawa's classic Japanese film, *The Seven Samurai.* A group of down-on-their-luck gunfighters are enlisted to help protect a poor Mexican village from a gang of Banditos led by Eli Wallach. Although it doesn't approach the stature of *Samurai,* a superior cast and well-directed action make for a fine film. You'll probably recognize Elmer Bernstein's score, for which he received an Oscar nomination.

MAJOR LEAGUE (1989)
** R 1:47
DIR: *David S. Ward* **CAST:** *Charlie Sheen, Corbin Bernsen, Tom Berringer, Wesley Snipes*
Major League is one of those movies perfectly suited to watching and forgetting about immediately. While there is absolutely nothing memorable about the film, it's entertaining enough to sit through. It is the story of the owner of a baseball

team who plots to destroy her team by hiring unqualified players. Featuring some hilarious acting by Charlie Sheen and his fellow performers, this movie is just plain fun.

MALCOLM X (1992)
**** R 3:21
DIR: *Spike Lee* **CAST:** *Denzel Washington, Spike Lee, Angela Bassett, Al Freeman, Jr.*
Spike Lee's triumphant epic does justice the legacy of the contorversial Civil Rights leader. Lee makes the wise decision of directing the movie as a chronicle of the changes within Malcolm X (*nee* Malcolm Little), showing each facet of his life in perspective with the others. Thus, the sequences when he is in jail are as important as the sequences when he is breaking from the Nation of Islam. Denzel Washington is dazzling, imbuing the character of Malcolm with all the depth and inner conflicts that the true man must have had. Washington received an Oscar nomination for the role. The various cameo performances are also very memorable, including Spike Lee himself as Malcolm's one-time street hustling partner.

THE MALTESE FALCON (1941)
**** NR 1:40
DIR: *John Huston* **CAST:** *Humphrey Bogart, Mary Astor, Peter Lorre, Sydney Greenstreet, Elisha Cook, Jr., Ward Bond*

The greatest detective film ever made. Bogart's portrayal of Dashiell Hammett's Sam Spade was different than any hero the screen had ever seen, and prefigured the anti-hero of the 1960s and '70s. Hired by Astor to find a valuable statuette, Bogart soon discovers that there are several unsavory characters who are interested in the piece. Huston's first attempt as a director—he had previously worked as a screenwriter—lay the groundwork for the slew of film noir pictures that would follow. Extraordinary supporting cast includes Lorre as the effeminate Joel Cairo and Greenstreet as the Fat Man.

A MAN CALLED HORSE (1970)
*** PG 1:54
DIR: *Elliot Silverstein* CAST: *Richard Harris, Judith Anderson, Corina Tsopei*
Long before the blockbuster hit *Dances With Wolves*, there was the small but equally beautiful *A Man Called Horse*. Starring Richard Harris in a truly remarkable performance, this film is a must-see. Harris, an uppity British aristocrat with definite Eurocentric attitudes sets out for the Americas in search of adventure. He is soon captured by a tribe of Native Americans and stripped of his so-called European dignity. He learns that the "savage natives" perhaps are more noble than he could ever be. The movie is rounded out with truly solid direction by Elliot Silverstein.

THE MANCHURIAN CANDIDATE (1962)
**** NR 2:06
DIR: *John Frankenheimer* **CAST:** *Frank Sinatra, Laurence Harvey, Janet Leigh, Angela Lansbury, Henry Silva*
Harvey is a Korean war veteran who has returned to the States as a hero. Problem is that he's actually been brainwashed and turned into a dangerous killer by the Communists and only his friend Sinatra suspects that anything is wrong with him. Part political satire, part suspenseful mystery, this is a unique and challenging film that works on many different levels. Landsbury is excellent as the mom from hell. Rereleased theatrically in 1987 after being kept off of television because of its controversial story.

A MAN FOR ALL SEASONS (1966)
**** G 2:00
DIR: *Fred Zinnemann* **CAST:** *Paul Scofield, Robert Shaw, Wendy Hiller, Orson Welles, Susannah York, Vanessa Redgrave*
Scofield leads a strong cast in this film adaptation of Robert Bolt's play about the conflict between King Henry VIII (Shaw) and Sir Thomas More (Scofield). A literate, honorable drama with excellent characterizations. The film won six Academy Awards, including Best Picture, Director, Actor, Screenplay, Cinematography, and Costumes.

MANHATTAN (1979)
**** R 1:36
DIR: *Woody Allen* CAST: *Woody Allen, Diane Keaton, Mariel Hemingway, Michael Murphy, Meryl Streep*

Allen's follow-up to his great *Annie Hall* is every bit as good as the previous film. Here, Allen plays a television writer whose wife (Streep) has left him for another woman. Allen has since taken up with teenager Hemingway, but he soon falls in love with Keaton. Only problem is that Keaton is in love with Allen's married friend Murphy. Beautifully shot in black and white and Panavision by Gordon Willis, and featuring a breathtaking score composed of old Gershwin tunes, this romantic-comedy is perfectly executed.

THE MANHATTAN PROJECT (1986)
** PG 1:57
DIR: *Marshall Brickman* CAST: *John Lithgow, Christopher Collet, Jill Eikenberry, John Mahoney*

This taut suspense drama, featuring John Lithgow's always superb performance as a military scientist working on the bomb, will push you to the edge of your seat. A young genius, eager to prove to the world just how dangerous the bomb really is, steals some plutonium from the plant where Lithgow works and then assembles an atomic device as his school science project. The government naturally cannot abide by this, so they chase him down for half the movie. The ending will take your breath away, as it's a race against time to turn off a ticking time bomb.

THE MAN WITH ONE RED SHOE (1985)
** PG 1:33
DIR: *Stan Dragoti* **CAST:** *Tom Hanks, James Belushi, Carrie Fisher, Dabney Coleman*
Based on the far superior French film *The Tall Blond Man with One Brown Shoe*, this is one of the many half-hearted movies Tom Hanks made after reaching superstar status with *Splash*. Hanks plays a concert violinist who is mistaken by the CIA as a spy because he shows up at the airport one day wearing one red shoe. The CIA spends the rest of the movie trying to find out what secrets he has to hide, only to realize in the end that they've been following a nobody. Despite an excellent cast, all of whom can be incredibly funny (including Carrie Fisher, as evidenced by her guest appearances on TV's *Saturday Night Live*), the movie probably won't make you laugh more than once or twice. It has none of the wit of the original, and since there is no humor, the implausibility of the situation becomes glaringly obvious. Good only for true fans of Tom Hanks.

THE MAN WHO FELL TO EARTH (1976)
*** R 2:20
DIR: *Nicolas Roeg* **CAST:** *David Bowie, Candy Clark,*

Buck Henry, Rip Torn
A strange, compelling film about a reptilian-eyed
alien (Bowie) who lands on earth in search of
water for his own dying planet. Bowie, just right
for the part of an E.T., becomes a science mogul
and is apparently corrupted by life away from
home. The scenes of life on Bowie's home planet
are poignant and surreal.

THE MAN WHO SHOT LIBERTY VALANCE
(1962)
**** NR 2:02
DIR: *John Ford* **CAST:** *James Stewart, John Wayne,
Vera Miles, Lee Marvin, Edmond O'Brien, Lee Van
Cleef, Strother Martin*
When greenhorn lawyer Stewart finds himself
facing the menacing Valance (Marvin), he turns to
macho man Wayne for help. Ford's vision is darker
here than in his past films, which may account for
the luke warm reaction the movie received upon
its release. It is now generally regarded as one of
the greatest works of the director, and one of the
finest Westerns ever made. The cast is uniformly
excellent.

THE MAN WHO WOULD BE KING (1975)
**** PG 2:07
DIR: *John Huston* **CAST:** *Sean Connery, Michael
Caine, Christopher Plummer, Saeed Jaffrey, Jack May,
Shakira Caine*

Connery and Caine play a pair of British soldiers who convince the locals of a small Himalayan country that they're gods in order to make off with the nation's treasure. When Connery's character goes overboard on his own Godliness, the two run into trouble. While this may sound like a familiar plot, (it's based on a short story by Rudyard Kipling) Huston turns it into a magnificent epic about the corrupting influence of power. The mountain scenery is stunning, as are the performances. Huston and co-writer Gladys Hill were nominated for their screenplay.

MAP OF THE HUMAN HEART (1993)
**** R 1:35
DIR: *Vincent Ward* **CAST:** *Jason Scott Lee, Patrick Bergen, Anne Parillaud*
One of the most praised films of 1993, *Map of the Human Heart* tells a story so unpredictable that even the most jaded movie-goer will be delighted by it. Avik, a young Canadian eskimo, is brought to Montreal by a dashing young pilot so that he can receive medical treatment in a modern hospital. Never able to return to his native ways, Avik decides to enter European culture as fully as possible, to the point of becoming a British bomber pilot during World War II! His success as a bombardier is astounding, and he even participates in the famed saturation bombing of Dresden. All the while, his love for a mysterious French Canadian woman grows ever stronger.

MARRIED TO THE MOB (1988)
*** R 1:44
DIR: *Jonathan Demme* **CAST:** *Michelle Pfeiffer, Matthew Modine, Dean Stockwell, Mercedes Ruehl*
Pfeiffer manages a thick Brooklyn accent for her role as a mob widow trying to get out from under the thumb of a lecherous mafioso (Stockwell) in this comedy about organized crime. Modine is funny as a dweeby F.B.I. agent who befriends Pfeiffer's character in the hopes of nailing a few thugs, but is soon entranced by her beauty and vulnerability. The real star is Demme's direction, which gives the film a vibrant comic energy. Rock star Chris Isaak has a funny cameo as a clown/hit man.

MARTY (1955)
*** NR 1:31
DIR: *Delbert Mann* **CAST:** *Ernest Borgnine, Betsy Blair, Joe Mantell, Jerry Paris, Esther Minciotti*
The moving story of a Bronx butcher (Borgnine, in an Oscar-winning turn) resigned to bachelorhood who meets and falls in love with a girl (Blair) who is just as plain and lonely as he. Paddy Chayefsky wrote the sensitive script, which goes a long way towards proving that love and romance are not the sole province of the beautiful and the popular. Academy Awards for Best Picture, Director, and Screenplay.

MARY POPPINS (1964)
**** G 2:20
DIR: *Robert Stevenson* **CAST:** *Julie Andrews, Dick Van Dyke, David Tomlinson, Glynis Johns, Ed Wynn*
This Disney classic combines live action and animated sequences to form a delightful musical fantasy. Julie Andrews, in her debut role, won an Oscar for her performance as the greatest nanny in the world. Along with chimney sweep and jack-of-all-trades Bert (Van Dyke), she brings a tremendous amount of happiness to the children in the Banks family. Memorable songs include "Chim Chim Cher-ee," "Supercalifragilisticexpialidocious," and "A Spoon Full of Sugar." Oscars for Best Score, Song, Visual Effects, and Editing.

M*A*S*H (1970)
*** PG 1:56
DIR: *Robert Altman* **CAST:** *Donald Sutherland, Elliott Gould, Sally Kellerman, Robert Duvall, Tom Skerritt, Jo Ann Pflug, Rene Auberjonois*
Director Robert Altman and Oscar-winning Screenwriter Ring Lardner, Jr., combined their extraordinary talents to create this hilarious film about the doctors at an unconventional American medical unit during the Korean War. Most of the black humor revolves around the jokes the doctors tell and the pranks they pull in an effort to relieve the tremendous amount of pressure they

are under. The film spawned an enormously successful television series.

MATEWAN (1987)
*** PG-13 2:12
DIR: *John Sayles* **CAST:** *James Earl Jones, Chris Cooper, Kevin Tige, Will Oldham, Ken Jenkins, Jace Alexander*
The true story of a bloody miner's strike in West Virginia in the 1920s. This low-budget, independent film has a gritty realism in its depiction of Appalachian poverty and corporate greed. Sayles sides with the striking miners as they battle infiltrators and the company's hired thugs. Cooper is excellent as an idealistic union organizer. The stunning visuals earned cinematographer Haskell Wexler an Academy nomination.

MCCABE AND MRS. MILLER (1971)
**** R 2:01
DIR: *Robert Altman* **CAST:** *Warren Beatty, Julie Christie, Rene Auberjonois, Keith Carradine, Shelley Duball, John Schuck.*
Robert Altman's stunning film turns the typical Hollywood Western—along with all of its myths and cliches—on its head. Beatty plays a small-time gambler who opens up a bordello with ambitious Christie. The rugged landscape of the turn-of-the-century Northwest adds to the bleak mood of the picture. A deeply-felt, haunting film

that is likely to stick with you long after the final credits roll.

MEAN STREETS (1973)
*** R 1:50
DIR: *Martin Scorsese* **CAST:** *Harvey Keitel, Robert De Niro, David Proval, Amy Robinson.*
This is the film that made Scorsese a hit with the critics. Keitel is a small-time crook who brings himself down by constantly trying to help out childhood friend and debt-ridden De Niro. The film is set in New York City's Little Italy—the neighborhood in which Scorsese grew up—and it shows. The director recreates the atmosphere of the area, with all of its attendant contradictions between family loyalty and fierce competitiveness, with startling truth and accuracy.

MEET ME IN ST. LOUIS (1944)
**** NR 1:53
DIR: *Vincente Minnelli* **CAST:** *Judy Garland, Margaret O'Brien, Lucille Bremer, Tom Drake, Mary Astor*
One of the great MGM musicals. The Ames family is preparing to move from St. Louis to New York just as their hometown is getting ready to host the 1903 World's Fair. Judy Garland and Margaret O'Brien (who won a special miniature Oscar for the year's best child actress) are outstanding. The memorable Ralph Blane-Hugh Martin score fea-

tures such marvelous tunes as "The Trolley Song," "Under the Babmoo Tree," "The Boy Next Door," "Have Yourself a Merry Little Christmas," and "You and I."

MELVIN AND HOWARD (1980)
*** R 1:35
DIR: *Jonathan Demme* CAST: *Paul LeMat, Jason Robards, Mary Steenburgen, Dabney Coleman, Michael J. Pollard*
The true story of Melvin Dumar, a Utah gas station attendant who made national headlines by claiming to be a beneficiary of Howard Hughes' will. Dumar says he encountered a bedgraggled Hughes wandering through the desert, and after a few hours in the car was promised part of his fortune. If this stylish film has a fault, it's that it presents Dumar's wild claim as truth. But that doesn't diminish the fun of watching a wide-eyed LeMat chase the American Dream. Steenburgen won a Best Supporting Actress Oscar for her role as Dumar's long-suffering wife. Goldman's fine script earned him an Academy Award as well. Robards was nominated for his supporting role as the spacey tycoon.

METROPOLIS (1926)
**** NR 2:00
DIR: *Fritz Lang* CAST: *Alfred Abel, Brigitte Helm*
If any science fiction movie deserves the label

"classic," then *Metropolis* is surely it. This silent film, recently restored to pristine picture quality, is now available accompanied by a soundtrack performed by some of the most successful rock stars of all time. Lang's direction can only be called brilliant, his prediction of a cold and inhuman society of the future seeming more accurate and compelling upon each viewing. The movie is visually impeccable, rivaling the so-called highly conceived visuals of most Hollywood movies made today.

MIDNIGHT COWBOY (1969)
**** R 1:53
DIR: *John Schlesinger* **CAST:** *Dustin Hoffman, Jon Voight, Sylvia Miles, Brenda Vaccaro, Barnard Hughes, Ruth White, Jennifer Salt, Paul Morrisey*
The classic story of an aimless young man from Texas (Voight) who wanders into Manhattan with the dream of becoming a high-paid gigolo. He hooks up with Ratso Rizzo, a desperate, ill street hustler played to perfection by Hoffman. Voight's vague notion of striking it big is soon thwarted as he and Ratso struggle to survive the mean streets of New York. Their relationship is one of the most memorable on film. The movie won an Oscar for Best Picture, as did Schlesinger and screenwriter Waldo Salt. Both Voight and Hoffman were nominated for Best Actor. Brenda Vaccaro received a nomination for Best Supporting Actress.

MIDNIGHT RUN (1988)
*** R 2:02

DIR: *Martin Brest* **CAST:** *Robert De Niro, Charles Grodin, Yaphet Kotto, John Ashton, Joe Pantoliano, Wendy Phillips*

De Niro and Grodin give the kind of performances needed to raise this film above its formulaic, predictable script. A cynical bounty hunter (De Niro) is sent to track down a mild-mannered accountant (Grodin) who has embezzled 15 million bucks from the mob. What ensues is an entertaining chase across most of the country, with both the mob and the F.B.I. pursuing the odd couple. Despite its conventions, this is a very enjoyable bit of film escapism.

MILLER'S CROSSING (1990)
*** R 1:55

DIR: *Joel and Ethan Coen* **CAST:** *Albert Finney, Gabriel Byrne, Marcia Gay Harden, John Turturro, Jon Polito, J.E. Freeman*

Finney is a good-hearted mob boss and Byrne is his right-hand man in this stylish 1930's gangster saga from the two brothers who brought us *Blood Simple* and *Barton Fink*. The story revolves around Byrne's effort to save Finney from competing mobsters, but his motives become questionable when he appears to double-cross his boss. This is a slick film with memorable action. But the Coens' seemed to have borrowed a bit too heavily from

The Glass Key, Dashiell Hammet's classic with a strikingly similar story line.

MIRACLE ON 34TH STREET (1947)
*** NR 1:36
DIR: *George Seaton* **CAST:** *Maureen O'Hara, John Payne, Natalie Wood, Edmund Gwenn, Gene Lockhart, William Frawley*

The enduring Christmas classic about Kris Kringle (Gwenn), who runs up against an unbelieving child (Wood) while working as Santa Claus at Macy's. He must go to court to prove the existence of St. Nick. A thoroughly entertaining and satisfying blend of comedy and fantasy. Oscars for Best Supporting Actor (Gwenn), Story and Screenplay.

MISERY (1990)
*** R 1:44
DIR: *Rob Reiner* **CAST:** *James Caan, Kathy Bates, Richard Farnsworth, Lauren Bacall, Frances Sternhagen*

Bates took home a well-deserved Best Actress Oscar for her portrayal of a demented fan who imprisons and tortures a romance novelist played by Caan. Bates' character rescues the injured writer after his car plunges off a snowy Colorado road. She appears at first to be a sympathetic nurse. But Caan soon realizes that he's dealing with a mercurial misfit who has no intention of letting him go.

Bates is brilliant as the obsessive loner who moves from psycho to sweetheart—sometimes within the same breath. Reiner manages to balance the script's dark humor with incredible tension. Along with *The Shining*, this is one of the best film versions of a Stephen King novel.

MISSING IN ACTION (1984)
** R 1:41
DIR: *Joseph Zito* **CAST:** *Chuck Norris, James Hong, M. Emmet Walsh, Lenore Kadorf*
Although the serious subject matter of this movie is treated far too lightly, it is still quite entertaining to watch. Chuck Norris plays a Vietnam veteran who returns to the far-off land in order to prove that American prisoners of war are still being held captive. The American government tries to prevent him from doing so, as his actions could damage pending diplomatic relations between the two countries. Featuring some great action scenes (Norris really knows how to choreograph those fight sequences!), this movie makes for a night of empty-headed, two-fisted fun.

MODERN TIMES (1936)
**** G 1:40
DIR: *Charlie Chaplin* **CAST:** *Charlie Chaplin, Paulette Goddard, Henry Bergman, Chester Conklin*
A sensational comedy in which Chaplin shows off his cinematic genius. Poking fun at the day to

day struggle of modern life, write-director-pro-ducer-star-scorer Chaplin created a masterpiece that has continued to be a favorite throughout the decades. The Little Tramp meets an orphan (Chaplin's lovely wife Goddard) and tries his hand at a series of jobs. Touching, funny, roman-tic—this film has it all.

MR. SMITH GOES TO WASHINGTON (1939)
**** NR 2:10
DIR: *Frank Capra* **CAST:** *James Stewart, Jean Arthur, Claude Rains, Thomas Mitchell, Guy Kibbee, Edward Arnold*
An effective slice of Frank Capra's populist ideal-ism. Stewart plays a naive young Senator who arrives in Washington only to discover corrup-tion and greed at work. Holding fast and hard to his own honest beliefs, he fights his own boss Arnold and his mentor Rains, while earning the love of hard-edged Arthur. Memorable scene: Stewart during his one-man fillibuster, tired and weak of voice, trying to beat the evil powers who control the Senate.

MONTY PYTHON AND THE HOLY GRAIL
(1974)
*** PG 1:30
Dir: *Terry Gilliam, Terry Jones* **CAST:** *Graham Chapman, John Cleese, Eric Idle, Michael Palin, Terry Gilliam, Terry Jones*

The gang from *Monty Python* takes on the legend of King Arthur with their usual irreverence. Diehard *Python* fans consider this film something of a holy grail itself—there's a classic fight scene between Arthur (Chapman) and a knight who refuses to give up the fight even after his arms and legs have been whacked off. And look for the killer rabbits. An enjoyable, albeit twisted, retelling.

THE MUMMY (1932)
*** NR 1:13
DIR: *Terence Fisher* **CAST:** *Boris Karloff, Zita Johann, Edward Von Sloan*
One of the best horror films of all time, *The Mummy* stars Boris Karloff as the walking undead who fulfills a curse on the greedy archaeologists who disturbed his slumber. Featuring brilliant performances all around, not to mention great effects and make-up, this movie is still creepy today! You're sure to enjoy this dandy little treat!

MUTINY ON THE BOUNTY (1935)
**** NR 2:15
DIR: *Frank Lloyd* **CAST:** *Clark Gable, Charles Laughton, Franchot Tone, Herbert Mundin, Donald Crisp*
Charles Laughton gives one of the great performances of all-time as the tyrannical Captain Bligh. Gable is Fletcher Christian, the leader of the mu-

tiny that takes place while sailing in the South Seas. A fantastic adventure tale that is much stronger than any of the subsequent remakes (including the one in 1962 starring Marlon Brando). Oscar for Best Picture. Remade as *The Bounty* with Mel Gibson in 1985.

MY DARLING CLEMENTINE (1946)
**** NR 1:37
DIR: *John Ford* **CAST:** *Henry Fonda, Walter Brennan, Linda Darnell, Victor Mature*
One of the most beloved Westerns of all time, John Ford's masterpiece *My Darling Clementine* is a must-see for any true film fan. This is perhaps still the best version ever recorded on celluloid of the legendary gunfight at the O.K. Corral between the Clantons and the Earps. The performances are incredible all around, Henry Fonda lending particular weight to his portrayal of Wyatt Earp, a man who saw the emotional conflict in killing in the name of justice. Not only is it a truly remarkable film, but it is also a delight to watch.

MY FAIR LADY (1964)
*** G 2:50
DIR: *George Cukor* **CAST:** *Rex Harrison, Audrey Hepburn, Stanley Holloway, Wilfrid Hyde-White*
The film version of the Broadway hit by Lerner and Lowe (which was based on George Bernard Shaw's *Pygmalion*). Harrison stars as Professor

Henry Higgins, the upper-class gentleman who turns the cockney flower girl Eliza Doolittle (Hepburn) into a woman of grace and charm. Of course, he falls in love with her during the transformation. Wonderful score includes "The Rain in Spain," "Just You Wait," and "On the Street Where You Live."

MY FAVORITE YEAR (1982)
**** PG 1:32
DIR: *Richard Benjamin* **CAST:** *Peter O'Toole, Joseph Bologna, Mark Linn-Baker*
This delightful sleeper comedy reminds the viewer of just how wonderful a good film can be to watch. A sentimental peek back into the world of live 1950's television comedy, *My Favorite Year* follows the antics of a young and idealistic TV writer who is thrilled to learn that his favorite movie star will be appearing as a guest star on his show. The only problem is, the star (Peter O'Toole) turns out to be a sniveling alcoholic with stage fright. Warm and touching, yet never hammy, this movie cannot be recommended highly enough.

MY LEFT FOOT (1989)
*** R 1:43
DIR: *Jim Sheridan* **CAST:** *Daniel Day-Lewis, Brenda Fricker, Ray McAnally, Hugh O'Conor, Fiona Sha*
Based on the autobiography of Irishman Christy Brown, who was born with cerebral palsy, yet

overcame his affliction to become an accomplished artist and writer. This remarkable film features Academy Award-winner Day-Lewis as Brown, in what can only be described as a tour-de-force by this brilliant young actor. Funny, warm, and touching, the picture also gains strength from the Oscar-winning performance of Fricker as Brown's loving, devoted mother.

MY LIFE AS A DOG (1986)
*** PG-13 1:41
DIR: *Lasse Hallstrom* **CAST:** *Anton Glanzelius, Tomas von Bromssen, Anki Liden, Melinda Kinnaman, Kicki Rundgren*
Glanzelius is a mischievious 12 year old boy sent off to live with his aunt and uncle when his mother falls ill. Lonely and confused, he identifies with a small Russian dog who has been sent into space by the Soviets. Set in Sweden in the 1950s, the film is an honest and poignant look at the highs and lows of childhood.
The foreign film was very popular with American audiences.

MY OWN PRIVATE IDAHO (1991)
*** R 1:42
DIR: *Gus Van Sant* **CAST:** *Keanu Reeves, River Phoenix, James Russo, Flea*
This movie is certainly not for everyone, but if you're in the mood for something different, then

this one is sure to satisfy. Reeves and Phoenix play gay male prostitutes in this updated version of Shakespeare's *Henry IV*. Although the very premise might be frightening enough to scare off most viewers, the two young stars (one of whose careers was so tragically cut short) give bravura performances, sure to entrance even the most cynical of viewers. After a few moments, you will get used to the occasional Shakesperean aside and realize that this is a movie about people and their frailties, and that prostitution and homosexuality are really not what the film is about. Highly recommended.

N

THE NAKED GUN (1988)
** PG-13 1:29
DIR: *David Zucker* **CAST:** *Leslie Nielsen, Priscilla Presley, Ricardo Montalban, George Kennedy, O.J. Simpson, Reggie Jackson, Nancy Marchand*
The creators of *Airplane!* return with this hilarious feature length film based on their unsuccessful television series *Police Squad*. Nielsen plays Lt. Frank Drebin, the dumbest yet luckiest cop this side of Peter Sellers' Inspector Clouseau. Drebin must break up the plot to kill the Queen of England during her visit to Los Angeles. The silly jokes come at such a fast clip, you'll barely have time to catch your breath.

NAKED GUN 2 1/2: THE SMELL OF FEAR (1991)
** PG-13 1:25
DIR: *David Zucker* **CAST:** *Leslie Nielsen, Priscilla Presley, George Kennedy*

Clutzy detective Frank Drebin takes on American big business interests. Finally realizing that America needs to adopt a new environmental policy, the government wants to switch to more environmentally friendly energy, but not without a fight from fossil fuel companies. Sound serious? It isn't! But, regrettably, it's also not as funny as the first film. If sight gags are your cup of tea, however, you might find some enjoyment in this lighthearted movie.

NAKED LUNCH (1992)
**** R 1:55
DIR: *David Cronenberg* **CAST:** *Peter Weller, Judy Davis, Julian Sands, Ian Holm*

This brilliant adaptation of William S. Burrough's nightmarish and hallucinogenic novel succeeds because of director David Cronenberg's decision to capture the book's feel, rather than its plot. The movie is about Burroughs himself, chronicling the drug-addicted writer's experiences in Northern Africa. Fantasy and reality blend grotesquely yet beautifully, and the viewer is never quite sure whether an incident is actually occuring, or if it exists only in Burroughs' (played magnificently by the low-key Peter Weller) mind. Featuring plots to take over the world through drug addiction, love triangles, accidental murders, and a whole host of bizarre creatures, *The Naked Lunch* is a must-see!

THE NAME OF THE ROSE (1986)
*** R 2:08
DIR: *Jean-Jacques Annaud* CAST: *Sean Connery, F. Murray Abraham, Christian Slater, William Hickey, Ron Perlman*
Although the film bombed in the States, this dark mystery set in a medieval Benedectine Abbey was a big hit overseas. Connery is excellent as a Franciscan monk who unravels a series of gruesome murders within the Abbey's spookey stone walls. The attention to medieval detail give an authentic portrayal of the monk's dreary lives. This is a unique thriller and as out of place as it may seem, Slater, playing a young novitiate, has a sex scene in here that helped make him a star.

NATIONAL LAMPOON'S ANIMAL HOUSE (1978)
** R 1:49
DIR: *John Landis* CAST: *John Belushi, Tim Matheson, John Vernon, Tom Hulce, Stephen Furst, Donald Sutherland, Karen Allen*
John Belushi shines as the biggest slob at Faber College. As a member of the Delta frat house, he

joins his brothers in a variety of pranks and stunts. A truly tasteless film, but at times very funny. In many ways it spawned a new style of raunchy humor in both television and film, aimed primarily at teenagers and young adults.

NATIONAL VELVET (1945)
*** G 2:05
DIR: *Clarence Brown* CAST: *Mickey Rooney, Elizabeth Taylor, Donald Crisp, Ann Revere, Angela Lansbury*
Enduring family favorite features Taylor as a young horsewoman who, with the help of Rooney, works hard to get her horse entered in the Grand National Steeplechase. It is perhaps Taylor's best-known role, and Rooney's finest performance. Ann Revere won the Oscar for Best Supporting Actress.

NAVIGATOR: A MEDIEVAL ODYSSEY (1989)
*** NR 1:31
DIR: *Vincent Ward* CAST: *Chris Haywood, Bruce Lyons*
Navigator: A Medieval Odyssey is one of those films that you see on video and wonder why it was never popular or widely released in the movie theatres. An action packed delight, it chronicles the efforts of several brave Medieval men who attempt to appease God in order to put an end to the devastating Black Plague. Guided by the pro-

phetic dream of a child, they enter a cave in England...and emerge in the 20th Century. They are then left to decide which time period is more chaotic and hellish. Funny, critical, and deeply moving, this is a film you won't want to miss.

NETWORK (1976)
**** R 2:00
DIR: *Sidney Lumet* CAST: *Peter Finch, Faye Dunaway, William Holden, Robert Duvall, Beatrice Straight, Ned Beatty*
A landmark film about the overwhelming power of television. Finch won an Oscar for his portrayal of a network news man who announces on live television that he intends to kill himself on air. When his ratings skyrocket, the network (personified by Dunaway in an Oscar-winning role) is more than happy to exploit his breakdown. He becomes a "mad prophet of the airwaves," and the film takes off into a wild, dark satire about greed and warped ambition. Straight won an Oscar for her role as Holden's wife, Paddy Chayefsky for his screenplay. The film was nominated for Best Picture, as were Lumet, Holden, Beatty and cinematographer Owen Roizman.

NEVER CRY WOLF (1983)
**** PG 1:45
DIR: *Carroll Ballard* CAST: *Charles Martin Smith, Brian Dennehy*

Acclaimed director and Francis Ford Coppola protege Carroll Ballard wrote and directed this fantastic movie based on the writings of Canadian author Farley Mowat. Charles Martin Smith plays a biologist researching the mysterious white wolves that inhabit the Yukon. Brian Dennehy plays the cynical pilot who flies him to the icy research site. Featuring some of the most memorable photography ever shot, this movie will leave you looking at animals in a whole new way.

NEVER GIVE A SUCKER AN EVEN BREAK (1941)
*** NR 1:11
DIR: *Edward Cline* **CAST:** *W.C. Fields, Gloria Jean, Leon Errol, Susan Miller, Margaret Dumont*
The last film to star W.C. Fields is an insane, essentially plot-less farce. It's a film within a film revolving around Fields' attempt to get a producer to back a picture about his life. Several wonderfully funny moments that only Fields' could pull off, including a classic chase scene.

NEVER SAY NEVER AGAIN (1983)
** PG 2:17
DIR: *Irvin Kershner* **CAST:** *Sean Connery, Max Von Sydow, Klaus Maria-Brandauer, Kim Bassinger*
The only James Bond film not produced by the usual team headed by veteran filmmaker Albert Broccoli, this is also the only Bond movie actually

based on a script by Ian Fleming. Although it is not a spectacular film, it is really exciting to see Sean Connery step back into the role that made him an international superstar. Featuring splendid action from beginning to end, including undersea fights and motorcycle chases, this tale will leave you breathless. In this adventure, Bond has to recover several nuclear devices stolen by an international terrorist group.

THE NEVERENDING STORY (1984)
*** PG 1:32
DIR: *Wolfgang Petersen* **CAST:** *Noah Hathaway, Barrett Oliver*
A movie that reminds you of the awesome powers of a child's imagination, *The Neverending Story* will take you on a journey to a far-off land that is threatened by the great Nothing—a lack of faith and dreams. The movie's protagonist is Bastian, a shy young boy who buries himself in the world of fantasy that can only be accessed through books. But his latest book seems to possess strange powers, as if it allows him to alter the story and help Atreyu, the brave warrior about whom he is reading. Soon he realizes that the world of the book and the "real" world he inhabits are only separated by his imagination, and he can cross from one to the other with ease. Superbly directed by acclaimed filmmaker Wolfgang Petersen.

NEW YORK, NEW YORK (1977)
** PG 2:44

DIR: *Martin Scorsese* **CAST:** *Robert De Niro, Liza Minelli, Mary Kay Place, Georgie Auld*

In making this film, brilliant director Scorsese proved that even geniuses have their off-days! Taking place in the days when Big Bands were at the top of the show biz ladder, *New York, New York* follows the on-again off-again love affair of a singer (Minelli) and a saxophonist (De Niro). The musical numbers (of which there are too many) are somewhat amusing, which is more than can be said for the storyline.

A NIGHT AT THE OPERA (1935)
**** NR 1:32

DIR: *Sam Wood* **CAST:** *Groucho Marx, Harpo Marx, Chico Marx, Kitty Carlisle, Allan Jones, Margaret Dumont*

The Marx Brothers' greatest triumph sees them create havoc with an opera production, only to save it in the end. Great music, romance, and, of course a continuous series of uproarious gags keep the film running in high gear. Memorable moments: the well-known overcrowded stateroom scene (perhaps their funniest bit ever), wearing pilot disguises during an official ceremony. A financial and critical success.

NIGHT GALLERY (1969)
*** NR 1:38
DIR: *Steven Spielberg, Barry Shear, Boris Sagal*
CAST: *Roddy McDowell, Ossie Davis, Joan Crawford*
One of writer / producer Rod Serling's most memorable acheivements after completing "The Twilight Zone" series was this horrific made-for-TV movie. Featuring three vignettes (one of which was Steven Spielberg's first professional project!), Serling narrates tales about Nazi fugitives, the nasty heir to a fortune, and a blind art collector. This one will certainly send shivers up and down your spine. It's worth it just to see a project that Spielberg and Serling, two of the greatest masters of fantasy and horror, worked on together.

NIGHT OF THE HUNTER (1955)
*** NR 1:33
DIR: *Charles Laughton* **CAST:** *Robert Mitchum, Lillian Gish, Shelley Winters, Evelyn Varden, Peter Graves*
Charles Laughton's only directorial effort is a stunning one. Mitchum plays a psychotic man posing as a preacher who marries widow Winters in order to find stolen money hidden by her dead husband. Mitchum and Gish are both excellent in this allegorical study of innocence and hypocrisy. Originally a commercial flop, the film has since built up a loyal and rabid cult following. James Agee wrote the script from a novel by Davis Grubb.

NIGHT OF THE LIVING DEAD (1968)
*** NR 1:36
DIR: *George A. Romero* **CAST:** *Duane Jones, Judith O'Dea, Russell Streiner, Karl Hardman, Keith Wayne, Judith Ridley*
Once considered to be outrageously graphic, this horror film now seems tame in the wake of the dozens of imitators that have followed in its footsteps. Flesh-eating zombies terrorize a group of people spending the night in a farmhouse. Shot in black and white, the movie achieves a hauntingly realistic effect that is strong enough to scare the most hardened horror film buff. Make sure you turn off the lights while watching this one!

A NIGHTMARE ON ELM STREET (1985)
*** R 1:31
DIR: *Wes Craven* **CAST:** *Robert Englund, Heather Langenkamp, Ronnee Blakely*
The first in the series of movies, *A Nightmare on Elm Street* is the only one of any worth. Under the solid direction of Wes Craven, this film contains some dream sequences that are truly frightening. The makeup and special effects are great, and although most of the cast couldn't act its way out of a hat, Robert Englund plays Freddy Krueger, the evil man who comes back to life and avenges his death by entering people's dreams, to a tee. Quite an entertaining flick.

NIGHT SHIFT (1982)
*** R 1:45

DIR: *Ron Howard* **CAST:** *Henry Winkler, Michael Keaton, Shelley Long, Richard Belzer, Kevin Costner*
This sleeper hit is a movie to seek out at the video store! Ron Howard's directorial debut features some truly outstanding performances. Mild-mannered Henry Winkler works the night shift at a morgue, hoping to maintain some peace and quiet in his life in the big city. But along comes Michael Keaton (in the role which made him famous) and pushes him into becoming a pimp. Soon the two are rich men, but their luck runs dry, and they are pursued by both the police and the mob.

NINE TO FIVE (1980)
*** PG 1:50

DIR: *Collin Higgins* **CAST:** *Jane Fonda, Lily Tomlin, Dolly Parton, Dabney Coleman*
Collin Higgins (*Harold and Maude*) wrote and directed this superb comedy about the lives of three single working women. Fonda, Tomlin, and Parton are all secretaries in a big corporation under fat cat Dabney Coleman. Coleman never misses an opportunity to harrass and wield power over them, until one day the tables are turned. This movie is more than just a non-stop laugh; it is warm and touching, dealing with many of the issues facing women today. Not only do they have to cope with returning to the workplace, but

they also have to handle hostile and sexist men in the office.

1984 (1984)
*** R 2:03
DIR: *Michael Radford* CAST: *Richard Burton, John Hurt, Cyril Cusack, Suzanna Hamilton*
This is one of those rare movies that captures fully the heart of the book upon which it was based. Director Michael Radford's intuitive understanding of the desperate, paranoid, and counter-productive society envisioned by novelist George Orwell has allowed him to craft a superb film, sure to last as long as the book. John Hurt plays the optimistic yet ultimately pathetic character of Winston Smith to a tee, and Sir Richard Burton's portrayal of the man who betrays him cannot be beat. Be warned, this movie is dark and desolate and not for the meek. If you feel like a fun movie, then *1984* isn't it!

NOISES OFF (1992)
** PG-13 1:44
DIR: *Peter Bogdanovich* CAST: *John Ritter, Carol Burnett, Michael Caine*
Internationally acclaimed director Peter Bogdanovich leads an all star cast in this mediocre adaptation of the play of the same name. Featuring very broad and slapstick comedy, this is the story of an acting troupe whose behind the scenes

conniptions are far more entertaining than anything they perform on stage. There is a great deal
of sexual innuendo, which will certainly make
you snicker, but there isn't much else, despite the
obviously remarkable talents of the cast and crew.

NORMA RAE (1979)
*** PG 1:53
DIR: *Martin Ritt* **CAST:** *Sally Field, Beau Bridges,
Pat Hingle, Ron Liebman*
This powerful, fact-based drama tells the story of
a lone woman who puts her entire livelihood on
the line in order to end unfair practices and union-
ize the mill in which she works. She receives
guidance from a big city man played by Ron
Liebman. Much of this film's success is due to the
remarkable ability of its cast, particularly Sally
Field, who took home an Oscar for her performance of the title role. Ritt's direction is also keen
and precise, wonderfully drawing out the talents
of his performers.

NORTH BY NORTHWEST (1959)
**** NR 2:16
DIR: *Alfred Hitchcock* **CAST:** *Cary Grant, Eva Marie
Saint, James Mason, Martin Landau, Jessie Royce
Landis, Leo G. Carroll*
Hitchcock's classic comedy-thriller about an in-
nocent advertising man (Grant) who is mistaken
for a CIA agent. The police and the crooks (with

Mason as the head honcho) are both after him as he leads them on a cross-country chase. Along the way he hooks up with Eva Marie Saint. The crop duster scene and the segment at Mount Rushmore are now part of the folklore of film. Bernard Hermann's score is especially memorable.

NO TIME FOR SERGEANTS (1958)
*** NR 1:51
DIR: *Mervyn LeRoy* **CAST:** *Andy Griffith, Myron McCormick, Nick Adams, Don Knotts, William Fawcett*
Long before there was a *Gomer Pyle,* Griffith starred in this tale of a Georgia farm boy who ends up in the Army, much to the chagrin of his rubbery-faced sergeant (McCormick). The interplay between Griffith's cluelesss soldier (his best screen role) and the apoplectic McCormick is priceless. This is a fine character comedy with dozens of roaring laughs. Much funnier than Gomer Pyle on his best day.

NOTORIOUS (1946)
**** NR 1:41
DIR: *Alfred Hitchcock* **CAST:** *Ingrid Bergman, Cary Grant, Claude Rains, Louis Calhern, Leopoldine Konstantin, Reinhold Schunzel*
Ben Hecht wrote this romantic thriller set in post-World War II Rio de Janeiro. Government agent Grant forces German Bergman into marrying a

Nazi (Rains) in order to trap the war criminal. When Rains catches on to their game, he begins to poison Bergman. In the meantime, Bergman and Grant have entered into a heated affair. Great suspense and romance, along with an edge-of-the-seat climax make this a top-notch Hitchcock.

NO WAY OUT (1987)
*** R 1:54
DIR: *Roger Donaldson* **CAST:** *Kevin Costner, Gene Hackman, Sean Young, Will Patton, George Dzundza, Howard Duff*
A superb spy thriller set in the Pentagon. Costner stars as an assistant to the Secretary of Defense (played with authority by Hackman). The two share both office space and a girlfriend (Young). When she ends up dead, Costner is set up as the fall guy. The superior plot bobs and weaves with a fast pace, and the performances are all top-notch. The backseat love scene between Costner and Young must have done wonders for the limousine biz.

═══════ O ═══════

THE OBJECT OF BEAUTY (1991)
*** R 1:37
DIR: *Michael Lindsay-Hogg* **CAST:** *John Malkovich, Andie MacDowell, Lolita Davidovich, Joss Ackland, Peter Riegert, Rudi Davies, Bill Patterson*

Malcovich is a sometimes-wealthy wheeler-dealer who's down on his luck. MacDowell is his spoiled long-time girlfriend. Together they live miles above their means, hopping from luxury suite to luxury suite with the misguided belief that the next Big Deal is just around the corner. When the bill comes due, they try to sell a small Henry Moore sculpture given to MacDowell by her ex-husband, but it's stolen from their hotel. The plotting that follows is clever enough, but the film is more about character than crime—when Macdowell orders a dozen bottles of Perrier to quench her delicate thirst, it's a classic example of Eighties excess.

THE ODD COUPLE (1968)
**** G 1:45
DIR: *Gene Sacks* CAST: *Walter Matthau, Jack Lemmon, Herb Edelman, John Fiedler*
Perhaps Neil Simon's finest play, *The Odd Couple* transfers superbly to the silver screen. Under the perfect direction of Gene Sacks, this story of two recently divorced men living with each other is hilarious from beginning to end. One was thrown out by his wife for being such a slob, the other for being so neat and anal. When forced to share an apartment with each other, all hell breaks loose. When they each start trying to date once again, then things get even more difficult—and hilarious. Warm and intelligent, this film is a definite must-see.

AN OFFICER AND A GENTLEMAN (1982)
** R 2:05
DIR: *Taylor Hackford* **CAST:** *Richard Gere, Debra Winger, Louis Gossett, Jr., David Keith, Robert Loggia*
Love story about a directionless young man (Gere) who enrolls in Naval Officer Candidate School and the woman who seeks his love (Winger). Gere must survive the hard-nose tactics of drill instructor Gossett (in his Oscar-winning role) in order to become a better person. Lots of sex and profanity "help" to modernize the overly-familiar, tired story. Strong performances also go a long way towards making this an enjoyable film. An old-fashioned crowd pleaser.

OH, GOD! (1977)
*** PG 1:44
DIR: *Carl Reiner* **CAST:** *George Burns, John Denver, Teri Garr, Ralph Bellamy*
The first in the long series of movies, this is also definitely the best! Fearing that the world has lost faith and spirituality, God (Burns) decides to use John Denver as his prophet. A lot of hilarious situations follow, none of which are madcap and zany (a problem which plagued all of the sequels). This is a touching tale of human interaction, sure to delight one and all.

THE OLD MAN AND THE SEA (1958)
*** NR 1:29
DIR: *John Sturges* **CAST:** *Spencer Tracy, Felipe*

Pazos, Harry Bellaver

It took an actor of Tracy's caliber to pull off Hemingway's story of a lone fisherman who does battle with a giant swordfish. Most of the action takes place on a skiff in the middle of a turbulent ocean, which presents a challenge to both actor and director to create something that holds water. But Tracy is riveting in this story of a man obsessed with conquering nature. His efforts paid off with an Oscar nomination. Cinematogrpher James Wong Howe was also pegged for a nomination.

OLIVER! (1968)
**** G 2:33
DIR: *Carol Reed* **CAST:** *Ron Moody, Oliver Reed, Mark Lester, Shani Wallis, Jack Wild, Hugh Griffith*
Carol Reed's excellent musical version of Dickens' novel *Oliver Twist*, featuring songs by Lionel Bart, who also penned the stage version of the familiar tale. Mark Lester plays the title role, an orphaned boy who joins a gang of young London theives, led by the evil Fagan (Moody). Several wonderful songs highlight the film, including "Food, Glorious Food," "Consider Yourself," and "As Long As He Needs Me." The re-creation of 19th century London is done to perfection. Six Academy Awards, including Best Picture, Director, Art Director, and Score.

THE OMEN (1976)
*** R 1:51
DIR: *Richard Donner* **CAST:** *Lee Remick, Gregory Peck, David Warner, Billie Whitelaw*

One of the truly fine horror films made before the genre was subverted into that of the slasher film, *The Omen* is sure to terrify and delight you. Directed by veteran action/suspense filmmaker Richard Donner (*Superman*), this is the tale of Satan's attempt to dominate mankind through the guise of a small boy named Damien. Gregory Peck is typically brilliant as the priest who wants to stop Damien's plan from succeeding. Chilling and gory, this is a classy movie that will scare the pants off of you.

ONCE UPON A TIME IN AMERICA (1984)
**** R 3:47
DIR: *Sergio Leone* **CAST:** *Robert De Niro, James Woods, Elizabeth McGovern, Tuesday Weld, Treat Williams, Bill Forsythe, Burt Young, Joe Pesci, Danny Aiello, Jennifer Connelly*

Sergio Leone's final film is a cinematic masterpiece. Unfortunately, the studio originally released the picture in a severely edited form that rendered the story all but impossible to follow. If you do rent this video, make sure that you rent the longer, fully restored version (both are available). The tale of two friends (De Niro and Woods) who rise up from their New York Jewish ghetto childhood to become top crime bosses in the 1930s is a fascinating, mesmerizing one. Misbegotten dreams, memory, and sorrow weave their way in and out of the movie's action. Beautifully acted and filmed, with a stunning re-creation of New York City in the first half of this century. Ennio Morricone's score is sure to play inside your head for days after viewing this remarkable work of art.

ONCE UPON A TIME IN THE WEST (1969)
**** R 2:45
DIR: *Sergio Leone* **CAST:** *Charles Bronson, Henry Fonda, Jason Robards, Keenan Wynn*
One of the best Westerns ever made, this one is a must-see. Charles Bronson comes to the aid of a widowed woman trying to make a home for herself in the Old West. It seems that a dastardly railroad company will do just about anything to kick her off her valuable land, right down to hiring a mercenary (played to a tee by Henry Fonda, who took the role just to break his type-casting as a nice guy). Two scenes that will stun you are when Fonda points his gun at a small child, and when some desperados ride into the train station at the movie's opening.

ONE CRAZY SUMMER (1986)
** PG 1:33
DIR: *Savage Steve Holland* **CAST:** *John Cusack, Demi Moore, Curtis Armstrong*

Pointless yet likeable story of a down-and-out teen who turns his life around during one summer vacation. He gains social and sailing skills he never had before, and he wins Demi Moore's heart. Although there's not much of a plot *per se*, the cast is populated with fairly talented young actors who put in decent performances, making this the kind of movie you just sit back and enjoy mindlessly.

ONE FLEW OVER THE CUCKOO'S NEST
(1975)
**** R 2:13
DIR: *Milos Forman* **CAST:** *Jack Nicholson, Louise Fletcher, Brad Dourif, Michael Berryman, Peter Brocco, Scatman Crothers, Danny DeVito*
This film adaptation of Ken Keysey's novel was the first movie in forty years to sweep the top five Academy Award categories—Best Picture, Director, Actor (Nicholson), Actress (Fletcher), Screenplay. When Nicholson enters an insane asylum, he clashes with icy head nurse Fletcher and exhorts the other patients to stand up for their rights. A dazzling paean to the strength of the human spirit. The cast is uniformly excellent, the direction stylish and crisp.

101 DALMATIONS (1960)
*** G 1:20
DIR: *Wolfgang Reitherman, Hamilton S. Luske, Clyde*

Geronimi **CAST:** *Voices of Rod Taylor, Betty Lou Gerson, J. Pat O'Malley, Martha Wentworth*
A Disney favorite. Pongo and Perdita are dalmations who arrange for their human owners to meet and marry. When Cruella De Ville steals Pongo and Perdita's puppies in order to fashion a fur coat, the dogs come to the rescue. Romantic, funny, and thrilling, it's family fun for all.

ON GOLDEN POND (1981)
*** PG 1:49
DIR: *Mark Rydell* **CAST:** *Katharine Hepburn, Henry Fonda, Jane Fonda, Doug McKeon, Dabney Coleman*
Sentimental drama with an outstanding cast. Henry Fonda, in his final, Academy Award-winning role (his first statue ever!), is wonderful as a retired professor whose summer vacation with his wife (Hepburn) at their New England lakefront home is disrupted when their resentful daughter (Jane Fonda) shows up. Family conflicts are eventually worked out, as elder Fonda learns to love. Hepburn and screenwriter Ernest Thompson also took home Oscars.

ON THE WATERFRONT (1954)
**** NR 1:48
DIR: Elia Kazan **CAST:** *Marlon Brando, Eva Marie Saint, Karl malden, Lee J. Cobb, Rod Steiger*
Hard-hitting drama about the world inhabited by New York City dockworkers. Brando stars as a

young man who, under the influence of his priest (Malden), decides to expose the corruption prevalent in the waterfront union. There is marvelous acting by everyone involved, but it is Brando who steals the film. His Oscar-winning performance is simply one of the greatest ever filmed. Particularly memorable is the "I coulda been a contender" scene. Eight Academy Awards, including Best Picture, Director, Story & Screenplay, Cinematography.

THE OSTERMAN WEEKEND (1983)
* R 1:42
DIR: *Sam Peckinpah* **CAST:** *John Hurt, Rutger Hauer, Burt Lancaster, Dennis Hopper*
Fans of Sam Peckinpah will be disappointed by the director's last effort. What makes the film especially hard to watch is that every performance is weak, despite the fact that the cast is populated by some of Hollywood's most talented performers. The plot is extremely complicated, filled with one double-cross after another. Let's just say that it opens with John Hurt's girlfriend being killed by lethal injection, and the violence keeps escalating nonsensically from there!

OTHELLO (1952)
**** NR 1:31
DIR: *Orson Welles* **CAST:** *Orson Welles, Fay Compton, Susan Cloutier, Robert Coote*

Considered by many to be the genius Welles' greatest film masterpiece (better even than *Citizen Kane*), *Othello* is an experience that will redefine film as an art form for the viewer. The movie was made in an extremely unorthodox manner; financed out of Welles' own pocket, he would shoot as much of it as he could before running out of money. He would then take on any acting job he could find, and use his salary to continue making the film! Despite this approach, the film seems flawlessly seamless, its expressionistic photography creating a sense of awe in the viewer.

OUTLAND (1981)
*** R 1:49
DIR: *Peter Hyams* **CAST:** *Sean Connery, Frances Sternhagen, James Sikking, Peter Boyle*
This wonderful science fiction movie, based loosely on the classic western *High Noon* has enough action and enough human drama to satisfy just about any viewer. Connery plays a marshall whose latest assignment is on a mining colony on Io, a small moon of Jupiter. He soon discovers a drug running conspiracy that is masterminded by the leaders of the colony, and he faces a moral crisis. Should he fight the conspiracy or become a part of it and retire a rich man? Connery's performance is dazzling, reminding the viewer of his unusual star appeal, and director Hyam's style builds the tension perfectly.

THE OUTLAW JOSEY WALES (1976)
*** R 2:15

DIR: *Clint Eastwood* **CAST:** *Clint Eastwood, Chief Dan George, Sam Bottoms, Sondra Locke*

Until 1993's critical and box-office hit *Unforgiven*, many considered this to be Eastwood's finest Western (which is quite high praise indeed, considering how many he made!). Eastwood, a mild-mannered farmer, turns to a life on the other side of the law after witnessing his family's death at the hands of some hoodlum Union soldiers. This tragic tale reminds the viewer that even the North, which entered the Civil War in opposition to slavery, was still a haven of bigotry and false morality.

THE OX-BOW INCIDENT (1943)
**** NR 1:15

DIR: *William Wellman* **CAST:** *Henry Fonda, Harry Morgan, Anthony Quinn, Francis Ford*

A truly brilliant movie, William Wellman's classic western chronicles the attempts of two men (Henry Fonda and Harry Morgan) to end mob terror in an Old Western town. Fonda and Morgan play their characters beautifully, capturing all of the fear and courage that occurs within the human spirit whenever someone is forced to face overwhelming odds. Anthony Quinn is also brilliant as a possibly innocent man targeted by the mob, and Wellman keeps you guessing as to whether or not he's guilty. A must-see!

P

PACIFIC HEIGHTS (1990)
*** R 1:47
Dir: *John Schlesinger* **CAST:** *Michael Keaton, Melanie Griffith, Matthew Modine, Laurie Metcalf, Tippi Hedren, Nobu McCarthy, Beverly D'Angelo, Dorian Harewood*

Keaton plays every landlord's worst nightmare in this pyscho-thriller about rent control laws run amok. Modine and Griffith play a perfect young couple who buy a perfect San Francisco Victorian (purists might notice that the house is actually on Portrero Hill, not Pacific Heights). They take in Keaton to help make ends meet, but soon discover that his checks bounce, he's into heavy-metal, and he's spreading cockroaches throughout the house. Worst of all, they can't get rid of him without a lengthy and expensive court battle. Things quickly degenerate into violence and, in a clever ending, vengance. Keaton is excellent as the sociopathic renter.

PAPILLON (1973)
*** PG 2:30
DIR: *Franklin J. Schaffner* **CAST:** *Steve McQueen, Dustin Hoffman, Victor Jory, Anthony Zerbe, Robert Deman, Don Gordon*

McQueen plays a Frenchman sent to Devil's Island for a murder he says he did not commit. Life at the penal colony is unbearable, and McQueen plots his escape with a bookish embezzler (Hoffman). While the plot may sound overly-familiar, the gritty realism and fine performances make this a spectacular film. It's based on the true story of Henry "Papillon" Charriere, the only man known to have ever escaped the terrible prison.

PASSENGER 57 (1992)
** R 1:24
DIR: *Kevin Hooks* **CAST:** *Wesley Snipes, Tom Sizemore, Bruce Payne, Elizabeth Hurley*
Although this film comes off as too coincidental and unlikely, it is still highly entertaining to watch. It is the story of a hijacker who is being trans-ported to his trial . . . on an airplane filled with innocent people. Wesley Snipes is a counterterrorist agent who happens to be on the same plane with him. You probably can figure out what happens next. What makes this movie really stand out are the fine performances, particularly that of Snipes, who is fast proving himself to be one of the best action film actors in the country.

PAT GARRETT AND BILLY THE KID (1973)
*** R 2:02
DIR: *Sam Peckinpah* **CAST:** *James Coburn, Kris Kristofferson, Bob Dylan, Katy Jurado*
For all you fans of the heroes and outlaws of the

Old West, this Sam Peckinpah masterpiece is
definitely for you! A beautiful and sentimental
look at the relationship between Garrett and the
Kid, which started off friendly but eventually
turned sour, is depicted, filled with the kind of
emotional complexities that make for great drama.
The acting is superbly hammy, and although Bob
Dylan doesn't appear much on camera, he provides the movie with one of the most passionate
and rousing scores of all time. If you rent this film,
be sure to rent the director's cut version, which is
far superior to the studio cut.

PATRIOT GAMES (1992)
**** R 1:58
DIR: *Phillip Noyce* CAST: *Harrison Ford, Anne
Archer, James Earl Jones, Patrick Bergen*
Based on the novel by Tom Clancy, Harrison Ford
steps into the role of CIA expert Jack Ryan (played
by Alec Baldwin in *The Hunt for Red October*). This
time, Ryan's family is in danger after he thwarts
an attempt by the Irish Republican Army to murder several lower members of the British Royal
family. In order to avenge the deaths of their
comrades, several other members of the IRA travel
to America to hunt him down. Excellently and
intelligently written, and featuring fine performances and solid direction, any action-buff is
sure to enjoy this movie.

PARENTHOOD (1989)
*** PG-13 2:04

DIR: *Ron Howard* **CAST:** *Steve Martin, Mary Steenburgen, Jason Robards, Dianne Wiest, Rick Moranis, Tom Hulce, Martha Plimpton, Keanu Reeves*

Robards plays the patriarch in this film about an extended family coping with the rigors and rewards of raising kids. Martin, in a somewhat forced performance, plays a stressed super-dad who tries to be everything his father (Robards) was not. Moranis is desperate for his young daughter to learn calculus and Japanese by the first grade. Wiest struggles with two teenagers and no father to help out. The film manages to be affecting without straying into sentimentality.

A PASSAGE TO INDIA (1984)
*** PG 2:43

DIR: *David Lean* **CAST:** *Alec Guinness, Judy Davis, Peggy Ashcroft, Victor Banerjee*

David Lean's marvelous adaptation of E.M. Forster's classic novel about the clash of British and Indian cultures in 1920s India. Davis plays an Englishwoman who accuses an Indian doctor (Banerjee) of rape. Impeccable performances and beautiful cinematography mark Lean's return to directing after a 14 year absence. Oscars for Best Supporting Actress (Ashcroft) and Score (Maurice Jarre).

PATHS OF GLORY (1957)
**** NR 1:26
DIR: *Stanley Kubrick* **CAST:** *Kirk Douglas, Ralph Meeker, Adolphe Menjou, Wayne Morris, George Macready, Richard Anderson*

An early classic from master director Kubrick. During World War I, French general Macready, ignoring Douglas's pleas to the contrary, orders his men to attack a German regiment despite the fact that they are hopelessly outnumbered. When the troops are slaughtered, the general chooses three men to be court-martialed and then executed on charges of cowardice as a means to cover up his own error. One of the finest anti-war films ever made.

PATTON (1970)
**** PG 2:50
DIR: *Franklin Schaffner* **CAST:** *George C. Scott, Karl Malden, Stephen Young, Michael Strong, Frank Latimore*

George C. Scott gives the greatest performance of his career in this screen biography of the temperamental World War II general. Aside from Scott's magnificent portrayal, the film features wonderfully staged battle scenes, and impressive work by Malden as General Omar Bradley, who would eventually relieve Patton of his command in Sicily. Winner of eight Oscars, including Best Picture, Director, Actor (an honor Scott refused to accept on the basis of his belief that actors should not compete with one another), and Screenplay (by Francis Ford Coppolla and Edmund H. North).

PEE-WEE'S BIG ADVENTURE (1985)
*** PG 1:30
DIR: *Tim Burton* **CAST:** *Pee-Wee Herman, Mark Holton, Diane Salinger*
Directed by the ever-brilliant Tim Burton (*Batman, Edward Scissorhands*), this movie turns out to be a surprising delight for both young and old! Follow valiant Pee-Wee Herman as he travels cross-country to find his beloved bicycle which was stolen by Francis, his greedy and spoiled acquaintance. Pee-Wee goes everywhere from the Alamo to Hollywood, meeting everyone on the road from an escaped convict to a woman in an unhappy marriage. Featuring some of the quirkiest and most original scenes in years, *Pee-Wee's Big Adventure* is big fun for the whole family.

PEGGY SUE GOT MARRIED (1986)
*** PG-13 1:43
DIR: *Francis Coppola* **CAST:** *Kathleen Turner, Nicholas Cage, Helen Hunt, Barry Miller, Catherine Hicks*
Turner stars as a woman in crisis who is magically transported back in time to high school, where she's able to make choices armed with 25 years of hindsight. The big question—should she marry the boy (Cage) who, 25 years hence, will walk out

on her? This is a funny, bittersweet film that's reminiscent of the old saying, "If you had it to do all over again, you'd have to do it all over again."

PET SEMATARY (1989)
** R 1:42
DIR: *Mary Lambert* CAST: *Denise Crosby, Dale Midkiff, Fred Gwynne*
This mildly entertaining movie based on the Steven King novel contains quite a few scares. It is the story of a young family who moves out to the countryside in order to avoid the violence of the city. But once there, they discover an eerie cemetery which the ancient tribe of Mick Mack Indians claimed possessed mysterious powers. One night the family is visited by a man they saw die a few days earlier... Well, you can probably guess what kinds of things come next. The acting is mediocre, but the script has enough surprises to divert your attention for a few hours.

PETER PAN (1953)
** G 1:16
DIR: *Hamilton Luske, Clyde Geronimi, Wilfred Jackson* CAST: *Voices of Bobby Driscoll, Hans Conried, Kathryn Beaumont, Heather Angel, Paul Collins*
Not the best of the Disney animated features, but still a lot of fun to watch. The classic James M. Barrie story features Peter taking three English children on an unforgettable adventure to

Neverland, where they come up against Captain Hook and meet Tinker Bell. Who can forget the singing of the song "You Can Fly," as the children are sailing over London?

THE PETRIFIED FOREST (1936)
*** NR 2:14
DIR: *Archie Mayo* CAST: *Humphrey Bogart, Leslie Howard, Bette Davis*
This is Bogart's first big part, and he shines as a menacing gangster holding a group hostage at a desert cafe. Davis, who was quite stunning as a young woman, plays the small-town waitress who falls in love with a wandering poet (Howard). The relationship between the two is magical, especially given the life-and-death setting. Bogart and Howard were in the original Broadway production of the Robert Sherwood play from which the film is adapted.

THE PHILADELPHIA EXPERIMENT (1984)
** PG 1:42
DIR: *Stewart Raffill* CAST: *Michael Pare, Nancy Allen, Eric Christmas, Kene Holliday*
Allegedly based on the true story of a World War II naval experiment gone awry, this is the tale of two men teleported to the present when the government uses their battleship as a guinea pig for a new cloaking device. Once they have arrived in the 1980s, they are shocked by the cultural differ-

ences, unable to understand how America could now be an ally of Germany and France, but an enemy of the Soviet Union. They quickly realize that they have to return to their own time, but they don't know how. Their only chance is to track down the scientist who masterminded the experiment. Featuring good performances by its leads, this imperfect movie is quite fun.

THE PHILADELPHIA STORY (1940)
*** NR 1:52
DIR: *George Cukor* CAST: *Katharine Hepburn, Cary Grant, James Stewart, Ruth Hussey, John Howard, Roland Young*
Film adaptation of Philip Barry's comedy about a wealthy Philadelphia socialite (Hepburn) who is preparing to marry for the second time when her ex-husband (Grant) and a reporter (Stewart) make an unexpected arrival. She's still in love with Grant, and Stewart is beginning to fall in love with her. Very witty dialouge and an Oscar-winning performance by Stewart highlight the film.

THE PICK-UP ARTIST (1987)
* R 1:21
DIR: *James Toback* CAST: *Robert Downey, Jr., Molly Ringwald, Dennis Hopper, Harvey Keitel*
Warren Beatty, fresh from *Ishtar*, refused to take credit for producing the film (one failure was enough!). Robert Downey, Jr. is the consumate

bachelor, possessing all of the pick-up lines that can't fail. But when he meets Molly Ringwald, his life takes a turn for the worse. Not only does he fall in love, but he realizes that he's become part of a family that is wanted by the mafia.

THE PINK PANTHER (1964)
*** PG 1:43
DIR: *Blake Edwards* CAST: *Peter Sellers, David Niven, Capucine, Claudia Cardinale, Robert Wagner* Sellers is hilarious as the incompetent Inspector Clouseau, who is trying to catch international jewel thief Niven. Sight gags, slapstick comedy, malapropisms, plot twists, and chase scenes provide dozens of hysterical moments. Henry Mancini's well-known score won an Oscar. Six sequels (and a popular television cartoon series) would follow in the footsteps of this magnificient comedy, including *A Shot in the Dark* and *The Pink Panther Strikes Again*.

PINNOCHIO (1940)
**** G 1:28
DIR: *Ben Sharpsteen, Hamilton Luske* CAST: *Voices of Dickie Jones, Evelyn Venable, Cliff Edwards, Christian Rub*
Disney favorite can be summed up in one word: magical. Based on the Carlo Collodi story about a wooden puppet who longs to become a little boy. The host of wonderous characters includes Jiminy

Cricket, Foulfellow, and J. Worthington (the fox). Included in the Oscar-winning score is the memorable "When You Wish Upon A Star." Aside from the humor and songs, there are also several downright frightening scenes, particularly when Lampwick is transformed into a donkey, and the chase sequence involving Monstro the whale.

PIXOTE (1980)
*** R 2:07
DIR: *Hector Babenco* **CAST:** *Fernando Ramos da Silva, Marilla Pera, Jorge Juliano, Gilberto Moura*
This is an unflinching, grim account of the thousands of abandoned children who roam the streets of San Paulo, Brazil. Babenco (*Kiss of the Spider Women*) tells the story through the eyes of an angel-faced ten year old (da Silva) as he encounters the degradation of life in the slums of this teeming city. He goes from purse-snatching to murder in short order. Babenco's documentary-like style raises the film from exploitation to a work of art that seeks solutions to the social ills it portrays. Not a film for the squeamish.

PLACES IN THE HEART (1984)
**** PG 1:50
DIR: *Robert Benton* **CAST:** *Sally Field, John Malkovich, Danny Glover, Ed Harris*
Robert Benton's masterpiece *Places in the Heart* is to film what John Steinebck's *The Grapes of Wrath*

is to literature. Sympathizing with the plight of southern farmers who are continually forced to hand their property over to large corporations, Benton's story chronicles the attempts of a strong-hearted widow (Field) who refuses to buckle to corporate pressure. Featuring an incredible cast— Field won her second Oscar and Malkovich was nominated for his first—this classic American tale is not to be missed. This is the kind of film that reminds you why you love to watch movies!

PLANES, TRAINS AND AUTOMOBILES
(1987)
*** R 1:30
DIR: *John Hughes* CAST: *Steve Martin, John Candy, Kevin Bacon, Michael McKean, Charles Tyner, William Windom*
Martin is an obsessive Chicago ad exec trying to make it home from New York for Thanksgiving. Candy is a sweet, slothful salesman who specializes in shower curtain rings. The two are thrown together after a blizzard diverts their plane to Wichita, and from there they become reluctant travel partners. Although the plot sounds light as air, Candy and Martin's comedic chemistry makes this an enjoyable romp through the Midwest. As the title implies, their travel plans do not go smoothly.

PLANET OF THE APES (1968)
*** R 1:48
DIR: *Franklin J. Schaffner* **CAST:** *Charlton Heston, Claude Akins, Roddy McDowell, Maurice Evans*
One of the finest science fiction films ever made, this tale of morality and destruction will fill you with hope and despair all at once. Featuring the intense acting of Charlton Heston and some revolutionary new makeup effects (which still look good to this day), you will be left wondering where you are until the last frames of the movie. Heston, an astronaut, crash lands on a strange planet inhabited by intelligent apes. These simians face many of the same dilemmas as humans do on Earth: the dichotomy between science and religion, the tension between light skinned and dark skinned, etc. Not to be missed!

PLATOON (1986)
*** R 2:00
DIR: *Oliver Stone* **CAST:** *Charlie Sheen, Willem Dafoe, Tom Berenger, Forest Whitaker, Francesco Quinn, Johnny Depp, Kevin Dillon*
Oliver Stone's powerful, if somewhat cold and distant, account of his own experiences in Vietnam. The story focuses on one soldier's (Sheen) experiences while fighting along the Cambodian border. The sequence that is essentially a reenactment of the Mai Lai massacre is especially potent. Great acting and vivid battle scenes highlight this

impressive antiwar film. Academy Awards for
Best Picture, Director, Editing (Claire Simpson).

PLAY MISTY FOR ME (1971)
*** R 1:42
DIR: *Clint Eastwood* **CAST:** *Clint Eastwood, Jessica
Walter, Donna Mills*
Clint Eastwood's first foray into the world of
directing is quite successful. Following a storyline
similar to that of *Fatal Attraction*, but made about
15 years prior to that mediocre film, this is the
story of a radio disc jockey being harassed by a
deranged fan. Why is she so maniacal? Why does
she always want him to play *Misty* for her? You'll
have to watch the film to find that out! Fun and
scary, this is one heck of a thriller.

POLICE ACADEMY (1984)
** R 1:35
DIR: *Hugh Wilson* **CAST:** *Steve Guttenberg, Kim
Catrall, Bubba Smith, G.W. Bailey, Michael Winslow*
The first in the long line of *Police Academy* films,
this is mildly amusing and quite watchable. It is
the story of a bunch of losers who have nowhere
to go, so they all join the police academy to
straighten out their lives. There are quite a few
humorous scenes, although some verge on being
truly distasteful, such as one involving a horse.
The movie is utterly predictable; the viewer is
subjected to a slew of good academy cadets and a

slew of bad academy cadets, and is expected to root for the good guys. Ten minutes into the film you already know how it is going to end, but it's still kind of funny. This is also the movie that made human sound effects man Michael Winslow a star.

POSSE (1993)
** R 1:47
DIR: *Mario Van Peebles* **CAST:** *Mario Van Peebles, Steven Baldwin, Blair Underwood*
Talented director/actor Mario Van Peebles leads an all-star cast in this fun little western told from an African-American perspective. A group of African-American men go absent without leave at the end of the Spanish-American War, and they spend the rest of the time trying to outwit the men who go after them. Although Peebles is not yet the surest of directors, he clearly draws his influence from Sergio Leone, the master Spaghetti Western director, and the results are quite enjoyable.

POSTCARDS FROM THE EDGE (1990)
*** R 1:46
DIR: *Mike Nichols* **CAST:** *Meryl Streep, Dennis Quaid, Shirley Maclaine, Rob Reiner, Gene Hackman, Richard Dreyfuss*
Veteran director Mike Nichols gives the orders to an all-star cast in this film based on the novel by Carrie Fisher (*Star Wars'* Princess Leia, and daugh-

ter of Debbie Reynolds and Eddie Fisher). Based loosely on Fisher's actual life, the story revolves around a young actress who has so many problems with her famous mother that she turns to drugs in order to seek refuge. Despite the seriousness of the topic, Nichols manages to keep the show warm and lighthearted, and it is a blast from beginning to end. You'll especially love the exceptional performances by all of the stars who seem to drift in and out of the story.

THE POSTMAN ALWAYS RINGS TWICE
(1981)
*** R 2:02
DIR: *Bob Rafelson* **CAST:** *Jack Nicholson, Jessica Lange, Michael Lerner, John Colicos, Angelica Huston*
The second adaptation of James M. Cain's classic potboiler about infidelity and murder. Nicholson is at his seedy best as a stranger who wanders into a California roadhouse and steals the owner's wife (Lange) out from under him. It doesn't take long for the two to start thinking less about sex and more about murder. The erotic chemistry between Nicholson and Lange is memorable.

PREDATOR (1987)
*** R 1:46
DIR: *John McTiernan* **CAST:** *Arnold Schwarzenegger, Carl Weathers, Bill Duke, Jesse Ventura, Shane Black*

It's hard to resist a movie that pits Arnold (as yet another Special Ops warrior) against a reptilian alien in a South American jungle. Arnold's squad has been sent on a military mission, but soon discover that they themselves are being hunted by a mysterious creature who can make itself invisible. Turns out that this space creature is an intergalatic sportsman, out for a few trophy heads from the small green planet near the sun. This is an extremely well-done sci-fi/action film with a big, big finish. Arnold looks cool in camouflage.

PRESUMED INNOCENT (1990)
*** R 2:07
DIR: *Alan J. Pakula* CAST: *Harrison Ford, Bonnie Bedelia, Brian Dennehy, Raul Julia, Paul Winfield, John Spencer, Greta Scacchi*
A first-rate adaptation of Scott Turow's best-selling courtroom drama about a straight-laced prosecutor (Ford) who finds himself on the wrong side of the courtoom aisle. Accused of murdering a fellow prosecutor (Scacchi) with whom he had an affair, Ford is excellent as the wronged man who sees his life and career slipping away. Bedelia shines as the pained wife who stands behind her husband, albeit reluctantly. As circumstantial evidence mounts, he enlists the help of a top defense attorney, played brilliantly by Julia. The film's strength is that we're never quite sure

whether Ford is a hero or a monster until the
startling resolution. Pakula's directing is tense as
a coiled spring.

PRETTY WOMAN (1990)
* R 1:57
DIR: *Garry Marshall* **CAST:** *Richard Gere, Julia
Roberts, Ralph Bellamy, Laura San Giacamo, Hector
Elizando*
Inexplicably mega-popular film in which Roberts
plays a hooker who is hired by wealthy businessman Gere to spend a week with him at the Beverly
Hills Hotel. Cliche-ridden, *Pygmalion* rip-off is
saved by an engaging performance from Roberts,
and a typically professional job from Gere. Cute
and heartwarming on one level, the film actually
provides a disturbing message to younger viewers about what qualities a woman needs to possess in order to be a success in today's world.

PRINCESS BRIDE (1987)
**** PG 1:38
DIR: *Rob Reiner* **CAST:** *Cary Elwes, Mandy Potankin,
Robin Wright, Andre the Giant*
This is a wonderful movie that lets you feel good
about yourself! A lighthearted romp through a
fantastical land in a fantastical time, it features
rhyming giants, devious albinos, beautiful princesses, and rodents of unusual size. Cary Elwes is
splendid as the hammy yet heroic heartthrob who

saves the day, and Robin Wright brings all the beauty possible to the Princess Buttercup. Featuring a host of cameos by famous performers, perhaps the finest is by Andre the Giant, who portrays one of the most loveable characters to hit the screen in years. There is even a great little prologue in which Peter Falk (a.k.a. Columbo) and Fred Savage (from TV's *The Wonder Years*) play off of each other.

PRIZZI'S HONOR (1985)
*** R 2:10
DIR: *John Huston* **CAST:** *Jack Nicholson, Kathleen Turner, Angelica Huston, William Hickey, John Randolph, Robert Loggia*

Nicholson is a devoted servant of a mob family, Turner a freelancer in this twisted comedy of love among hit men (or hit person, in Turner's case). They marry after a whirlwind courtship but soon run into trouble when career opportunities collide. Nicholson must chose between La Familia and his blushing, gun-toting bride. Hickey plays a sweet, menacing Godfather. A fine allegory about the problems faced by double-income couples. Huston took home a Best Supporting Actress Oscar for her role as a neurotic mob daughter who pines for Nicholson. Huston, Hickey and Nicholson were all nominated, as were screenwriters Richard Condon and Janet Roach.

THE PRODUCERS (1968)
*** NR 1:28

DIR: *Mel Brooks* **CAST:** *Zero Mostel, Gene Wilder, Dick Shawn, Kenneth Mars, Estelle Winwood, Renee Taylor*

Outrageously funny tale about a Broadway producer (Mostel) and his accountant (Wilder) who conspire to sell well over 100 percent of the interest in a musical to a group of investors. In order for them to succeed, the show must flop, so they hire a writer (Mars), director (Hewett), and star (Shawn) who will ensure the musical's failure. The show-within-a-show, "Springtime for Hitler," provides many of the laughs. Brooks received an Academy Award for his screenplay.

PSYCHO (1960)
**** R 1:49

DIR: *Alfred Hitchcock* **CAST:** *Anthony Perkins, Janet Leigh, Vera Miles, Simon Oakland, John Gavin, Martin Balsam*

Hitchcock is at the top of his game in this story about the young man (Perkins) who runs the Bates motel and the young secretary/embezzler (Leigh) who ends up spending a terrifying night there. Hitchcock's storytelling method—the main character is killed very early on in the film—and blending of black humor and terrifying suspense set the tone for a generation of horror-filmmakers. He also kept thousands of moviegoers out of their showers! Listen for Bernard Hermann's legendary musical score.

PUBLIC ENEMY (1931)
*** NR 1:25
DIR: *William Wellman* **CAST:** *James Cagney, Jean Harlow, Joan Blondell, Beryl Mercer, Donald Cook, Mae Clarke*
This is the film that made Cagney a star. He plays a prohibition gangster, and the movie tells of his rise and fall. Though a bit dated, the film remains a classic because of Cagney's magnificient performance. Watch for the famous "grapefruit scene," in which the star smashes the fruit into Clarke's face.

PUMPING IRON (1977)
*** PG 1:25
DIR: *Robert Fiore, George Butler* **CAST:** *Arnold Schwarzenegger, Lou Ferrigno*
A funny, insightful documentary about the fierce competition for the Mr. Universe weightlifting championship. Although not a drama, Schwarzenegger's performance as he struts before the cameras should have earned him an Oscar nomination. It's no wonder that a pumped-up, greasy Arnold won the coveted title for many years in a row. There's an espcially revealing moment when Arnold psyches out Ferrigno (later of Incredible Hulk fame), who seems unprepared

for his competitor's brash confidence. If it weren't so painful, it would be funny. The filmmakers manage to keep an effective ironic distance from the action.

PUNCHLINE (1988)
*** R 2:08
DIR: *David Seltzer* CAST: *Tom Hanks, Sally Field, John Goodman, Kim Griest*
Beautifully written and tragically funny, *Punchline* is the story of people who want to make their mark on the world by making others laugh. Featuring excellent performances, the viewer identifies easily with the pain felt by the characters as they struggle to make their dreams come true. Director David Seltzer guides the story along effortlessly. And watch for a number of humorous cameos by real comedians and other show biz types.

THE PURPLE ROSE OF CAIRO (1985)
*** PG 1:22
DIR: *Woody Allen* CAST: *Mia Farrow, Jeff Daniels, Danny Aiello, Edward Herrmann, Dianne Wiest*
Allen takes a flight of fancy here in the story of Farrow, an abused, depression-era housewife, and Daniels, a dashing film hero who literally walks off the screen and into Farrow's sad little life. Farrow is excellent as a mousey woman who yearns for the kind of excitement depicted in

madcap musicals. Daniels is charming as a fictional character confronting real life (including a funny encounter with a group of prostitutes) for the first time. Trouble starts when the actor who created the character shows up to try and talk his creation back onto the screen, where the other characters await his return. Allen received an Oscar nomination for his bittersweet screenplay about the chasm between life and art.

Q

Q (1982)
** R 1:33
DIR: *Larry Cohen* CAST: *David Carradine, Michael Moriarty, Richard Roudtree*
Q is a campy yet attractive homage to horror films. New York City is visited by the ancient Aztec god Quetzalcoatl after some strange death rituals have occurred. The lizard god can't quite match the dinosaurs of *Jurassic Park* in terms of realness, but the special effects are good enough. The movie is quite fun and entertaining, and it's not a bad way to kill a few hours.

Q PLANES (1939)
*** NR 1:28
DIR: *Tim Whelan* CAST: *Ralph Richardson, Laurence Olivier, Valerie Hobson, George Merritt*

Featuring some of the finest British actors of all time, this World War II-era movie is absolutely hilarious. Ralph Richardson portrays an inspector hunting down Lawrence Olivier, whom he suspects of selling secrets about the British military's air capabilities to the Nazi army. If you love old movies, or if you just like to laugh and be thrilled at the same time, then this film is definitely for you.

QUACKSER FORTUNE HAS A COUSIN IN THE BRONX (1970)
*** R 1:28
DIR: *Warris Hussein* **CAST:** *Gene Wilder, Margot Kidder, Eileen Colga*
A delightful little sleeper not to be missed, *Quackser Fortune has a Cousin in the Bronx* stars the ever-hilarious Gene Wilder and Margot Kidder (*Superman*'s Lois Lane). Kidder is an American student attending the University of Dublin, and Wilder is the zany Irishman who falls in love with her. Their escapades make for a wonderfully entertaining comedy.

QUADROPHENIA (1979)
*** R 1:55
DIR: *Franc Roddam* **CAST:** *Phil Daniels, Sting, Leslie Ash, Mark Wingett, Garry Cooper*
One of the finest rock and roll movies ever made, *Quadrophenia* tells the story of two British gangs,

the Rockers and the Mods. Featuring some fine performances, particularly that of Sting (former lead singer for the Police), the viewer catches a glimpse of some of the true anger and angst experienced by young people in England at the time. Not to be missed.

QUEEN OF HEARTS (1989)
*** R 1:42
DIR: *John Amiel* **CAST:** *Vittorie Duse, Joseph Long, Vittori Ammandola, Tat Whalley*
One of the few films that successfully combines elements of different genres, this funny and poignant movie about an Italian husband and wife who venture to England to open a restaurant will touch your heart. Featuring fine performances and direction, this small gem is a must-see.

QUEST FOR FIRE (1982)
*** R 1:37
DIR: *Jean-Jacques Annaud* **CAST:** *Everett McGill, Rae Dawn Chong, Ron Perlman, Nameer El-Kadi, Gary Schwartz*
Remarkable tale about a prehistoric tribe who are attacked and lose their fire. Unaware of how to make fire, they send three members on a search to find the flame. Anthony Burgess developed a special language for the characters to speak, and Desmond Morris created a unique body language and gestures for them to use. A fascinating adventure-fantasy.

QUICK CHANGE (1990)
*** R 1:28
DIR: *Murray and Howard Franklin* **CAST:** *Bill Murray, Geena Davis, Randy Quaid, Bob Elliot, Phillip Bosco, Jason Robards*

Murray, Davis and Quaid play a trio of bank robbers who pull off a flawless heist. The real challenges come as they try to make their way from Midtown Manhattan to the airport. Murray is low-key and funny as a mastermind overwhelmed by foreign taxi drivers, hold-up men, mafia thugs, and serious parking problems. Davis plays his girlfriend, Quaid the anxiety-ridden crime partner who's not cut out for this kind of work. A clever script and fast pace makes this an enjoyable farce.

THE QUIET EARTH (1985)
*** R 1:31
DIR: *Geoff Murphy* **CAST:** *Alison Routledge, Bruno Lawrence*

Although this movie starts to lose energy about halfway through, it is still quite an experience to watch. Bruno Lawrence portrays a scientist who believes that he is the last man alive on earth after some freak disaster. To make matters worse, he thinks that one of his scientific projects might have been responsible for the disaster! The first twenty minutes of the film are exceptionally gripping, and they are well worth the price of the rental alone. Although the acting leaves something to be desired, the direction is very good.

THE QUIET MAN (1952)
**** NR 2:09
DIR: *John Ford* CAST: *John Wayne, Maureen O'Hara, Barry Fitzgerald, Victor McLaglen, Ward Bond, Arthur Shields, Mildred Natwick*
Extremely popular John Ford film about an American ex-boxer (Wayne) who retires to his native Ireland and woos local lass O'Hara. Standing in his way, however, is O'Hara's overprotective brother (McLaglen). Wayne is excellent in the title role, and Ford and cinematographers Winton Hoch and Archie Stout won Oscars for their work (the film takes marvelous advantage of the gorgeous Irish setting).

QUIGLEY DOWN UNDER (1990)
*** PG 1:46
DIR: *Simon Wincer* CAST: *Tom Selleck, Alan Rickman, Laura San Giacomo*
Although this movie is nothing special, it is still a lot of fun to watch! A rough and tough 1800s Texas cowboy (Selleck) takes a job in Australia. There, he not only has to deal with his own culture shock, but also with nasty ranchers and beautiful women. Entertaining and funny, it's good for a laugh. Selleck is particularly charming, as usual.

QUO VADIS? (1958)
**** R 2:40

DIR: *Franco Rossi* **CAST:** *Frederic Forrest, Klaus Maria Brandauer, Francesco Quinn*

One of the finest epics ever filmed about ancient Rome, this is the story of a Roman legionary who loves a Christian woman. The two plot throughout the film to meet secretly, in order to avoid execution for their sinful love. One of their biggest adversaries in the movie is the Emperor Nero himself. Slow moving yet still worth watching, especially for the acting.

R

RAGING BULL (1980)
**** R 2:08

DIR: *Martin Scorsese* **CAST:** *Robert De Niro, Cathy Moriarty, Joe Pesci, Frank Vincent, Nicholas Colasanto, Theresa Saldana*

Martin Scorsese's masterpiece about the rise and fall of middleweight champion Jake La Motta. De Niro, in an Oscar-winning performance, is mesmerizing as the fighter. Filmed in black and white, the boxing scenes are pure poetry *and* violence (Academy Award-winning editor Thelma Schoonmaker is also largely responsible for their effectiveness). Joe Pesci and Cathy Moriary shine in their first major roles. Voted the best film of the decade in a national poll of film critics.

RAIDERS OF THE LOST ARK (1981)
*** PG 1:55

DIR: *Steven Spielberg* **CAST:** *Harrison Ford, Karen Allen, Wolf Kahler, Paul Freeman, Denholm Elliott, John Rhys-Davies*

Blockbuster action-adventure movie from the team of Steven Spielberg and George Lucas. Ford plays Indiana Jones, an archeologist trying to find the Ark of the Covenant before the Nazis get to it. Great music (by John Williams) and special effects combine to create loads of excitement, thrills and chills in this thoroughly entertaining movie.

RAIN MAN (1988)
*** R 2:20

DIR: *Barry Levinson* **CAST:** *Dustin Hoffman, Tom Cruise*

Hoffman took home a well-deserved Best Actor Oscar for his stunning portrayal of a middle-aged autistic man with the memory of a personal computer. Cruise is superior as his sleazy younger brother who kidnaps Hoffman to get part of a three million dollar inheritance. As the two travel across the country, Cruise begins to bond with his strange traveling companion, even as he uses his special gifts to count cards in Vegas. This is a touching, funny film which challenges our preconceptions about mental illness. Winner of the Academy Award for Best Picture, Director, and Screenplay. Also nominated for Cinematography, Art Direction, Editing and Original Score.

THE RAIN PEOPLE (1969)
*** R 1:42
DIR: *Francis Ford Coppola* **CAST:** *Shirley Knight, James Caan, Robert Duvall*

One of brilliant director Francis Ford Coppola's first truly independent films, and possibly even one of his earliest masterpieces, *The Rain People* is the story of a woman (Knight) who runs away from her confining life upon discovering her pregnancy. Coppola's gift for directing actors is already obvious in this remarkable little gem, which, although flawed, is still thoroughly engrossing. Knight is joined on her journey to nowhere by James Caan, an orphaned college athlete who received brain damage during a college football game. Containing many of the same themes of *Thelma & Louise* , *The Rain People* pre-dates that film by over 20 years!

RAISE THE RED LANTERN (1991)
**** NR 2:05
DIR: *Zhang Yimou* **CAST:** *Gong Li, Ma Jingwu, He Caifei, Cao Cuifeng, Kong Lin*

Beautiful film about a college educated girl (Gong Li) who is sent to a nobelman's home in 1920's China to become one of his wives. The story examines the relationships between Li, her master, their servants, and the other wives—all of whom still live in the same household. It may be slow-going at times, but the gorgeous cinematography and the exceptional performance by Li make this film a must-see.

RAISING ARIZONA (1987)
*** PG-13 1:34
DIR: *Joel and Ethan Coen* **CAST:** *Nicholas Cage, Holly Hunter, Trey Wilson, John Goodman, William Forsythe, Frances McDormand, Randall Cobb*
The Coen brothers are better known for stylish thrillers like *Blood Simple* and *Miller's Crossing*, but this first venture into comedy is a success. Cage plays a good-hearted ex-con who marries a cop (Hunter). When they find out she's "barren", they decides to kidnap one of the quintuplets born to a wealthy Arizona couple. The rest of the film is a wild romp as the couple tries to hold on to their ill-gotten gain. The ending is as far-fetched and funny as the rest of the movie.

A RAISIN IN THE SUN (1961)
*** NR 2:08
DIR: *Daniel Petrie* **CAST:** *Sidney Poitier, Ruby Dee, Claudia McNeil, Diana Sands, Louis Gossett, Jr.*
Essentially a note-for-note filmed version of Lorrain Hansberry's Pulitzer Prize-winning play about a black family living in a Chicago ghetto who want to move to an all-white neighborhood. Outstanding performances by everyone involved. Even after all these years, Hansberry's dialouge

still stings, and the story remains a contemporary one.

RAMBLING ROSE (1991)
**** R 1:52
DIR: *Martha Coolidge* **CAST:** *Laura Dern, Dianne Ladd, Robert Duvall, Lukas Haas*
Based on the novel by Calder Winningham, this movie beautifully evokes the culture and heritage of the South in the 1930s. Duvall plays the head of a household who agrees to take in a young woman named Rose (Dern), who has proven to be difficult for her parents to handle. Duvall agrees to try to straighten her out, but in return she must work for the family. She clicks immediately with Ladd, who seems to view Rose as the daughter she never had (Ladd is, in fact, Dern's mother in real life, and the two performed so well together that they both earned Oscar nominations). But problems start to arise when the men in the family, both Duvall and 13-year old Haas, grow more intimate with Rose. The intimacy becomes so extreme that the film was actually quite controversial. A delight by any standards, this is a movie you don't want to miss.

RAMBO: FIRST BLOOD PART II (1985)
* R 1:35
DIR: *George P. Cosmatos* **CAST:** *Sylvester Stallone, Richard Crenna, Charles Napier*

The movie that reminded the world of Sylvester Stallone's superstar status, *Rambo: First Blood Part II* seems even more ridiculous today than it did a few years ago. Stallone plays a Vietnam vet who has run into bad luck. But the U.S. Government cuts a deal with him: if he goes back to Vietnam and finds proof of any Prisoners of War still being held, he will be able to start his life anew. The offer is too tempting to refuse, and he makes his way to Southeast Asia. Once there, he encounters thousands of the stupidest Russian, Chinese, and Vietnamese soldiers ever depicted on celluloid, destroys more foliage than the entire U.S. army did during the actual war, and shows off his bulging muscles. There are some neat scenes with a bow and arrow, however, and you have to admire Stallone for doing a film about a subject that was so unpopular at the time. It's just a pity he did it so badly.

RAPID FIRE (1992)
** R 1:35
DIR: *Dwight H. Little* **CAST:** *Brandon Lee, Powers Booth, Nick Mancuso*
This splendid action film was the last one Brandon Lee completed before his tragic death. Lee displays what could have been a great deal of promise, and the viewer can't help but feel that he could have had a career as successful as that of his late father, martial arts expert Bruce Lee. The best

performance is surely that of Nick Mancuso, who brings a delightful whit to the antagonist. Although the script is quite thin and self-serving, the action scenes make the movie worth viewing.

RAN (1985)
**** R 2:40
DIR: *Akira Kurosawa* **CAST:** *Tasuya Nakadai, Satoshi Terao, Jinpachi Nezu, Daisuke Ryu, Mieko Harada*
Awe-inspiring epic adaptation of Shakespeare's *King Lear* by master Japanese filmmaker Akira Kurosawa. Gorgeous cinematography and stunningly choreographed battle scenes highlight this story about a foolish old warlord who divides his kingdom among his three sons. When his only loving son objects to the plan, he banishes him to the harsh wilderness.

RASHAMON (1951)
**** NR 1:28
DIR: *Akira Kurosawa* **CAST:** *Toshiro Mifune, Machiko Kyo, Masayuki Mori, Takashi Shimura*
Four people in a forest who witness a rape-murder—the three participants and a woodcutter—give differing accounts of the circumstances surrounding the crime. Kurosawa is exploring the nature of truth in this work, the great filmmaker's first international success (it won the Oscar for Best Foreign Film). Beautiful cinematography and poetic filmmaking make this a movie not to be missed.

THE RAVEN (1963)
*** NR 1:26

DIR: *Roger Corman* **CAST:** *Vincent Price, Boris Karloff, Jack Nicholson, Peter Lorre*

One of Roger Corman's finest directorial efforts, this film transforms Edgar Allen Poe's classic poem of chills and suspense into a narrative. Corman's direction is tight and potent, utilizing every meager penny of the tight budget to its fullest effect. The interaction between the characters is just dandy, particularly Jack Nicholson in one his first performances. Funny and scary, this is a great movie to sit back and watch on a stormy night.

THE RAZOR'S EDGE (1984)
*** PG-13 2:10

DIR: *John Byrum* **CAST:** *Bill Murray, Theresa Russell, Catherine Hicks, Denoholm Elliot, Brian Doyle Murray, James Keach*

This is a competent, well-meaning rendition of Somerset Maugham's classic novel of a young man (Murray) in search of meaning. The film has a real intelligence and integrity about it, but Murray seems to underplay the character's quest as he goes from the battlefields of World War I to the mountain tops of India. In the end, we don't care as much about his fate as Maugham intended.

REAR WINDOW (1954)
**** PG 1:52
DIR: *Alfred Hitchcock* **CAST:** *James Stewart, Grace Kelly, Raymond Burr, Wendell Corey, Thelma Ritter, Judith Evelyn*
A perfect film from the master of suspense. Stewart plays a photographer stuck in his Greenwich Village apartment because of a broken leg. With nothing to do but spy on his neighbors through their rear windows, he begins to suspect that the man across the way (Burr) has murdered his wife. A superb blending of suspense, humor, and psychological study. Stewart is remarkable as the unwholesome voyeur. Kelly is as gorgeous as ever as Stewart's girlfriend.

RE-ANIMATOR (1985)
*** R 1:26
DIR: *Stuart Gordon* **CAST:** *Jeffrey Combs, Bruce Abbott, Stuart Gordon, Barbara Crampton*
This wonderful little gem is a low-budget delight not to be missed by horror movie fans. Based loosely on the classic macabre tales of H.P. Lovecraft, this is the tale of a brilliant medical student who learns the key to eternal life. He starts injecting his wonder potion into the cadavers in the medical school, with terrifically gruesome results. There are plenty of twists and turns that will leave you guessing, the dark humor is great, and you'll get a blast out of the scenes involving severed heads.

REBECCA (1940)
**** NR 2:10
DIR: *Alfred Hitchcock* **CAST:** *Laurence Olivier, Joan Fontaine, Judith Anderson, George Sanders, Nigel Bruce, C. Aubrey Smith*
Hitchcock's first American film (and only Oscar winner) is an adaptation of Daphne du Maurier's Gothic Romance novel. Newlywed Fontaine is forced to live up to the memory of brooding husband Olivier's dead first wife, the beautiful Rebecca. Award-winning cinematography by George Barnes and Franz Waxman's mysterious score combine with Hitchcock's direction to create a haunting atmosphere. Impeccable performances all around.

REBEL WITHOUT A CAUSE (1955)
*** NR 1:51
DIR: *Nicholas Ray* **CAST:** *James Dean, Natalie Wood, Sal Mineo, Jim Backus, Ann Doran, Dennis Hopper*
Tragic story about a delinquent teenager (Dean) who feels out of place in a world dominated by the values of his parents and the adults surrounding him. At the time of its release, the film managed to hook into a generation who were beginning to develop their own popular culture and sense of values. Impressively, this somewhat dated look at teen alienation has continued to touch the lives of disaffected youths throughout the following decades. The sensitive performance by Dean is

his most famous, but one can't overlook the excellent supporting cast, especially Mineo and Wood as Dean's friends and confidants.

RED RIVER (1948)
**** NR 2:13
DIR: *Howard Hawks* CAST: *John Wayne, Montgomery Clift, Walter Brennan*
One of the finest Westerns ever made, this is a tribute to the talents of director Howard Hawks and star John Wayne. Wayne plays the overseer of a cattle drive, and Montgomery Clift is the idealistic young man who doesn't like the way his tyrannical boss runs the show. The two clash, but only one will be victorious. Tense until the chilling end, this is a must-see! This is one of the few movies where it is hard to find fault with anyone's performance in the project. Not only are all the actors perfect, including Clift (even though this is his debut role), but the direction is tight and economical, the script is emotional, and even the photography is great.

REMO WILLIAMS: THE ADVENTURE BEGINS (1985)
** PG 2:01
DIR: *Guy Hamilton* CAST: *Fred Ward, Joel Grey, Wilford Brimley, Charles Cioffi*
This fun adventure is the perfect movie to rent on video on restless nights with nothing else to do.

Based on "The Destroyer" series of books, you will be thrilled by some of the incredible stunts and feats of balance, many of which were performed by Fred Ward (Remo Williams) himself. Ward is a cop whose death was faked so that he could become a government-licensed vigilante. He learns incredible new skills of agility and combat from an ancient Korean martial arts expert. Watch for the amazing fight over the Statue of Liberty, which was still covered in scaffolding, due to its refurbishing, while the movie was being filmed.

REPO MAN (1984)
*** R 1:32
DIR: *Alex Cox* CAST: *Emilio Estevez, Harry Dean Stanton, Vonetta McGee, Sy Richardson*
A cult classic by the same director who gave us the brutal *Sid and Nancy*. Estevez plays a car repossessor who's taught the tricks of the trade by his slimy boss (Stanton). The plot involves the pursuit of an old Chevy Malibu containing the remains of dead space aliens. There are enough spot-on cultural references and sight gags to keep this from flying into the ozone. A punk version of a screwball comedy.

REPOSSESSED (1990)
* PG-13 1:24
DIR: *Bob Logan* CAST: *Linda Blair, Leslie Nielson,*

Ned Beatty, Lana Schwab
What should have been a wonderful comedy turns out to be a confused and sober jumble of a movie. Linda Blair plays a role similar to the one she portrayed in *The Exorcist*, only instead of being a young girl, she's now a housewife. Nielson plays the priest who is going to exorcise the demons from within her. The premise is funny, but the film never pays off. It tries to be another *Airplane!*, but it does not succeed.

REPULSION (1965)
**** NR 1:45
DIR: *Roman Polanski* **CAST:** *Catherine Deneuve, Ian Hendry, Yvonne Furneaux*
Polanski's dark vision of a beautiful woman's descent into schizophrenia. Deneuve stars as a young English woman who shuts herself into a small, filthy apartment. Her hallucinations, including arms coming out of the wall to attack her, are horrifying. When friends try to help, her psychosis leads to murder. One of the most frightening psycho-thrillers ever made.

RETURN OF THE JEDI (1983)
*** PG 2:13
DIR: *Richard Marquand* **CAST:** *Mark Hamill, Harrison Ford, Carrie Fisher, David Prowse, James Earl Jones*
The final installment of George Lucas' breathtak-

ing *Star Wars* trilogy, this film wraps it all up with a bang and sends you out of the movie theatre with a smile on your face that stretches from ear to ear! Featuring dazzling special effects, a satisfying script, delightful-looking monsters, and fine performances, this really is one of the finest science fiction movies ever made. You will follow Luke Skywalker on his missions to free his comrade Han Solo, vanquish the evil from Darth Vader (or die trying), and ultimately destroy the new Death Star Space Station. Winner of the Academy Award for Special Effects.

REVENGE OF THE NERDS (1984)
** R 1:30
DIR: *Jeff Kanew* **CAST:** *Anthony Edwards, Robert Carradine, Ted McGinley, John Goodman*
Superior performances all around save this movie from being just another teen comedy. After being pushed too far too long, the nerds at a local college decide to get even with the jocks. They steal their women, steal their popularity, and even steal their frat house. Although the subject matter is mindless, it never becomes distasteful (as with so many other similar movies), and the performances by its stars almost make it touching at moments. *Revenge of the Nerds* isn't great, but it certainly isn't disappointing.

REVERSAL OF FORTUNE (1990)
**** R 1:50

DIR: *Barbet Schroeder* **CAST:** *Jeremy Irons, Glenn Close, Ron Silver, Anabella Sciorra*

Irons won an Oscar for his remarkable transformation into Claus von Bulow, the snobby Austrian aristocrat accused of attempting to murder his wealthy wife. The story is told from the point of view of Sonny von Bulow (played beautifully by Close), who as of publication still langours in a coma in an east coast hospital. Silver plays Alan Dershowitz, the Harvard attorney who enlisted an army of law students to appeal Von Bulow's conviction. This is masterful story-telling that presents the facts but leaves it to the viewer to decide guilt or innocence. Schroeder was nominated for Best Director, Nicholas Kazan for Best Adapted Screenplay.

THE RIGHT STUFF (1983)
**** PG 3:13

DIR: *Philip Kaufman* **CAST:** *Sam Shepard, Scott Glenn, Ed Harris, Dennis Quaid, Fred Ward, Barbara Hershey, Veronica Cartwright, Pamela Reed, Levon Helm, Jeff Goldblum*

Adapted from Tom Wolfe's best-selling book, this story chronicles the beginnings of America's space program, from Chuck Yeager's (Shepard) attempt to break the sound barrier to the first astronauts who orbited the Earth. For such a

potentially, large, epic subject, Kaufman has fash-
ioned a compelling film more concerned with the
human side of those involved. We watch the
behind-the-scenes triumphs and disappointments
of the public heroes, as well as how the media
create the myths that surround them. At three
hours plus, the film is never boring, and many
scenes, particularly when the camera goes air-
borne, are thrilling.

RISKY BUSINESS (1983)
*** R 1:39
DIR: *Paul Brickman* CAST: *Tom Cruise, Rebecca
DeMornay, Curtis Armstrong, Richard Masur*
This is the movie that made Tom Cruise a star! He
gives a bravura performance as a lonely young
man alienated from his affluent parents, hoping
to become successful through his own hard work.
One week, when his parents go away on vacation,
he hopes to satisfy his budding sexual curiosity
by hiring a call girl for a night. The only problem
is, she steals the most valuable item in the house!
Featuring a cast of young and talented actors, you
can really understand why most of these performers have gone on to become stars. Funny and
sad, *Risky Business* is wonderfully entertaining.

RIVER'S EDGE (1987)
*** R 1:39
DIR: *Tim Hunter* CAST: *Crispin Glover, Keanu*

Reeves, Dennis Hopper, Ione Skye, Jim Metzler, Roxana Zal, Daniel Roebuck

A disturbing film about a group of teenagers who remain silent after one member of their group is killed by another. Worse still, they go out in carloads to view the corpse lying on a river bank, as if it were there for their entertainment. The saddest part of all is that this is based on a true case in Northern California. Screenwriter Neil Jimenez and this fine young cast takes an unflinching look at moral failure and a society numbed to violence.

THE ROAD WARRIOR (1982)
*** R 1:34
DIR: *George Miller* CAST: *Mel Gibson, Bruce Spence, Vernon Wells, Emil Minty, Mike Preston, Virginia Hey*

This sequel to *Mad Max* is actually far superior to the original. Gibson is a cop in a post-apocalyptic universe fighting off theives who are trying to take over a commune's home-made refinery. Lots of action, highlighted with breathtaking chase scenes, combines with skillful direction to make this film a winner.

ROBOCOP (1987)
*** R 1:43
DIR: *Paul Verhoven* CAST: *Peter Weller, Nancy Allen, Ronny Cox, Miguel Ferrer, Daniel O'Herlihy*

A wildy entertaining action sci-fi film about a semi-human robot who patrols the street of next-century Detroit. Weller plays the steel cop who has vauge, fleeting images of having once been alive. He's the last hope against ravaging packs of street hoodlums destroying the city, and the film revolves around his pursuit of the thugs who took his life, condemning him to an existence neither human nor machine. There's enough biting humor to keep this film from taking itself too seriously.

THE ROCKETEER (1991)
**** PG 1:50

DIR: *Joe Johnston* **CAST:** *Bill Campbell, Timothy Dalton, Alan Arkin, Jennifer Connelly*

This delightful Disney film pays homage to the cliffhanger serials of the 1930s almost as well as Steven Spielberg's *Raiders of the Lost Ark* does. Taking place during World War II, a Howard Hughes-like character invents a jet pack in order to insure America's defeat of the Nazis. After almost falling into enemy hands, an all-American pilot finds it and becomes *The Rocketeer*. He soon learns to harness the power of the jet pack and uses it to fend off a Nazi invasion. Featuring a spectacular fight on a zeppelin and a deliciously devilish performance by Timothy Dalton, this is one not to be missed.

ROCKY (1976)
** PG 1:59

DIR: *John G. Avidsen* **CAST:** *Sylvester Stallone, Talia Shire, Burgess Meredith, Burt Young, Carl Weathers, Thayer David*

Immensely popular underdog tale about a down and out fighter (Stallone) who is given a chance to fight for the championship by a publicity-hungry title holder (Weathers). Stallone brings a great deal of sincerity to this familiar story, and he receives a substantial amount of help from both Shire and Meredith. The boxing scenes are tremendously exciting, and you're sure to be cheering for Stallone by the end of the fight. Four uneven, yet still popular, sequels would follow.

ROLLERBALL (1975)
*** R 2:08

DIR: *Norman Jewison* **CAST:** *James Caan, Maud Adams, John Houseman*

In a nondescript time (presumably the near future), all war and violence has been irradicated from the planet. At first this sounds great, but the viewer quickly realizes the price that mankind has had to pay in order to achieve this ideal: complete submission to major corporations which now act as governments. In order to allow society some kind of release for its violence, the corporations have created a sport called Rollerball, which has all of the action of motorcross and football in one! The only problem is that one loner Rollerball star, played brilliantly by James Caan, threatens to destroy the status quo.

ROMANCING THE STONE (1984)
*** PG 1:46
DIR: *Robert Zemeckis* **CAST:** *Kathleen Turner, Michael Douglas , Danny DeVito*
A lively adventure starring Turner as a mopey Manhattan romance writer and Douglas as a ne'r-do-well bird smuggler. Together they search for Turner's kidnapped sister and a priceless jewel, fighting off Colombian soldiers, con men, and alligators along the way. This is a breezy, fun romp where the bad guys aren't that bad and a happy ending is pretty much insured.

A ROOM WITH A VIEW (1986)
*** NR 1:55
DIR: *James Ivory* **CAST:** *Maggie Smith, Helena Bonham Carter, Denholm Elliott, Julian Sands, Daniel Day-Lewis, Simon Callow, Judi Dench*
Exquisite adaptation of E.M. Forster's novel about a young, proper Englishwoman's (Bonham Carter) coming of age during a trip to Florence, Italy. Despite her upper-crust boyfriend back home (Day-Lewis), she falls in love with an "unsuitable" boy (Sands) she meets on her trip, much to the horror of chaperon Smith. A beautiful film to behold, and the winner of three Academy Awards.

ROSEMARY'S BABY (1968)
**** R 2:16

DIR: *Roman Polanski* **CAST:** *Mia Farrow, John Cassavetes, Ruth Gordon, Maurice Evans, Charles Grodin, Ralph Bellamy*

Roman Polanski's terrifying film based on Ira Levin's best-selling novel. Farrow plays a naive pregnant woman whose husband (Cassavetes) becomes involved with the devil-worshippers who live next door. Gordon took home an Oscar for her alternately humorous and frightening portrayal of an evil witch posing as a concerned and helpful friend to Farrow. A truly harrowing take on motherhood.

'ROUND MIDNIGHT (1986)
*** R 2:10

DIR: *Bertrand Tavernier* **CAST:** *Dexter Gordon, Francois Cluzet, Gabrielle Haker, Sandra Reaves-Philips, Lonette McKee, Herbie Hancock, Martin Scorsese*

Legendary real-life saxophonist Dexter Gordon gives a startling and tremendously affecting performance as Dale Turner, a talented musician whose alcohol and drug-abuse problems plague his otherwise brilliant career. Inspired by the lives of famous jazz musicians Bud Powell and Lester Young, this touching film is a must for jazz fans, as it features some fantastic music played Gordon, Hancock and other professionals. Cluzet is wonderful as the devoted jazz buff who nurses both Gordon and his music back to health in the musician's later years. The saccharine subplot involving Cluzet's relationship with his estranged wife and daughter is the only thing keeping this great film from reaching four star level.

ROXANNE (1987)
*** PG 1:47
DIR: *Fred Schepisi* **CAST:** *Steve Martin, Daryl Hannah, Rick Rossovich, Michael J. Pollard, Fred Willard, Shelley Duvall*

Martin and Schepisi have a great time updating Cyrano de Bergerac in this faithful, yet original retelling of Edmond Rostand's classic tale of a suave Frenchman whose one major flaw sat smack in the middle of his face. Martin, playing a small-town fire chief, suffers from the same attribute. He falls hard for a beautiful astronomer (Hannah), who in turn falls for a hunky fireman (Rossovich). Martin helps the dull fireman woo her with an extraordinary soliloquy, and must then suffer the consequences. This film has an endearingly light touch. Martin is excellent as the bright, talented fire chief who lets birds perch on his nose.

RUBY (1992)
** R 1:50
DIR: *John Mackenzie* **CAST:** *Danny Aiello, Sherilyn Fenn, Arliss Howard*

Fresh on the coattails of controversial filmmaker Oliver Stone's *JFK*, the producers of this movie tried to cash in on the resurgence of interest in the late president by examining one of the lesser-known figures in his life, Jack Ruby. Needless to say, the movie is far from eventful. It doesn't really tell the viewer much about the late nightclub owner who shot Lee Harvey Oswald, nor does it even elevate the mystery of Kennedy's death to yet another dimension. It's just pretty boring. Aiello and Fenn do their best to keep things interesting, and they deserve praise for that, but not even their talents can overcome such a thin script and Mackenzie's feeble direction.

THE RULES OF THE GAME (1939)
**** NR 1:41
DIR: *Jean Renoir* **CAST:** *Marcel Dalio, Nora Gregor, Mila Parely, Jean Renoir, Roland Toutain, Julien Carette*
A tremendously rich comedy-drama about the lives and loves of a group of aristocrats who are spending the weekend at the home of Dalio and his wife Gregor. A biting, satiric look at the morals and pretensions of the upper crust. Beautifully shot and well-acted, this film has often been imitated, but rarely equalled.

RUNAWAY TRAIN (1985)
*** R 1:51
DIR: *Andrei Konchalovsky* **CAST:** *Jon Voight, Eric*

Roberts, Rebecca DeMornay
A pair of convicts (Voight and Roberts) jump a train after escaping from an Alaskan prison. When the conductor dies of a heart attack, there's no way to stop the train. Voight and Roberts are excellent as two desperate men rushing pell-mell towards an uncertain fate. DeMornay, in a refreshingly unglamorous role, plays a railroad worker who needs the help of the criminals to stay alive. This is a taut thriller with wonderful acting.

THE RUNNING MAN (1987)
** R 1:41
DIR: *Paul Michael Glaser* **CAST:** *Arnold Schwarzenegger, Richard Dawson*
One of Arnold Schwarzenegger's less interesting movies, *The Running Man*, based on an early novel by Steven King, still packs enough action and laughs to be entertaining. "The Running Man" is a game show of the future in which alleged criminals are given the chance to fend for their life on national television. Schwarzenegger gets caught up in the whole show, and soon realizes that these "Runners" are not criminals at all, but merely people who possess a viewpoint that differs with the status quo. The one really memorable thing from this movie is Richard Dawson's magical and scene-stealing performance as the game show host.

RUTHLESS PEOPLE (1986)
*** R 1:33
DIR: *Jim Abrahams, David Zucker, Jerry Zucker*
CAST: *Bette Midler, Danny DeVito, Helen Slater, Judge Reinhold, Anita Morris*
The trio who brought us *Airplane* also offers up this black comedy about a kidnapped woman (Midler) whose slimy husband (DeVito) refuses to pay ransom in the hope that his wife will be iced. Reinhold and Slater play the sweet, sympathetic kidnappers who were cheated by DeVito in a business deal. What ensues is a very clever, near-gymnastic plot. Morris is funny as DeVito's conniving mistress.

―――――――― **S** ――――――――

SALVADOR (1986)
** R 2:03
DIR: *Oliver Stone* **CAST:** *James Woods, Jim Belushi, Elpedia Carrillo, Colby Chester, Cynthia Gibb, Michael Murphy*
Woods plays real-life journalist Richard Boyle, a grungy leftist who's at his best when reporting from the world's hot spots. He travels to El Salvador where he covers the brutal civil war. Although Stone, as usual, climbs up on a soapbox to make his movie, this is still a compelling and enlightening look at political repression. The film's biggest flaw is that at the same time it cries out

against the injustice perpetrated on the peasants, it also presents them as lazy and immoral. Stone and Boyle shared an Oscar nomination for their script. Woods was nominated for Best Actor.

SAY ANYTHING (1989)
*** PG-13 1:40
DIR: *Cameron Crowe* **CAST:** *John Cusack, Ione Skye, John Mahoney, Eric Stoltz, Lili Taylor*
A well-done Romeo and Juliet story of a charming high school misfit (Cusack) who falls for the shy class valedictorian (Skye). While the plot may sound overly-familar, Cusack and Skye are absolutely believeable as young lovers from different sides of the tracks. The film takes a numbing turn when it starts dealing with crimes committed by Skye's father, but until then *Say Anything* has an understated appeal.

SCANDAL (1989)
*** R 1:46
DIR: *Michael Canton-Jones* **CAST:** *John Hurt, Joanne Whalley-Kilmer, Bridget Fonda, Ian McKellen, Jeroen Krabbe*
A powerful, erotically-charged true story of a destructive affair in the early 1960s between a young English woman (Whalley-Kilmer) and John Profumo (McKellen), the British war minister. When it's revealed that the woman was also sleeping with a Russian spy (Krabbe), the ensuing

scandal brought down the government. Hurt gives a wonderful performance as a social-climbing doctor who acts as a purveyor for government officials. Whalley-Kilmer and Fonda are first-rate as party girls who unwittingly usher in the fall of the conservative government.

SCARFACE (1983)
** R 2:50
DIR: *Brian De Palma* CAST: *Al Pacino, Steven Bauer, Michelle Pfeiffer, Robert Loggia, F. Murray Abraham*

This is an ambitious, flawed remake of the 1932 classic about the rise of a Chicago mobster. Here, the setting is 1980's Miami, where a boat lift has just brought thousands of Cuban criminals into the country. Pacino stars as a petty Cuban thief who works his way up to become a big-time dope smuggler. De Palma tries to show that Tony's story is a somewhat skewed version of the American Dream. It works well to a point, but the incredibly bloody shoot-out at the end of the movie seems almost laughably gratuitous. Pacino goes a bit over the top in his portrayal of a would-be crime boss.

SCROOGED (1988)
*** PG-13 1:41
DIR: *Richard Donner* CAST: *Bill Murray, Alfre Woodard, Karen Allen, Carol Kane, Robert Mitchum, David Johansen*

Murray plays a memorable Scrooge in this modern-day remake of the Dicken's classic. Instead of a miserly banker, Murray plays a comically cruel Network boss busy making a Christmas special. The story shares the same structure as the original, with the ghosts visiting Murray to show him the err of his ways. Kane is funny as a pugilistic ghost of Christmas present. Woodard plays the Bob Cratchit role, and her silent son is the film's Tiny Tim. This is a funny, heartwarming re-telling of one of the world's favorite stories.

SEA OF LOVE (1989)
*** R 1:52
DIR: *Harold Becker* **CAST:** *Al Pacino, John Goodman, Ellen Barkin, Patricia Barry*
This is a wonderful police-thriller not to be missed! Pacino is a cop who has hit middle-age, and he is not reacting well to it. It is affecting his work and his home life, and he actually falls for one of his own suspects (Ellen Barkin). Featuring excellent performances all around (this is the film that reminded viewers John Goodman could play more than just *Roseanne*'s husband) and an intelligent plot, you will be glad you rented *Sea of Love*.

THE SEARCHERS (1956)
**** NR 1:59
DIR: *John Ford* **CAST:** *John Wayne, Natalie Wood, Vera Miles, Jeffrey Hunter, Ward Bond, Harry Carey, Jr*

A psychologically complex drama that is considered by many to be the most accomplished Western ever made. Wayne stars as a Civil War veteran who goes on a seven year search for his niece (Wood), who has been kidnapped by savage Indians. Wayne embodies both the light and dark qualities of a Western hero—on the one hand, he is relentless in his courageous pursuit; on the other, he insists on killing his niece when he finds her because she has been defiled. Beautifully directed by Ford with plenty of stunning photography of the desert landscapes.

SECRET OF NIMH (1982)
*** G 1:22
DIR: *Don Bluth* **CAST:** *Derek Jacobi, Elizabeth Hartman, Dom Deluise, John Carradine*
Based on the famed book by author Robert C. O'Brien, this is the splendid tale of a recently widowed field mouse who needs the help of some strange and mischievous rats to move her house before the farmer plows it up. The mouse, Mrs. Brisby, soon learns that she has many furry friends in the woods, as her late husband, Jonathan, was well liked by other creatures. What exactly is the secret of NIMH? Why do these rats seem so intelligent? You'll have to watch the movie to find out, and you won't be disappointed. Featuring animation that would put Disney to shame, and the voices of some of the most talented actors working today, this is a remarkable cartoon.

SEMI-TOUGH (1977)
*** R 1:47
DIR: *Michael Ritchie* CAST: *Burt Reynolds, Krist Kristofferson, Jill Clayburgh, Robert Preston, Bert Convy*

Kristofferson and Reynolds play aging N.F.L. heroes in this smart send-up of professional sports and the touchy-feely self-improvement glut of the 1970s. Both men, who compete for the affections of Clayburgh, seek the counsel of a group therapy guru (a la Werner Erhard) played by Convy. His advice to seek "It" without ever defining "It" leaves Kristofferson entranced and Reynolds beffudled. This is a time-capsule of one of the weirder periods in recent history.

THE SERPENT AND THE RAINBOW (1988)
** R 1:33
DIR: *Wes Carven* CAST: *Paul Winfield, Bill Pullman, Cathy Tyson, Theresa Merrit*

Allegedly based on true events, this horror film is certainly an interesting and unpredictable movie to watch. An American anthropologist ventures to Haiti in search of the key to the black magic which turns people into zombies. He comes across a cult claiming to possess such power, but he almost becomes a victim to it himself. There are some wonderful and frightening dream sequences which make this movie stand out a little from most generic horror fare.

THE SERVANT (1963)
*** NR 1:55
DIR: *Joseph Losey* **CAST:** *Dirk Bogarde, Wendy Craig, James Fox, Sarah Miles*
This stunning British masterpiece will leave you biting your fingernails long after the credits have finished rolling! Borrowing the plot of a vampire film, but placing it within the context of normal human interactions, this movie analyzes the ways in which people prey off of each other for their own gain. Enormously entertaining, you can't help but feel sorry for the aristocratic protagonist (Fox) who is virtually devoured by his own servant (Bogarde). Some of the most interesting drama unfolds between Bogarde and Fox's lover, Wendy Craig.

THE SEVEN-PERCENT SOLUTION (1976)
*** PG 1:53
DIR: *Herb Ross* **CAST:** *Nicol Williamson, Alan Arkin, Robert Duvall, Vanessa Redgrave, Laurence Olivier, Joel Grey*
Sherlock Holmes (Williamson) and Sigmund Freud (Arkin), pair up to track down the ruthless Dr. Moriarty. Based on the book by Nicholas Meyer, this is an ingenious story about the interaction of real and fictional characters. Williamson is excellent as the brilliant detective who must confront, with the help of the father of psychoanalysis, his own drug addiction before continu-

ing to hunt for clues. Duvall is funny and low-key as Dr. Watson. An Oscar nomination for Meyer's screenplay of his own book.

THE SEVEN SAMURAI (1954)
**** NR 3:28
DIR: *Akira Kurosawa* CAST: *Takashi Shimura, Toshio Mifune, Seiji Miyaguchi, Yoshio Inaba.*
The greatest samurai film ever produced, Kurosawa's action-adventure masterpiece was later remade by Universal Studios as *The Magnificient Seven*. Samurai Shimura is hired by the citizens of a 16th century village to protect them from invaders, so he gathers together six other samurai, trains the villagers in warfare, and succeeds in fighting off the bandits. Epic battle sequences, humor, suspense ... this film has it all.

THE SEVENTH SEAL (1957)
**** NR 1:45
DIR: *Ingmar Bergman* CAST: *Max von Sydow, Gunnar Bjornstrand, Nils Poppe, Bibie Andersson*
Ingmar Bergman's masterpiece takes place in 14th century Sweden, where a knight (von Sydow) returns from the Crusades only to find the black plague ravaging his homeland. When Death comes to claim him, von Sydow engages the Grim Reaper in a game of chess, thus giving von Sydow a reprieve and allowing him to meditate on the meaning of life. A haunting, beautifully shot allegorical film.

THE SEVENTH SIGN (1988)
** R 1:38
DIR: *Carl Schultz* CAST: *Demi Moore, Peter Friedman, Michael Biehn, John Heard*
This interesting little thriller conjures up a fairly unique vision of the apocalypse. A pregnant woman (Demi Moore) is being stalked by a strange man who leaves death in his wake wherever he goes. Religious experts believe the man is the reincarnation of Christ, and that Judgment Day is near. Moore simply thinks that he's nuts and has targeted her unborn baby. But as the plot progresses, she starts to believe that the child within her might not be just like everyone else.

SEX, LIES AND VIDEOTAPE (1989)
*** R 1:44
DIR: *Steven Soderbergh* CAST: *James Spader, Andie McDowell, Peter Gallagher, Laura San Giacomo*
In this impressive debut, writer/director Soderbergh tells the story of a neurotic young man (Spader) whose honesty is so pervasive that he discusses his impotence with anyone willing to listen. His only brush with intimacy comes from videotaping women as they discuss their sex lives. When he wanders into town to visit an old friend (Gallagher), his presence acts as a powerful catalyst. MacDowell is Gallagher's obsessive wife who spends her days thinking of garbage. Her husband is a world-class sleaze who's sleeping

with MacDowell's sister (San Giacomo). In the midst of all this emotional impotence, Spader's own habits seem relatively normal. This is an exceedingly well-written and directed drama about love, friendship and betrayal. Soderbergh earned an Oscar nomination for his script.

SHANE (1953)
**** NR 1:58
DIR: *George Stevens* **CAST:** *Alan Ladd, Jean Arthur, Van Heflin, Jack Palance, Brandon de Wilde, Ben Johnson, Emile Meyer*
This extremely popular western has a very simple story: an ex-gunfighter (Ladd) now working for Wyoming homesteaders (Arthur and Heflin) is forced to pick up a gun once again in order to protect his bosses from a ruthless cattle baron (Meyer). Palance plays Meyer's hired gun. Loyal Griggs won an Academy Award for his gorgeous cinematography.

SHE-DEVIL (1989)
** PG-13 1:39
DIR: *Susan Seidelman* **CAST:** *Meryl Streep, Roseanne Barr, Ed Begley, Jr., Linda Hunt, Sylvia Miles*
A forgettable comedy about a housewife's revenge. Barr stars as a singularly unattractive women whose accountant husband (Begley) dumps her for an ostentatious romance writer (Streep). The rest of the movie revolves around

Barr destroying both of their lives. That's all clever enough, but the problem is that Barr has so few redeeming qualities, it's easy to understand why her husband walked. The movie is more annoying than funny.

SHE'S GOTTA HAVE IT (1986)
*** R 1:24
DIR: *Spike Lee* **CAST:** *Tracy Camilla Johns, Tommy Redmond Hicks, John Canada Terrell, Spike Lee*
Spike Lee's first feature film, this lighthearted look at the sexual revolution within the black community verges on brilliance. This is the story of three different men vying for the affection of one incredibly alluring woman. Shot in a black and white semi-documentary style that lends urgency to its theme, this movie is as moving as it is funny. Unlike most of Lee's other films, this one explores the complexities inherent to all human beings, rather than the differences between the races.

THE SHELTERING SKY (1991)
*** R 2:17
DIR: *Bernardo Bertolucci* **CAST:** *Debra Winger, John Malkovich, Campbell Scott, Timothy Spall, Jill Bennett*
A lush, languid film version of Paul Bowle's novel about a young, rootless American couple (Malkovich, Winger) who travel through North

313

Africa with a friend (Scott). Like this aimless trio, the film moves without much deliberation or sense of destination. But as in *The Last Emperor*, the beauty of Bertolucci's direction is enough to make this an engrossing experience. Just don't expect car chases. Or a happy ending.

THE SHINING (1980)
**** R 2:23
DIR: *Stanley Kubrick* **CAST:** *Jack Nicholson, Shelley Duval, Danny Lloyd, Scatman Crothers*
Everything works in this fine, frightening adaption of the Stephen King novel about a writer with a severe case of cabin fever. Nicholson stars as a mild-mannered novelist who, with his wife and son (Duval, Lloyd), become caretakers at a large Colorado resort closed for the winter. Kubrick is masterful at building tension as Nicholson goes progressively mad, until he puts down his type-writer and picks up an ax. There are a few scenes in here that have become part of pop culture. Ever hear the phrase "Here's Johnny!!" Verrrrry Spoooky.

SHOAH (1985)
**** NR 9:30
DIR: *Claude Lanzmann*
It took 10 years for Lanzmann to track down the survivors and nazi guards who witnessed the horrors of the Holocaust. In this gripping docu-

mentary, they act as witnesses to a history that must never be repeated nor forgotten. Lanzmann doesn't use the common technique of intersplicing news footage of goose-stepping Germans. Instead, we must imagine the horrors of genocide from the vivid re-telling by those who were there. The power of this documentary is that we are left to our own mind's eye to conjure up the nightmare of it. This is a documentary for the ages.

A SHOCK TO THE SYSTEM (1990)
*** R 1:30
DIR: *Jan Egleson* CAST: *Michael Caine, Elizabeth McGovern, Peter Riegert, Swoosie Kurtz, Will Patton*
Caine stars as an ad exec who gets passed over by a young upstart (Riegert) for an expected promotion. When he discovers that murder can be a shortcut to career advancement, his star within the company rises quickly. This is a biting satire that teeters between dark comedy and murder mystery, with Caine turning in his usual fine performance as a disgruntled middle aged man who gets a new lease on life through a few simple homicides. It's a testament to the quality of the screenplay that we actually sympathize with a serial killer.

SHOOT THE PIANO PLAYER (1960)
**** NR 1:32
DIR: *Francois Truffaut* CAST: *Charles Aznavour,*

Nicole Berger, Marie Dubois
Considered by many to be acclaimed director Francois Truffaut's greatest work, this film brilliantly intermingles a variety of styles made famous by the Hollywood directors he so admired. It is the tale of a one-time famous concert pianist who has now lost all, and somehow manages to get wrapped up in a murder mystery. Openly and proudly melodramatic, this film can make you laugh and cry at the same time. If you are a fan of movies that are simply about people, then it is very hard to beat this one!

SHORT CIRCUIT (1986)
*** PG 1:35
DIR: *John Badham* **CAST:** *Steve Guttenberg, Ally Sheedy, John Cryer, G.W. Bailey*
This movie is way too cutesy, but it still has enough spirit to make even the most cynical viewer smile. *Short Circuit* is the story of a robot developed by the military who becomes "alive" after a freak accident. The robot, named Johnny 5, decides that he no longer wants to be a fighter, and quickly falls in love with a beautiful woman. Featuring warm performances by Sheedy and Guttenberg, this film is especially well-suited to children, but adults who want to smile will enjoy it as well.

A SHOT IN THE DARK (1964)
*** PG 1:41
DIR: *Blake Edwards* **CAST:** *Peter Sellers, Elke Sommer, George Sanders, Herbert Lom, Tracy Reed, Burt Kwouk*
The funniest of the Pink Panther movies features Sellers once again as bumbling Inspector Clouseau. This time around he is convinced that Parisian maid Sommer is innocent of murder despite evidence which suggests otherwise. The scene at the nudist colony is a certifiable comedic classic.

SID AND NANCY (1986)
*** R 1:51
DIR: *Alex Cox* **CAST:** *Gary Oldman, Chloe Webb*
This is a strange, twisted romance of our times. Oldman stars as Sid Vicious, a punk rocker with the Sex Pistols. Webb is his groupie girlfriend. What's remarkable about this film is that despite the couple's punk depravity, drug indulgence and sado-masochism, director Cox (*Repo Man*) brings out something sympathetic and human in them. This is a true story about the star-crossed lovers and their tragic end, but it's also about the punk movement, an important part of rock history that burnt out like a shooting star. It's an injustice that neither Oldman nor Webb received Oscar nominations for their remarkable performances.

SILENCE OF THE LAMBS (1991)
**** R 1:58
DIR: *Jonathan Demme* **CAST:** *Jodie Foster, Anthony Hopkins, Scott Glenn, Ted Levine, Brooke Smith, Anthony Heald*

Outstanding performances by Foster and Hopkins mark this terrifying thriller, crisply directed by Jonathan Demme, in what was a clear departure from his earlier work. Foster plays a rookie FBI agent who is enlisted in the search for a serial killer. Prisoner Hopkins, a former psychiatrist convicted of murder (and cannibalism), provides Foster with clues to the killer's psychology which ultimately lead to his capture. This was the first film to capture the top five Academy Awards (Best Picture, Actor, Actress, Director, Screenplay) since *One Flew Over the Cuckoo's Nest*

SILENT RUNNING (1971)
*** G 1:30
DIR: *Douglas Trumbull* **CAST:** *Bruce Dern, Cliff Potts, Ron Rifkin, Jesse Vint*

Given society's increased concern about the ozone and rain forests, this sci-fi film about the environment is as topical today as it was 20 years ago. Dern stars as a sensitive space captain in charge of a huge ship containing the last surviving vegetation from Earth. This space-age Noah is accompanied by two cute robots, Huey and Dewey, who prefigure R2D2 by about six years. Trumbull's special effects are as breathtaking here as those he did for *2001*.

SILVER BULLET (1985)
*** R 1:30
DIR: *Daniel Attias* **CAST:** *Gary Busey, Corey Haim, Everett McGill, Megan Follows*

This is one of the finest movie adaptations of a Stephen King book yet! Breathtakingly frightening, it is the story of two courageous souls who do battle with a band of sinister werewolves. Featuring a cast of talented actors, most notably Academy Award-nominee Gary Busey, this film has a general air of quality that most Stephen King films lack. Moreover, the special effects sequences are spectacular (and certainly not for the meek!).

SINGIN' IN THE RAIN (1952)
**** NR 1:43
DIR: *Gene Kelly, Stanley Donnen* **CAST:** *Gene Kelly, Debbie Reynolds, Donald O'Connor, Jean Hagen, Cyd Charisse, Douglas Fowley, Rita Moreno*

Most fans of musicals consider this to be the greatest of all time. Set in Hollywood when the industry was making the transition from silents to talkies, the story concerns silent stars Kelly and Hagan trying to make a successful leap into sound. When Hagan's voice proves to be a problem, and when Reynolds shows up as Kelly's new love interest, Hagan begins to scheme. Great dancing—especially Kelly and O'Connor—and many musical gems ("Make "Em Laugh," "Singin' In the Rain," and "Good Morning," among others) highlight this thoroughly entertaining film.

SISTER ACT (1992)
** PG 1:40
DIR: *Emile Ardolino* CAST: *Whoopi Goldberg, Maggie Smith, Harvey Keitel*
This vehicle perfectly shows off the multi-faceted talents of comedienne Whoopi Goldberg: she sings, she dances, she acts, she tells jokes! A wonderful crowd pleaser, this is the story of a woman running from the mob. She decides to hide in a convent where no one could possibly find her, but once inside she finds life far too stifling, so she decides to introduce her new "Sisters" to some of life's pleasures that they have never experienced. If you want to have a really good time, then *Sister Act* is the perfect movie for you!

SLAPSHOT (1977)
*** R 2:03
DIR: *George Roy Hill* CAST: *Paul Newman, Lindsay Crouse, Michael Ontkean, Melinda Dillon, Strother Martin*
Newman stars as a near-has been hockey coach whose motley minor league team finally finds success when they resort to violence. This is a

biting comedy with fine performances and quirky characters, especially the three gruesome brothers whose on-ice behavior makes them heroes to their fans.

SLAUGHTERHOUSE FIVE (1972)
*** R 1:44
DIR: *George Roy Hill* **CAST**: *Michael Sacks, Ron Leibman, Sharon Gans, Valerie Perrine, Eugene Roche*
Kurt Vonnegut fans will not be disappointed by this fine adaptation of his anti-war/sci-fi novel about an optometrist (Sacks) who's able to hop back and forth through his life, from a German P.O.W. camp to his stay on an alien planet to his own death. It seemed an impossible book to bring to the screen, but Hill and the cast have succeeded. The scenes of the horrific fire bombing of Dresden come from Vonnegut's own experiences as a P.O.W. (The title of the film refers to the building where he was kept prisoner).

SLEEPER (1973)
*** PG 1:28
DIR: *Woody Allen* **CAST**: *Woody Allen, Diane Keaton, John Beck, Mary Gregory, Don Keefer*
A dweebish health food fanatic goes into the hospital for a simple operation and wakes up 200 years later. Although vegetables have grown to the size of Buicks, Allen is still disappointed by the future. He finds himself involved in a futuris-

tic rebellion against a facist government, and in a desperate act, takes the leader's nose hostage. Watch the movie. This is Allen before he got serious, and the belly laughs come nonstop.

SLEEPING BEAUTY (1959)
*** G 1:15
DIR: *Clyde Geronimi, Eric Larson, Wolfgang Reitherman, Les Clark* **CAST:** *Voices of Eleanor Audley, Verna Felton, Bill Shirley, Barbara Jo Allen, Barbara Luddy, Mary Costa*
Enduring classic fairy tale with music adapted from Tchaikovsky. The animation was based on Medieval French manuscripts. Good and evil fairies, a prince and a princess, fiery battles . . . all in all a memorable animated feature.

SLEUTH (1972)
*** PG 2:18
DIR: *Joseph L. Mankiewicz* **CAST:** *Lawrence Olivier, Michael Caine*
Based on the play of the same name by Anthony Shaffer, this is a stirring vehicle for both of its stars. Olivier and Caine are at their fiendish best, as each tries to outwit the other in a real-life game of murder. Just when you think you've figured out who is going to beat whom, the movie turns around on itself (over and over again). As well as being incredibly tense, the film also has many moments of genuine humor.

SMILE (1975)
*** PG 1:53
DIR: *Michael Ritchie* **CAST:** *Bruce Dern, Barbara Feldon, Melanie Griffith, Geoffrey Lewis, Nicholas Pryor*

Ritchie goes behind the scenes of a small California beauty pageant to reveal the backbiting and desperation of the young women who want desperately to make it to the big time. Like Robert Altman's *Nashville*, this satire uses a documentary, roving style to create a biting comedy of small-town values and competition.

SOME LIKE IT HOT (1959)
**** NR 2:01
DIR: *Billy Wilder* **CAST:** *Tony Curtis, Jack Lemmon, Marilyn Monroe, Joe E. Brown, Pat O'Brien, George Raft*

Curtis and Lemmon play two musicians who are innocent, and unfortunate, witnesses to the St. Valentine's Day Massacre. When the gangsters come after them, they disguise themselves as women and join an all-female band. An extraordinarily funny film, with sterling performances from Curtis and Lemmon, as well as from Monroe as the absolutely delicious Sugar Kane. Joe E. Brown also adds fine support, including the movie's hilarious final line.

SOMETHING WILD (1986)
*** R 1:53
DIR: *Jonathan Demme* **CAST:** *Melanie Griffith, Jeff Daniels, Ray Liotta*

Daniels is a boring accountant whose only brush with crime is walking out on a check. Griffith is a wild girl who inexplicably picks up Daniels on a Manhattan street, then proceeds to take him on the ride (including a few minutes with a pair of handcuffs) of his life. The first part of the film has a bouncy road-picture feel to it. But when Griffith's ex-husband, played menacingly by Liotta, shows up on the scene, the movie detours unexpectedly into gruesome violence. An energetic bout of filmmaking

SOPHIE'S CHOICE (1982)
*** R 2:37
DIR: *Alan J. Pakula* **CAST:** *Meryl Streep, Kevin Kline, Peter MacNicol*

Streep won an Oscar for her magnificent portrayal of a Holocaust survivor who bears a terrible burden because of a torturous decision forced upon her by Nazi captors. Trying to rebuild her life in Brooklyn, she befriends a young writer (MacNicol) and a manic-depressive (Kline). From William Styron's best-selling novel comes this gut-wrenching film. Pakula received a nomination for his script.

SOUNDER (1972)
*** G 1:45
DIR: *Martin Ritt* **CAST:** *Cicely Tyson, Paul Winfield, Kevin Hooks, Carmen Matthews, Taj Mahal*
A moving story about a family of black sharecroppers struggling for survival during the depression, and the hound dog who helps bind them together. Tyson and Winfield both received Oscar nominations for their fine performances in this classic family film.

THE SOUND OF MUSIC (1965)
*** G 2:54
DIR: *Robert Wise* **CAST:** *Julie Andrews, Christopher Plummer, Eleanor Parker, Richard Haydn, Peggy Wood, Angela Cartwright*
One of the most popular films ever produced was once actually a rather mediocre Broadway musical. Based on the true story about Austria's Von Trapp family, who fled the terror of the Nazis in 1938 and went to Switzerland. Andrews plays Maria Von Trapp, the nun-turned-nanny who led her flock of children to safety. Rodgers and Hammerstein songs include "Do-Re-Mi," "My Favorite Things," and the title track. Winner of five Academy Awards, including Best Picture.

SOYLENT GREEN (1973)
*** PG 1:35
DIR: *Richard Fleischer* **CAST:** *Charlton Heston,*

Edward G. Robinson, Leigh Taylor-Young, Chuck Connors

An entertaining, thought-provoking sci-fi film about a not-so-distant future where natural resources are running dry and the population explosion is out of control. Heston plays a sweaty cop investigating the murder of an executive of a shadowy corporation. Robinson, in his final role, plays Heston's intellectual assistant. Together, they track down the motive for the killing and the secret behind the Soylent Corporation, a secret that drives Robinson to suicide. Although the film's eco-message is a bit heavy handed, the movie still packs an environmental punch.

SPARTACUS (1960)
*** NR 3:16
DIR: *Stanley Kubrick* **CAST:** *Kirk Douglas, Laurence Olivier, Peter Ustinov, Charles Laughton, Jean Simmons, Tony Curtis, John Gavin, Nina Foch, John Ireland*

A sweeping epic about a rebellion of Roman slaves led by Spartacus (Douglas). This is a massive, beautifully conceived film full of great acting and beautiful cinematography. Although the film's length may be daunting, Dalton Trumbo's fine script keeps things zipping along. Make sure to rent the film's 1991 re-issue, in which several key scenes (including a famous flirtation between Olivier and Curtis) were restored, and the film as a whole was digitally enhanced.

SPLASH (1984)
*** PG 1:51
DIR: *Ron Howard* **CAST:** *Tom Hanks, Darryl Hannah, John Candy, Eugene Levy*

This is the movie that cemented Ron Howard's reputation as a first rate director and made Tom Hanks a superstar! This touching story of a man unable to find love in the big city will delight you to no end. Hanks is so lonely and desperate that he almost contemplates suicide, but then he finds the woman of his dreams (Hannah), who turns out to be a mermaid. Featuring a cast of brilliant comic performers, and filled with unexpected and humorous plot twists, this movie is hilarious from start to finish.

STAGECOACH (1939)
**** NR 1:40
DIR: *John Ford* **CAST:** *Claire Trevor, John Wayne, Andy Devine, Thomas Mitchell, Louise Platt, John Carradine, George Bancroft*

John Ford's highly influential Western about a group of stagecoach passengers traveling into dangerous Indian territory. This was Ford's first Western since the silent era, and was the film that made Wayne a star. Shot in Monument Valley, *Stagecoach* would become the Western to which all other Westerns would aspire. Oscars for Best Supporting Actor (Mitchell) and Best Score.

STALAG 17 (1953)
**** NR 2:00
DIR: *Billy Wilder* **CAST:** *William Holden, Otto Preminger, Don Taylor, Peter Graves, Robert Strauss*
An engaging story of a disparate group of American G.I.'s sharing the same shack in a German P.O.W. camp. Holden won an Oscar for his portrayal of a slick operator wrongly accused of being a snitch. Much of the film deals with his efforts to make sure the real spy is caught, but this is more a movie about how men survive and bond in the harsh conditions of war. Although there's plenty of comedy here, don't expect any of the silly antics of "Hogan's Heros." Wilder received an Academy nomination, as did Strauss for Best Supporting Actor.

STAND AND DELIVER (1988)
*** PG 1:42
DIR: *Ramon Mendez* **CAST:** *Edward James Olmos, Lou Diamond Phillips, Andy Garcia, Rosana De Soto, Will Gotay, Ingrid Oliv, Virginia Paris*
The compelling true story of Jamie Escalante, an idealistic high school math teacher in East Los Angeles who cajoled and inspired his disadvantaged students into taking advanced placement calculus. Although there are some minor discrepancies between fact and fiction (most of the kids are creations of the writer), a majority of Escalante's students did pass the a.p. calculus test—a re-

markable feat for an inner-city school. Olmos earned an Academy nomination for his performance.

STARDUST MEMORIES (1980)
*** PG 1:29
DIR: *Woody Allen* **CAST:** *Woody Allen, Charlotte Rampling, Jessica Harper, Marie-Christine Barrault*
Allen walks a fine line in this semi-autobiographical tale of the price of fame and the rabid devotion of fans transfixed by celebrity. Allen essentially plays himself, a writer/director attending a festival of his works. Like Fellini's *8 1/2*, Allen's fans are often portrayed as bubble-eyed geeks who should be told to get a life. Some critics thought Allen was being a condescending jerk who ridiculed the same people who made him rich and famous. But this is still a diverting look at the very mixed blessing of fame. Daniel Stern has a funny cameo as an adolescent fan who is moved to sophmoric blabbering by one of the director's films.

STARMAN (1984)
*** PG 1:55
DIR: *John Carpenter* **CAST:** *Jeff Bridges, Karen Allen, Charles Martin Smith*
This is a surprisingly gentle sci-fi film from the same director who gave us *Halloween*. Bridges stars as a kindly, chameleon space man who takes

on the shape of Allen's dead husband. Pursued by government agents, the pair head across country to rendevous with the space man's brethren. Like *E.T.*, this alien has magical powers that help Allen reconcile the death of her husband. It's fun to watch Bridges learn to be human.

STAR WARS (1977)
*** PG 2:01
DIR: *George Lucas* **CAST:** *Harrison Ford, Mark Hamill, Carrie Fisher, Peter Cushing, Alec Guinness, David Prowse, voice of James Earl Jones (as Darth Vader)*
Fun-filled science fiction film is one of the most popular movies of all time. This homage to B-movies and the sci-fi Saturday matinees of the Flash Gordon era features some of the most elaborate and technically impressive special effects you're ever likely to see. There are plenty of good guys and bad guys, along with a princess and a couple of young male heroes. Sure to be a family favorite for decades.

THE STING (1973)
*** PG 2:09
DIR: *George Roy Hill* **CAST:** *Paul Newman, Robert Redford, Robert Shaw, Charles Durning, Eileen Brennan, Harold Gould*
When big-time crook Shaw has one of their friends murdered, Chicago con men Newman and

Redford set up a sting in order to get revenge. Director Hill keeps the action moving and the complex story understandable, while the two stars charm the pants off of the ladies, the audience, and each other. There's great chemistry at work here! Stay on your toes for the exciting and unpredictable ending. Winner of seven Academy Awards, including Best Picture, Director, Screenplay, and Music (Marvin Hamlisch's adaptation of Scott Joplin's ragtime).

STICK (1985)
** R 1:49
DIR: *Burt Reynolds* **CAST:** *Burt Reynolds, Candace Bergen, Charles Druning, George Segal*
A light-hearted yet often annoying action drama based on the Elmore Leonard book of the same name, this movie quickly grows tiresome. Reynolds, whose direction has seldom reached above average, tells an unfocused story of a high class car thief hired by an eccentric millionaire with a taste for the dangerous and illegal. Reynold's never seems to know if he wants to make a pure action film or a comedy, and, predictably enough, he fails at both.

STRAIGHT TIME (1978)
*** R 1:54
DIR: *Ulu Grosbard* **CAST:** *Dustin Hoffman, Theresa Russell, Gary Busey, Harry Dean Stanton, M. Emmet Walsh*

This is an overlooked gem about the futile struggle of a paroled convict (Hoffman) to go straight after release onto the streets of L.A. The film is based on the life of ex-con Edward Bunker, and has a gritty realism that puts this far above other films of its ilk. Walsh, one of the best character actors in the world, excels here as a manipulative probation officer. Stanton and Busey play Hoffman's crime partners in a botched heist. But it's Hoffman's self-destructive criminal who steals the show. This is first-rate work.

STRANGERS ON A TRAIN (1951)
**** NR 1:41
DIR: *Alfred Hitchcock* **CAST:** *Robert Walker, Ruth Roman, Farley Granger, Marion Lorne, Leo G. Carroll.*
The master of suspense strikes again with this tale of two strangers (Walker and Granger) who meet on a train and discuss a hypothetical plan by which they exchange murders. Only problem is, Walker decides to take the talk seriously, and then demands that Granger keep up his half of the bargain. Raymond Chandler's script (from Patricia Highsmith's novel) is first rate, as is Lorne's performance as Walker's mother. Watch for the famous merry-go-round sequence.

STRANGER THAN PARADISE (1984)
*** R 1:30
DIR: *Jim Jarmusch* **CAST:** *John Lurie, Ezter Balint, Richard Edson*

There's not much plot to Jarmusch's off-beat films, but they never fail to beguile. Lurie and Edson star as a couple of low-rent card sharks who don't seem to do much of anything. Lurie's Hungarian cousin (Balint) comes for a visit, and the trio wander aimlessly from New York to Cleveland to Florida. If you're not used to Jarmusch's rhythm, this might be a bit slow. But keep an open mind— Jarmusch has a unique, amusing vision of life in America.

A STREETCAR NAMED DESIRE (1951)
**** PG 2:02
DIR: *Elia Kazan* **CAST:** *Marlon Brando, Vivien Leigh, Kim Hunter, Karl Malden.*
A landmark production of Tennessee Williams' Pulitzer Prize-winning play, not only for bringing serious, adult material to the screen, but for the unforgettable performance by Brando (ironically, he was the only one of the four major stars who did not win an Oscar). The story concerns faded and desperate Southern belle Blanche DuBois' (Leigh) visit to her sister's (Hunter) dreary home in New Orleans and her run-in with brother-in-law Stanley Kowalski (Brando). Listen for Alex North's brilliant jazz score.

THE STUNT MAN (1980)
*** R 2:09
DIR: *Richard Rush* **CAST:** *Peter O'Toole, Steve Railsback, Barbara Hershey*

Railsback is an outlaw who becomes a stuntman and, unwittingly, the pawn of a svengali director (O'Toole) in this skilled piece of filmmaking. O'Toole is wonderful as the dreamy, manipulative auteur whose vision comes before safety. But the movie is also about the travails of filmmaking, and the obviously self-conscious, over-the-top direction is almost a character unto itself. An absorbing, energetic work of art which earned Rush a Best Director nomination. Nominations for O'Toole (Best Actor), and Lawrence Marcus and Rush for Best Adapted Screenplay.

SULLIVAN'S TRAVELS (1941)
**** NR 1:30
DIR: *Preston Sturges* **CAST:** *Joel McCrea, Veronica Lake, William Demarest, Franklin Pangborn, Margaret Hayes*
One of the wisest and funniest films ever made about the movie business. McCrea stars as a disgruntled-yet-idealistic film director who yearns to get away from the glitz of Hollywood to explore the guts of Depression-era America. The pampered director goes undercover as a hobo and hooks up with a struggling actress (Lake), who helps him navigate in the unfamiliar world of poverty. The film moves effortlessly from slapstick to gritty realism under Sturges' masterful touch.

SUNSET BOULEVARD (1950)
**** NR 1:50
DIR: *Billy Wilder* **CAST:** *Gloria Swanson, William Holden, Erich von Stroheim, Jack Webb, Fred Clark, Hedda Hopper, Buster Keaton, Cecil B. DeMille, Nancy Olson*

Gloria Swanson delivered the performance of her career as a former silent film star still living off past glories. Struggling screenwriter Holden becomes her lover and the writer of the film she hopes will launch her comeback. A dark, cynical look at Hollywood and its glorification of youth, powered by great acting and an unbeatable script (it won the Oscar).

SUPERMAN (1978)
*** PG 2:23
DIR: *Richard Donner* **CAST:** *Christopher Reeve, Marlon Brando, Gene Hackman, Margot Kidder, Ned Beatty, Glenn Ford*

Over a decade before movies like *Batman* and *Dick Tracy* made comic book movies the buzzword in Hollywood, *Superman* hit the big screen. A glorious and spectacular adventure film, this one is great for the whole family. Directed solidly from start to finish by Richard Donner, you get to see how the last son of Krypton matures and becomes Superman, standing for truth, justice, and the American way! Even after all these years, your first glimpse of Christopher Reeve in the blue and red suit will make your heart soar. Featuring an incredible cast, most of whom are Academy Award winners, *Superman* is perhaps the best comic book movie of all time.

SUSPECT (1987)
*** R 1:58
DIR: *Peter Yates* **CAST:** *Cher, Dennis Quaid, Liam Neeson, John Mahoney, Joe Mantegna, Phillip Bosco*
Quaid is a high-powered Washington lobbyist who's called for jury duty. Cher is the attorney defending a homeless man accused of murder. Dissatisfied with the evidence he's receiving, Quaid strikes out on his own to investigate the crime. The ethics of such behavior are at the heart of this intelligent, stylish thriller. Neeson is superior as the deaf Vietnam vet overwhelmed by the charges.

SUSPICION (1941)
*** NR 1:39
DIR: *Alfred Hitchcock* **CAST:** *Cary Grant, Joan Fontaine, Cedric Hardwicke, Nigel Bruce, Leo G. Carroll*
Not a great Hitchcock, but suspenseful and entertaining nonetheless. Fontaine (in an Oscar-winning role) plays a naive woman from a wealthy family who marries playboy Grant despite the scandalous rumors that surround him. When he wreaks havoc with their finances, she fears that he

is going to murder her for the insurance money.
Bruce is excellent as Grant's best friend.

SWIMMING TO CAMBODIA (1987)
*** NR 1:27
DIR: *Jonathan Demme* CAST: *Spalding Gray*
A remarkably vivid film which consists of Gray
sitting behind a desk talking. It's a testament to
Gray's monolouge that this limited setting is never
less than riveting. He tells the story of his bizarre
experiences as an actor on the set of *The Killing
Fields,* the Academy Award-winning tale of the
brutal communist take-over in Cambodia. His
keen eye for ironic detail, and his compassion for
the people of Cambodia make for a memorable
film. The sparse music was composed by performance artist Laurie Anderson.

―――――――― T ――――――――

TAKE THE MONEY AND RUN (1969)
*** PG 1:25
DIR: *Woody Allen* CAST: *Woody Allen, Janet
Margolin, Lonny Chapman, Marcel Hillaire, Jackson
Beck (narrator)*
Hysterically funny farce from Allen in his first
film as writer / director / star. Using a mock-docu-
mentary style, the film tells of the life of a bumbling
small-time crook (Allen) as he fumbles his way
through a series of crimes. A non-stop joke-fest

with some great one-liners and sight gags. The bank robbery scene, when the teller argues about what the stick-up note says ("gun or gub?") is one of the many hilarious highlights.

TAKING OFF (1971)
*** R 1:33
DIR: *Milos Forman* **CAST:** *Buck Henry, Lynn Carlin, Linnea Heacock, Paul Benedict*

Milos Forman, the brilliant Oscar-winning director of *One Flew Over the Cukoo's Nest* and *Amadeus*, leads an all-star cast in this warm-hearted comedy about parents and their children. Staging a role reversal that has now become trite and overused, Forman was one of the first filmmakers to explore the possibility of teenage children teaching their parents something new, namely, how to live life again! Not as serious as many of his other films, *Taking Off* is a lovely movie to see.

TALK RADIO (1988)
*** R 1:50
DIR: *Oliver Stone* **CAST:** *Eric Bogosian, Alec Baldwin, Ellen Greene, Leslie Hope, John Pankow*

Bogosian is center-stage as an acerbic late-night radio talk show host whose callers range from white supremacists to dumb teenagers. He has a collection of enemies who call and threaten his life, and as the night proceeds the threats become more and more unnerving. The film is based on

Alan Berg, the Denver radio man who was murdered in 1984 for his outspoken hatred of neonazis and hatemongers. Bogosian is riveting in this adaption of his one-man play.

TAPS (1981)
** PG 1:58
DIR: *Harold Becker* **CAST:** *Timothy Hutton, Sean Penn, Tom Cruise, George C. Scott*
Hutton is the chief cadet at a military academy. When the academy's headmaster, George C. Scott, passes away suddenly, Hutton takes over the institution by force to prevent it from being torn down. So commences a standoff between the armed students, trained in military tactics, and the U.S. Army forces outside, awaiting for the order to storm the campus by force. Although the script is implausible and the direction stolid, the performances by its young actors make this film worth watching. Cruise shows much of the promise he later fulfilled in such movies as *Risky Business* and *Born On the 4th of July*. Sean Penn, in his first starring role, is superb, and Timothy Hutton proves that his Oscar for *Ordinary People* was no fluke.

TAXI DRIVER (1976)
**** R 1:53
DIR: *Martin Scorsese* **CAST:** *Robert De Niro, Cybill Shepherd, Jodie Foster, Harvey Keitel, Albert Brooks, Peter Boyle*

Scorsese, screenwriter Paul Schrader, and De Niro acheived perfection is this chilling and disturbing tale of modern day angst and alientation. De Niro plays a psychotic Vietnam marine veteran turned taxi driver who becomes obsessed with a presidential candidate, a pimp (Keitel), a teen prostitute (Foster), and a beautiful woman who has rejected him (Shepherd). His anger mounts until it finally explodes in a violent fury. Harrowing score by Bernard Herrmann was his last. The most incisive look at the post-Vietnam, post-Watergate era ever recorded on film.

THE TEMP (1993)
* R 1:40
DIR: *Tom Holland* **CAST:** *Timothy Hutton, Lara Flynn Boyle, Dwight Schultz*
How can a movie with such a talented cast turn out so bad? *The Temp*, one of the most lackluster attempts at a thriller in recent years is, quite simply, a waste of time. It is the story of a new woman in the office who seems to be trying to climb up the ranks by murdering her superiors ... Or are her superiors merely imagining things? The premise is quite good, but the pay off is very poor.

TENDER MERCIES (1983)
**** PG 1:33
DIR: *Bruce Beresford* **CAST:** *Robert Duvall, Tess*

Harper, Betty Buckley, Ellen Barkin
It took an Australian director (Beresford) to make this classic film about a down-and-out American Country singer as he picks up the pieces of his broken life. Duvall won an Oscar for his moving portrayal of the drunken, divorced musician whose voice has left him. He finds a new dignity when he marries a young widow (Harper) and takes her son under his wing. The film not only tells the poignant story of Duvall, but also brilliantly defines a slice of American life. Horton Foote won an Oscar for Best Screenplay. The film received a Best Picture nomination, as did Beresford for his direction.

THE TERMINATOR (1984)
*** R 1:48
DIR: *James Cameron* CAST: *Arnold Schwarzenegger, Linda Hamilton, Michael Biehn, Paul Winfield, Lance Henriksen*
A science fiction thriller featuring the perfectly cast Schwarzenegger as a cyborg sent back from the 21st century to murder Hamilton, the future mother of a man who will one day save the human race. Lots of great action sequences and some terrific one-liners from Schwarzenegger. *The Terminator* set the standard for a host of imitators which would follow in its footsteps.

TERMINATOR II: JUDGMENT DAY (1992)
*** R 2:15
DIR: *James Cameron* **CAST:** *Arnold Schwarzenegger, Linda Hamilton, Edward Furlong*

Veteran action director James Cameron outdid himself with this sequel to *The Terminator*. *T2* will scare the pants off of you and make you stand up and cheer from beginning to end. Linda Hamilton's performance is an improvement of incredible magnitude over the prior film. Arnold doesn't let his end down, either; he's better than ever as the big bully from the future with an attitude. Even Edward Furlong, the young actor playing Hamilton's son, seems remarkably comfortable in front of the camera. For those of you who haven't seen the movie yet, here's a little teaser: this time there are two terminators from the future!

TESTAMENT (1983)
*** PG 1:30
DIR: *Lynne Littman* **CAST:** *Jane Alexander, William Devane, Roxana Zal*

Alexander stars as a suburban housewife in this devastating story of a small town struggling for survival after a nuclear attack. But don't confuse this with a mediocre post-nuclear action film. The people of this small town react with fear and amazing dignity as they wait for help that never comes. This is a gut-wrenching tale of a woman who watches as her children and the people around her slowly die from radiation poisoning. A powerful anti-nuke statement that now seems happily dated.

THAT'S ENTERTAINMENT! (1974)
**** G 2:12
DIR: *Jack Haley, Jr.* **CAST:** *Gene Kelly, Fred Astaire, Ginger Rogers, Bing Crosby*

If you're a fan of those great old Hollywood musicals, then this is a must-see! Hosted by some of the greatest entertainers of all-time, this retrospective traces the most memorable moments in musical history. You'll relive beautiful scenes from classics like *An American in Paris* and over 100 of your other favorites. You'll even see such unlikely highlights as Clark Gable singing. This movie certainly lives up to its title!

THELMA & LOUISE (1991)
*** R 2:08
DIR: *Ridley Scott* **CAST:** *Susan Sarandon, Geena Davis, Michael Madsen, Harvey Keitel*

This fine road movie, helmed by acclaimed director Ridley Scott, redefines the genre of the buddy picture by having the buddies be women. Thelma and Louise go on the run after killing a man who tries to rape them. Once they discover the freedom and exhilaration of the open road, they realize that they had been imprisoned for their whole lives simply because they were women in a men's world. Thrilling right up to the tragic end, screenwriter Callie Khouri's script garnered her an Oscar.

THEM! (1954)
*** NR 1:33
DIR: *Gordon Douglas* **CAST:** *James Whitmore, Edmund Gwenn, Joan Weldon, Fess Parker, James Arness*

This is the best in an endless series of movies about animals and people who have major growth spurts after a bit of radiation. Here, thousands of giant ants roam the southwest disturbing picnics and toppling buildings. Whitmore plays a bedraggled soldier whose training did not include 50-foot insects. The climax in the L.A. sewer system is extremeley well-done. Another fine effort on the part of Hollywood to exploit America's fear of Russia and nuclear war.

THE THIN BLUE LINE (1988)
*** NR 1:36
DIR: *Errol Morris*

This is a good example of the power of the documentary film. Morris takes a second look at a 1976 murder of a Dallas policeman and, after years of interviews and research, suggests that the wrong man is in jail for the crime. Morris uses some dramatization to re-enact the crime, but the real tension here comes from the dozens of interviews of eye-witnesses and the alleged killer. Largely because of this film, the man was freed after 11 years in a Texas prison. And, in an ending worthy of O. Henry, the alleged killer then sued Morris for part of the film's profits.

THE THIN MAN (1934)
*** NR 1:33
DIR: *W.S. Van Dyke* **CAST:** *William Powell, Myrna Loy, Maureen O'Sullivan, Nat Pendleton, Cesar Romero*
The first and best in the series of comic-mysteries featuring Nick and Nora Charles (Powell and Loy), the sparkling and sophisticated couple who spend a good deal of their time having fun solving whodunits. The two stars are brilliant together, playing off one another with a witty repartee that keeps the laughs rolling as the suspense surrounding their search for the Thin Man builds. If you enjoy this film, then check out its sequels, particularly *After the Thin Man* and *The Thin Man Goes Home*.

THE THIRD MAN (1949)
**** NR 1:45
DIR: *Carol Reed* **CAST:** *Orson Welles, Joseph Cotten, Alida Valli, Trevor Howard*
Classic thriller about a pulp writer (Cotten) searching through the streets of post-World War II

Vienna for his old pal, the mysterious Harry Lime (Welles). Despite the fact that he is only on screen for a limited amount of time, Welles' engaging performance truly dominates the film (and while he portrays a despicable character, it's difficult to not like him). Graham Greene's script is extremely tight, Reed's direction is consistently striking, and Robert Krasker's Oscar-winning cinematography creates endlessly fascinating visuals. Top it off with Anton Karas' disconcerting zither music and you have one great film.

THE 39 STEPS (1935)
**** NR 1:29
DIR: *Alfred Hitchcock* **CAST:** *Robert Donat, Madeleine Carroll, Lucie Mannheim, Peggy Ashcroft*
An early classic from Hitchcock features some terrific acting from Donat and Carroll, whose repartee while they are handcuffed together for a good portion of the film is wonderfully entertaining. Donat is an innocent man who inadvertantly gets involved in an international spy ring. Carroll believes he is a criminal as they try to escape from the police and the true spies.

THIS IS SPINAL TAP (1984)
*** R 1:22
DIR: *Rob Reiner* **CAST:** *Michael McKean, Christopher Guest, Harry Shearer, Rob Reiner, Paul Schaeffer*
A wickedly funny look at the pretensions of both

rock & roll and those who take it too seriously. Reiner is the visionary behind this "mock-umentary" which follows a has-been heavy metal band on a disasterous U.S. tour. McKean and Guest play the not-so-bright band leaders who've been together since childhood and now share a raging case of Herpes. This film is chock full of hysterical bits—including drummers who spontaneously combust, an amplifier that goes to "11," and a bimbo girlfriend who makes plans for the band according to their astrological signs. This is satire at its best.

THREE DAYS OF THE CONDOR (1975)
*** R 1:58
DIR: *Sydney Pollack* **CAST:** *Robert Redford, Faye Dunaway, Cliff Robertson, Max Von Sydow, John Houseman*
Redford is a bookish C.I.A. analyst who finds himself on the run from his own agency in this taught thriller based on James Grady's novel. Coming back to work after lunch he finds all his co-workers murdered. He enlists the help of a passerby (Dunaway) who becomes more and more involved in his desperate escape from assasins. The chemistry between Dunaway and Redford is excellent. Von Sydow is superior as a low-key bureaucratic assasin in this story of crosses and double crosses.

THREE MEN AND A BABY (1987)
* PG 1:39
DIR: *Leonard Nimoy* **CAST:** *Ted Danson, Tom Selleck, Steve Guttenberg, Nancy Travis, Margaret Colin, Philip Bosco, Celeste Holm.*
Remake of the 1985 French film *Three Men and a Cradle* was a huge box office hit. Trite plot concerns three single roomates (Danson, Selleck, Guttenberg) who must take care of a baby girl who is left on their doorstep. Warm, light-hearted entertainment.

THE THREE MUSKETEERS 1974
*** PG 1:45
DIR: *Richard Lester* **CAST:** *Richard Chamberlain, Oliver Reed, Michael York, Frank Finlay, Raquel Welch*
A masterful blend of comedy and rousing adventure; internationally acclaimed director Richard Lester has created a classic for all-time. We all know the story of the three French musketeers who rebel in the name of the true king, and miraculously seem to be able to take on the entire royal forces. But there's never a dull moment in this movie, and it breathes new life into the old plot. Featuring some of the finest swordsmanship in film since the fifties, you won't want to miss this one!

THREE WOMEN (1977)
*** PG 2:05
DIR: *Robert Altman* **CAST:** *Sissy Spacek, Janice Rule, Shelly Duvall, Robert Fortier*
A disturbing, surreal look at the lives of three alienated women as they trudge through life. Duvall plays a woman who survives by imagining herself to be more popular and sophisticated than she really is. Spacek plays an immature girl who moves in with Duvall and then steals not only clothes, but her identity. Rule is a quiet, somber woman who speaks through her strange paintings. This is a unique film that shouldn't be passed over. Along with *Short Cuts* and *Nashville*, one of Altman's finest works.

THROW MOMMA FROM THE TRAIN (1987)
*** PG-13 1:28
DIR: *Danny DeVito* **CAST:** *Billy Crystal, Danny DeVito, Anne Ramsey, Kate Mulgrew*
Crystal stars as a bitter writing teacher whose ex-wife makes a fortune stealing his book. DeVito plays an emotionally-stunted writing student whose dictatorial mother (Ramsey) makes him miserable. Through a major miscommunication, DeVito plots to kill Crystal's wife under the assumption that Crystal will knock off his mother. With a nod to Hitchcock's *Strangers on a Train*, the plot takes a number of twists and tumbles before reaching its overly-sentimental conclusion. Crys-

tal and DeVito both turn in fine performances, but it's Ramsey as the gravel-voiced, terrifying Momma who steals the show. Her performance earned her an Academy nomination for Best Supporting Actress.

THX-1138 (1971)
*** PG 1:28
DIR: *George Lucas* CAST: *Robert Duvall, Donald Pleasence, Johnny Weissmuller, Jr., Maggie McOmie*
A somber early effort from sci-fi king George Lucas. Duvall plays a citizen of a dictatorial 25th century country. When he rebels, he is caught by robot police and tortured. Although the plot may sound too Orwellian, Lucas' unique vision and Duvall's fine performance makes this an impressive film. Lucas did a short version of the film for his Master's degree from U.S.C., then later expanded it into a feature.

TIME BANDITS (1981)
*** PG 1:50
DIR: *Terry Gilliam* CAST: *John Cleese, Iam Holm, Shelley Duvall, Sean Connery, Michael Palin, Katherine Helmond, Ralph Richardson, David Warner*
A young boy journeys through rips in the fabric of time with a gang of kindly dwarves in this magical fantasy from ex-*Monty Python* member Terry Gilliam. As the motley crew traverses history they encounter Robin Hood (Cleese), Agamemnon

(Connery), and Napoleon (Holm). They also meet up with Good and Evil. This is a visually-stunning work that will delight and inspire the whole family.

TIN MEN (1987)
*** R 1:48
DIR: *Barry Levinson* **CAST:** *Richard Dreyfuss, Danny DeVito, Barbara Hershey, Jackie Gayle, John Mahoney*

DeVito and Dreyfuss play Baltimore aluminum siding salesmen in the early 1960s whose escalating feud leads to infidelity. This is a first-rate character-driven comedy about a pair of hucksters trying to make a buck in a corrupt business. Levinson (*Diner, Rain Man*) is a Baltimore native, so the attention to period detail is first-rate.

TO BE OR NOT TO BE (1942)
**** NR 1:39
DIR: *Ernst Lubitsch* **CAST:** *Jack Benny, Carole Lombard, Robert Stack, Felix Bressart, Lionel Atwill, Stanley Ridges, Sig Ruman*

A great black comedy. Benny, in his finest moment as a movie actor, plays Joseph Tura, the leader of a Polish Shakespearean troupe fleeing from the terror of the Nazis. Lombard, in her last film role, is exquisite as Benny's wife. Some very funny moments when Benny does his impersonations, particularly of Hitler and Hamlet! Fine direction by Lubitsch.

TO KILL A MOCKINGBIRD (1962)
*** NR 2:09
DIR: *Robert Mulligan* **CAST:** *Gregory Peck, Mary Badham, Philip Alford, Brock Peters, Robert Duvall, John Megna*
A penetrating look at race relations from screenwriter Horton Foote, who won an Oscar for his adaptation of Harper Lee's novel. Peck, in one of his finest performances, stars as a widowed lawyer defending a black man (Peters) accused of rape in 1930s Alabama. Child actor Badham was nominated for her excellent performance as Peck's daughter, while Peck took home the Oscar.

TOM JONES (1963)
**** NR 2:09
DIR: *Tony Richardson* **CAST:** *Albert Finney, Susannah York, Edith Evans, Diane Cilento, Joan Greenwood, Joyce Redman, Rachel Kempson, Hugh Griffith*
Finney is the over-sexed rebel in this adaptation of Henry Fielding's novel about the stuffy class system of 18th-century England. Forced to leave home after a scandalous tryst, the young man embarks on a series of bawdy adventures. The now-famous seduction scene between Finney and York, in which they tease each other with roast chicken and oysters, is worth the price of a rental in itself. This took home the Best Picture Oscar, as did Richardson for his direction and John Osborne

for his adapted screenplay. Nominations for Finney (Best Actor) and Griffith (Best Supporting Actor).

TOP GUN (1986)
* PG 1:50
DIR: *Tony Scott* **CAST:** *Tom Cruise, Kelly McGillis, Anthony Edwards, Tom Skerritt, Val Kilmer, John Stockwell, Tim Robbins, Meg Ryan*
Huge box office hit feels more like a recruitment ad for the Navy than a movie. Cruise stars as a macho fighter pilot who is assigned to a prestigious training program where he tries to become the number one pilot. McGillis plays his love interest despite the total lack of chemistry between the two stars, and Kilmer is his rival. Slick, empty headed film is saved by some breathtaking flight footage as well as Edwards engaging performance as Cruise's friend.

TOPKAPI (1964)
*** NR 2:02
DIR: *Jules Dassin* **CAST:** *Peter Ustinov, Melina Mercouri, Maximillian Schell, Robert Morley*
Ustinov won a Best Supporting Actor Oscar for his portrayal of an international jewel thief in this tight, clever tale of the ambitious heist of an Istanbul museum. This rollicking film works best when detailing the gang's plotting, planning and squabbles. The actual robbery is extremeley well-

done. This movie led to a number of copy-cats, but none had as much class and style.

TOUCH OF EVIL (1958)
**** NR 1:48
DIR: *Orson Welles* **CAST:** *Orson Welles, Charlton Heston, Janet Leigh, Joseph Calleia, Dennis Weaver, Akim Tamiroff, Marlene Dietrich, Zsa Zsa Gabor, Valentin de Vargas*

Welles' last Hollywood film is another triumph for the great director. Welles plays a corrupt detective in a border town who locks horns with good guy Heston, a narcotics agent. Leigh, as Heston's new bride, ends up caught in the middle of the sordid struggle. Highly stylized film opens with one of the most famous sequences in movie history, a three minute tracking shot that sets the tone for the remainder of the film. A masterful merging of style and subject matter.

TREASURE OF SIERRA MADRE (1948)
**** NR 2:04
DIR: *John Huston* **CAST:** *Humphrey Bogart, Walter Huston, Tim Holt, Bruce Bennett*

Fine performances from Bogart and Huston highlight this engrossing depiction of greed. The two actors, along with Holt, play down and out prospectors who hit it big in the Mexican mountains, only to be done in by their own human weaknesses. Thoroughly entertaining action-adventure film won Oscars for Best Director, Screenplay (John Huston, adapted from B. Travers story), and Supporting Actor (Walter Huston).

TRUE GRIT (1969)
*** G 2:08
DIR: *Henry Hathaway* **CAST:** *John Wayne, Glen Campbell, Kim Darby, Jeff Corey, Robert Duvall, Dennis Hopper, Strother Martin*

Wayne won the first Oscar of his distinguished forty year career for his performance as Rooster Cogburn, a one-eyed marshall who goes off in search of the murderer (Corey) of Darby's father. Fine family entertainment. Darby is impressive as a teenage tomboy. Wayne would reprise the role six years later in *Rooster Cogburn*.

TURTLE DIARY (1986)
*** PG 1:37
DIR: *John Irvin* **CAST:** *Ben Kingsley, Glenda Jackson, Michael Gambon*

This heart-warming sleeper is a must-see! Directed by acclaimed British filmmaker John Irvin, *Turtle Diary* tells the story of two lost souls in England who share a passion for undersea life. One is an author, the other a book clerk, but both are highly idealistic and scheme to release the turtles from the local zoo into the ocean. Kingsley and Jackson are both in their usual brilliant form, making this a hilarious comedy to watch. You will cry tears of joy as the story progresses and the two would-be thieves grow closer to each other.

TWIN PEAKS: FIRE WALK WITH ME (1992)
*** R 2:15
DIR: *David Lynch* CAST: *Sheryl Lee, Kyle MacLachlan, Ray Wise, David Bowie, Chris Isaak, Kiefer Sutherland*
While this movie certainly isn't for everybody, if you're a fan of David Lynch, then you will not be disappointed. Taking place before the TV series started, in the last week that Laura Palmer was seen alive, we finally learn all of the complexities of her family life and exactly how her father became so evil. We are also introduced to some of the FBI's more unusual agents; the ten minute sequence which opens the film, featuring Chris Isaak and Kiefer Sutherland as two such agents, is absolutely hilarious.

TWINS (1988)
** PG 1:52
DIR: *Ivan Reitman* CAST: *Arnold Schwarzenegger, Danny DeVito, Kelly Preston*
Acclaimed filmmaker Ivan Reitman (*Meatballs, Ghostbusters*) directed this uproarious tale of two twins separated at birth: Schwarzenegger and DeVito! The two were conceived as part of a government genetic experiment to breed super warriors, but things went awry when one got all

the brains and the other all the braun. 35 years after their separation, Julius (Schwarzenegger) discovers his twin's existence and goes out into the big world to find him. Featuring wonderful comic performances, this movie is a lot of fun.

TWO OF A KIND (1982)
** NR 1:42
DIR: *Roger Young* **CAST:** *George Burns, Robby Benson, Cliff Robertson, Ronny Cox*
One of the better made-for-TV movies available on videocassette, this film follows the lives of an elderly man (Burns) and his mentally retarded grandson (Benson). Benson's parents have the patience to deal with neither of the two, so they naturally turn to each other for support. Their relationship grows as each discovers the untapped potential within himself, and learns how to express himself fully in the hostile world. A touch hammy at times, but still quite rewarding nonetheless.

2001: A SPACE ODYSSEY (1968)
**** G 2:18
DIR: *Stanley Kubrick* **CAST:** *Keir Dullea, Gary Lockwood,William Sylvester, Daniel Richter, Douglas Rain (as the voice of HAL)*
A mind-bending film; there is simply no other movie like it. The story is essentially the tale of human kind, from pre-historic man's first interac-

tion with a heavenly power to man's voyages into space. The astronaut footage, featuring the uncontrollable computer, HAL, was years ahead of its time and remains stunning to this day. Complex, disturbing, and extremely moving.

U

THE UNBEARABLE LIGHTNESS OF BEING
(1988)
**** R 2:51
DIR: *Philip Kaufman* CAST: *Daniel Day-Lewis, Juliette Binoche, Lina Olin, Erland Josephson, Derek de Lint, Pavel Landowsky.*
Passionate adaptation (by Jean-Claude Carriere) of highly regarded Milan Kundera novel. During the 1968 Russian invasion of Czechoslovakia, a promiscuous doctor (Day-Lewis) more interested in love than politics romances two beautiful, but very different, women (the innocent Binoche and the sexy Olin) at the same time. As the political events of the time play themselves out, Day-Lewis becomes more and more involved in his country's turmoil, while at the same time facing the deeper issues that confront him in his personal life. An extremely sensual, intelligent, and thought-provoking film.

UNCLE BUCK (1989)
** PG 1:46
DIR: *John Hughes* **CAST:** *John Candy, Amy Madigan, Jean Kelly*

This delightful comedy is sure to please the whole family. John Candy plays the inept title role of the film, who agrees to babysit his sister's three children after their father is hospitalized. The results are predictable, but funny nonetheless. Buck screws up anything that can or can't go wrong, the children show him how things are done, and the whole family grows closer and more understanding as a result of the mischief. Perhaps a little too cutesy for its own good, *Uncle Buck* is still quite effective.

UNCOMMON VALOR (1983)
** R 1:40
DIR: *Ted Ketchoff* **CAST:** *Gene Hackman, Randall "Tex" Cobb, Robert Stack, Fred Ward, Patrick Swayze*

One of the first movies to seriously analyze America's role in the Vietnam conflict (particularly regarding its apathetic attempts to search for MIA's and POW's), this movie features some fine performances by its stars. Hackman, whose son never returned from Vietnam, rounds up some of his old army buddies and plans an illegal mission to rescue American POW's in Vietnam. The government tries to thrwart their plans at every turn, right down to stealing all of their high tech military equipment, yet they still attempt to carry through with the plan. Although the movie is not stellar, it is still worth watching due to the moral questions it raises.

UNDER THE VOLCANO (1984)
*** R 1:49
DIR: *John Huston* **CAST:** *Albert Finney, Jacqueline Bissett, Anthony Andrews*
One of John Huston's finest achievements, this is the dark tale of an American diplomat in South America coping with his alcoholism. Set in the Great Depression era, the film is very moving, and features a wonderful cast. Finney is dead on in his portrayal of the alcoholic, arousing pity and anger in the viewer. Definitely not for the weak-hearted.

UNFAITHFULLY YOURS (1948)
*** NR 1:45
DIR: *Preston Sturges* **CAST:** *Rex Harrison, Linda Darnell, Barbara Lawrence, Rudy Vallee, Kurt Kreuger, Lionel Stander, Robert Greig*
Harrison plays the conductor of a symphony who believes his wife (Darnell) is having an affair with his male secretary (Kreuger). While leading his orchestra through three symphonies, Harrison fantasizes about three different—and very funny—ways to handle the situation, including murder. A fine farce, in the grand tradition of other Sturges comedies. Harrison is outstanding.

UNDER SIEGE (1992)
*** R 1:43
DIR: *Andrew Davis* **CAST:** *Steven Seagal, Tommy Lee Jones, Gary Busey, Colm Meaney*

Your reaction to this film will depend entirely upon how you perceive it after the first few minutes. If you think it is a serious action film, then you will hate it; but if you believe it to be a comedy spoof, then you will enjoy it immensely. Seagal plays a Navy Seal demoted to being a cook on a battleship carrying nuclear warheads. Tommy Lee Jones is a former US Intelligence agent who hijacks the ship in order to start a nuclear war, which he feels is adequate punishment for the sins of mankind. Featuring some remarkably hammy dialogue, over-the-top action, and some fine acting, this is a film to enjoy and *not* to think about.

UNFORGIVEN (1992)
**** R 2:07
DIR: *Clint Eastwood* **CAST:** *Clint Eastwood, Morgan Freeman, Gene Hackman, Richard Harris*

Considered one of the best films of the last five years, *Unforgiven* is the story of a vigilante hired to get revenge on the men who permanently disfigured a prostitute in the Old West. Eastwood made this film in attempt to rewrite Hollywood's glamorous portrayal of the period, realizing that most movies have idealized the violence and individually enforced justice. As such, none of the characters in this movie can truly be considered the good guys, and no one wears white hats. A deep and moving film, it won Oscars for Best Picture, Best Director, Best Supporting Actor (Gene Hackman's portrayal of a small town sheriff is one of the film's highlights), and Best Editing.

AN UNMARRIED WOMAN (1978)
**** R 2:04
DIR: *Paul Mazursky* CAST: *Jill Clayburgh, Alan Bates, Michael Murphy*
Clayburgh plays a woman dealing with her sudden divorce from her husband in this gripping drama. We see her transform herself from a dependent housewife to a self-sufficient woman as she rebuilds her life through relationships with other men. The preformances are spectacular all around, particularly that of Clayburgh, and the direction is superb and forceful. Exploring many of the same themes as *Thelma & Louise*, although possibly in a more mature manner, *An Unmarried Woman* is a wonderful adult drama.

UNTAMED HEART (1993)
*** PG-13 1:42
DIR: *Tony Bill* CAST: *Christian Slater, Marissa Tomei, Rosie Perez, Kyle Secor*
This standard yet still entertaining love story between a waitress and a bus boy stars Marisa

Tomei and Christian Slater. Led by veteran director Tony Bill, the two actors, noted more for their physical attractiveness than for their stage technique, actually put in bravura performances! Slater is uncharacteristically low key, and Tomei turns a standard character (the lost young woman, alienated by a cold world) into something fresh and three-dimensional. Overall, this is a very good film.

THE UNTOUCHABLES (1987)
*** R 1:59
DIR: *Brian DePalma* **CAST:** *Kevin Costner, Sean Connery, Andy Garcia, Robert DeNiro*
One of inconsistent director Brian DePalma's better films, this remake of the 1950's television show is not to be missed. Featuring stellar performances all around (Sean Connery finally earned an Oscar for his portrayal of an Irish beat cop), this edge-of-your-seat adventure will leave you cheering for the good guys! Kevin Costner plays Elliot Ness, a crusader fighting a war against gangland head Al Capone (DeNiro) in the midst of prohibition. With some incredible photography—the scene in which DeNiro compares a corporation to a baseball team is particularly effective—this film is one you'll probably want to watch over and over again.

V

THE VANISHING (1993)
** R 1:50
DIR: *George Sluizer* CAST: *Jeff Bridges, Kiefer Sutherland, Nancy Travis*
Sutherland plays a man whose girlfriend disappeared one day while the two were on vacation with each other. Understandably, he cannot deal with the inexplicable occurence, and he spends the next three years of his life searching in vain for her. He finally meets up with a man, claiming to be her abductor, who offers to reveal her fate to him. But there's one important catch: in order fully to understand her fate, Sutherland must actually undergo the same experience! Well acted but a bit too gruesome and unbelievable.

VENOM (1982)
** R 1:38
DIR: *Piers Haggard* CAST: *Klaus Kinski, Sterling Hayden, Oliver Reed, Sarah Miles*
In the best tradition of Hitchcock, this movie will have you biting your nails from beginning to end. A group of kidnappers plan to hold the young son of a rich American couple living in London hostage while his parents are away. But their plans go awry when they discover the boy to be an animal lover. Due to a mix up at the local pet shop, the most recent addition to his menagerie is one of the

most venomous snakes in the world, rather than a harmless garden snake! Things get even more complicated when one of the kidnappers, in a fit of nervousness, shoots a police officer.

THE VERDICT (1982)
*** R 2:09

DIR: *Sidney Lumet* **CAST:** *Paul Newman, Charlotte Rampling, Jack Warden, James Mason, Milo O'Shea, Lindsay Crouse, Edward Binns, Roxanne Hart*
David Mamet-scripted courtroom drama features a top-notch performance from Newman as a down-and-out lawyer trying to redeem himself when he fights both the medical establishment and the Catholic Church in a malpractice suit. Lumet's sure handed direction and an excellent supporting cast—highlighted by Mason as the smooth-as-silk defense attorney who opposes Newman—help to make this a compelling drama.

VERTIGO (1958)
**** PG 2:08

DIR: *Alfred Hitchcock* **CAST:** *James Stewart, Kim Novak, Barbara Bel Geddes, Tom Helmore, Henry Jones, Raymond Bailey, Ellen Corby*
Considered by many to be the greatest Hitchcock film of all-time. The masterfully (and psychologically) complex plot has Stewart playing a retired cop whose fear of heights once caused the death of another police officer and a beautiful woman.

Riddled with guilt, he begins to withdraw from any contact with people, until an old friend convinces him to follow his wife (Novak), whom he suspects is having an affair. The dream-like story continues to spin a weave of deception, derangement, and obsession, building to a shattering climax. The haunting score by Bernard Herrmann adds a great deal to this thrilling masterpiece.

VICTOR/VICTORIA (1982)
*** PG 2:13
DIR: *Blake Edwards* CAST: *Julie Andrews, Robert Preston, James Garner, Lesley Ann Warren, Alex Karras, John Rhys-Davies*
Stylish comedy featuring Andrews as a down-on-her-luck singer in 1930s Paris who becomes a star when she begins pretending to be a gay female impersonator! Trouble ensues when a Chicago gangster (Garner) falls in love her. Preston does a wonderful turn as Andrews' gay cohort, and Warren is very funny as Garner's bimbo girlfriend. A well done comedy of errors.

VICTORY (1981)
** PG 1:50
DIR: *John Huston* CAST: *Michael Caine, Sylvester Stallone, Max von Sydow, Pele*
This well-meaning but muddled film never quite scores a goal, but it does come close. In order to prove yet again that the Germans are engineering

a superior race, the Nazi army organizes a soccer match between some of their soldiers and some Allied prisoners of war. The Allies realize that this soccer game will result in lowered protection of some of their more important men who are being held prisoner, so they send Sylvester Stallone in to rescue them. The only problem is that the prisoners don't want to leave; they want to finish the soccer game instead.

W

WAGES OF FEAR (1952)
**** NR 2:36
DIR: *Henri Clouzot* CAST: *Charles Vanel, Yves Montand, Peter Van Eyck, Vera Clouzot*
One of the best action thrillers ever made, this French movie chronicles the adventures of a gang of n'er-do-wells who have fled from all corners of the Earth to a remote South American town. After having stayed there until they have been forgotten by the rest of the world, they can finally return to their homelands. The only problem, however, is how to raise the money in order to do so. One day, a big American corporation advertises for four brave men to drive truckloads of explosives across hazardous terrain. Will the men survive? This movie will keep you on the edge of your seat!

WAR AND PEACE (1968)
**** NR 6:13

DIR: *Sergei Bondarchuk* **CAST:** *Ludmila Ivanov-Golovko, Irina Gubanova, Sergei Bondarchuk*

This film is truly an experience to see! Perhaps larger in scope than even the greatest of Hollywood epics, this six hour (!) adaptation of Tolstoy's most famous novel is a marvel to behold. Regrettably, many copies of the video come only dubbed in English, but if you are really interested in seeing this film, then look for one in Russian with English subtitles (the dubbed version is so much poorer!). This movie won the Best Foreign Film Oscar of 1968.

WAR OF THE WORLDS (1953)
**** NR 1:25

DIR: *Byron Haskin* **CAST:** *Gene Barry, Les Tramayne, Ann Robinson, Henry Brandon*

George Pal's monumental production of the H.G. Wells' classic is every bit as exciting today as it was 40 years ago. Following much the same formula as *Star Wars*, it employs a vast array of special effects and a powerful story of good and evil. This tale of invasion will knock you out, and if you don't already know how it ends, then get ready for a doozy!

WARGAMES (1983)
*** PG 1:50

DIR: *John Badham* **CAST:** *Matthew Broderick, Ally*

Sheedy, Dabney Coleman, Barry Corbin
Featuring excellent performances all around, this is one of the finest movies ever to come out of the Cold War. Matthew Broderick plays a young hacker who accidentally stumbles into the Defense Department's nuclear tactics files while trying to steal some games electronically from a software producer. Thinking he's a Russian spy, the Pentagon sends people out after him, but in the end only he can save the world from destroying itself. Fiercely anti-war, yet never condescending to preachiness, this box-office blockbuster is a treasure to watch again and again.

WAYNE'S WORLD (1992)
*** PG-13 1:35
DIR: *Penelope Spheeris* **CAST:** *Mike Meyers, Dana Carvey, Tia Carrerre, Rob Lowe, Ed O'Neill*
One of the best slapstick movies of recent years, *Wayne's World* successfully transfers the concept of a sketch for the *Saturday Night Live* TV show to a feature-length movie on the big screen. Featuring hundreds of little sight gags and one-liners (you'll probably have to see the movie more than once to get them all), this movie will make you laugh until you "hurl!" Wayne Campbell, an idealistic young teenager from Aurora, Illinois, has dreams of taking his public access TV show big time. Opportunity finally comes knocking on his door, but he soon discovers that Hollywood isn't

as welcoming as it first seemed. Does Wayne successfully run his show *and* win the girl? You decide for yourself with the multiple endings!

WEEDS (1987)
*** R 1:55
DIR: *John Hancock* **CAST:** *Nick Nolte, William Forsyth, Enrine Hudson, Joe Mantegna*
Nick Nolte plays a man serving a life sentence in a maximum security prison. A hopeful playwright, Nolte spends all of his time behind bars creating dramatic pieces about his experiences. When a literary agent finds merit in some of his work, Nolte somehow finds himself out of prison and commencing life as an artist. He forms a theatre company populated entirely by ex-convicts. Featuring amazing performances and solid direction, this is an intense and interesting film.

WE'RE NO ANGELS (1989)
** PG-13 1:46
DIR: *Neil Jordan* **CAST:** *Robert DeNiro, Sean Penn, Demi Moore, Bruno Kirby*
What do you get when the director of *The Crying Game*, the writer of *Glenn Garry Glenn Ross*, and the stars of *Raging Bull* and *Bad Boys* team up? A really bad film! Based loosely on the 1950s movie of the same title starring Humphrey Bogart and directed by Michael Curtiz (both of whom showed their brilliance with *Casablanca*), this remake is no

match for an already mediocre original. De Niro and Penn play two escaped convicts on the run. When they reach a nearby church, they learn that two new priests are expected to join shortly. They decide that masquerading as the priests would be the perfect cover. While in the church, Penn discovers a spirituality within himself that he never knew of before, and De Niro rediscovers love (with Demi Moore). While the premise sounds touching and exciting, the payoff certainly is not!

WEST SIDE STORY (1961)
*** NR 2:35
DIR: *Robert Wise, Jerome Robbins* **CAST:** *Natalie Wood, Richard Beymer, Rita Moreno, George Chakiris, Russ Tamblyn, Simon Oakland, John Astin*
Excellent film adaptation of the classic Broadway musical about two rival New York City gangs— one white, the other Puerto Rican—and the modern Romeo (Beymer) and Juliet (Wood) caught in the middle of the struggle. Robbins' dazzling choreography is enhanced by the authentic New York City locations. Outstanding Leonard Bernstein and Stephen Sondheim score ("Maria," "Tonight") remains wonderous. Winner of ten Academy Awards, including Best Picture, Director, Supporting Actor (Chakiris), and Supporting Actress (Moreno). A special Oscar was presented to Robbins for his choreography.

WESTWORLD (1973)
*** PG 1:28
DIR: *Michael Crichton* **CAST:** *Richard Benjamin, Yul Brynner, James Brolin*

Michael Crichton (of *Jurassic Park* fame) directed this futuristic tale of a world in which robots have finally been perfected. Crichton explores the moral ramifications of the advancement of technology (much as he does in his dinosaur film) within an exhilerating and entertaining context. Benjamin and Brolin play two tired executives who go to an adult amusement park where they can live out their wildest fantasies. The two want to play cowboys for a while, so they choose to visit Westworld, where they can get into shootouts with robots and never get hurt. But what happens if one of the machines went a little haywire . . . ? Featuring a terrific script and outstanding acting, *Westworld* is a fine example of science fiction.

WHAT EVER HAPPENED TO BABY JANE? (1962)
*** NR 2:12
DIR: *Robert Aldrich* **CAST:** *Joan Crawford, Bette Davis, Victor Buono*

A superb character study of two elderly women lamenting their lost youth, this suspense yarn will scare you silly. Davis, an ex-child movie actor, hounds her sister, Crawford, from beginning to end, trying to overcome her insecurities by hurting those around her. This movie features fine performances all around, and Aldrich's direction is taut and forceful.

THE WICKER MAN (1973)
*** R 1:35
DIR: *Robin Hardy* **CAST:** *Edward Woodward, Christopher Lee, Britt Ecklund*
A truly terrifying movie, you will want to watch *The Wicker Man* over and over again! Edward Woodward, in a bravura performance, plays an English cop investigating the disappearance of a young child in a cult-like community that lives in isolation on an island. The cultists are, to put it mildly, rather odd, and as the tension builds, you start to sympathize entirely with Woodward and his attempts to discover what is going on. In the end, you share his point of view so much that you feel like a victim yourself! A must-see. Can be very hard to find, so grab it when you get the opportunity.

WILD AT HEART (1990)
*** R 2:07
DIR: *David Lynch* **CAST:** *Nicholas Cage, Laura Dern, Willem Dafoe, Dianne Ladd, Harry Dean Stanton*
While it is common knowledge that the films of controversial director David Lynch are not suited for everybody, *Wild at Heart* seems to polarize viewers even more than usual; for example, the

film was so praised at the famous Cannes festival that it actually won the Grand Prize, but it was also booed by the audience at many screenings. In other words, if you're a Lynch fan, you'll enjoy it, but otherwise you won't. Loosely based on a movie starring Marlon Brando, it features some fantastic performances by Cage and Dern, who portray two wild young kids who celebrate life and love in the strangest and (sometimes) most violent ways. Ultimately this is a love story, and a very beautiful one at that, in which all the ugliness of a violent world cannot keep two lovers apart. If you don't mind being subjected to some scenes of graphic violence, then you might enjoy this movie.

THE WILD BUNCH (1969)
*** R 2:22
DIR: *Sam Peckinpah* **CAST:** *William Holden, Ernest Borgnine, Edmond O'Brien, Robert Ryan, Warren Oates, Ben Johnson, Strother Martin*
Outstanding modern western about a band of aging outlaws who, unable to adapt to early 20th century life, head off to Mexico for one final score. At the Texas-Mexican border, they join a revolutionary Mexican general in his fight against the Mexican army. The violent action scenes are photographed gorgeously, and the innovative editing only adds to the excitement. A visual treat featuring several great performances, particularly Holden as an honorable gunfighter.

WILD HEARTS CAN'T BE BROKEN (1991)
*** G 1:28
DIR: *Steve Miner* **CAST:** *Gabrielle Anwar, Michael Schoefling, Cliff Robertson*

Featuring one of the most wildly implausible (yet true!) plots ever to grace a film, this movie is sure to uplift your spirits in a way that few can. Set in the Depression of the 1930s, Anwar plays a young woman who runs off to join the travelling circus. She learns how to high dive off a platform while riding a horse, and her unusual act steals the show. But one day something goes wrong, and she is blinded. Will this stop her? Of course not, because *Wild Hearts Can't Be Broken*! The movie is also a love story that is sweet yet never too sentimental. If you want to rent a movie that the whole family will enjoy, that will bring a warm smile to your face, then this might be just the right one.

WILD STRAWBERRIES (1957)
**** NR 1:30
DIR: *Ingmar Bergman* **CAST:** *Victor Sjostrom, Ingrid Thulin, Bibi Andersson, Gunnar Bjornstrand, Folke Sundquist.*

Sjostrom stars as an elderly college professor who reviews his life while taking an automobile trip to get an honorary degree. Bergman's brilliant direction (he also wrote the script) includes an assortment of flashbacks and dream sequences as Sjostrom looks at the meaning of life, from childhood to death. An extraordinarily powerful film, this classic is a must for anyone remotely interested in expanding their film vocabulary and knowledge.

WILLOW (1988)
** PG 2:00
DIR: *Ron Howard* **CAST:** *Val Kilmer, Warwick Davis, Billy Barty, Joanne Whalley*
One of the most juvenile action films of the 1980s, you probably won't enjoy this movie if you are over the age of thriteen. It is the story of a small man with a big heart who saves an entire kingdom by keeping the heir to the throne out of the clutches of an evil witch. The story is old, the special effects second-rate, and the acting nothing to write home about. Save this one for your kids.

WINGS OF DESIRE (1988)
**** PG-13 2:10
DIR: *Wim Wenders* **CAST:** *Bruno Ganz, Solveig Dommartin, Otto Sander, Curt Bois, Peter Falk*
Beautiful fantasy about two angels (Ganz and Sander) who float around West Berlin, watching over the citizens of the city. When Ganz falls in love with a circus performer (Dommartin), he becomes infatuated with the idea of becoming a human being. Among the many breathtaking concepts and techniques employed by Wenders is the unusual look to the movie—as Ganz gets closer to

humanity, the film gradually turns from black and white to color. Falk, playing himself, gives one of the finest performances of his distinguished career. A yearning, haunting, lyrical masterpiece from a director unknown to most Americans.

THE WIZARD OF OZ (1939)
**** G 1:42
DIR: *Victor Fleming* **CAST:** *Judy Garland, Roy Bolger, Frank Morgan, Bert Lahr, Jack Haley, Margaret Hamilton, Billie Burke*
A family classic for the ages. Musical fantasy features Garland as a Kansas farm girl who takes a trip to the magical land of Oz. Once there, she meets numerous unforgettable characters, including the cowardly lion, the tin man, the scarecrow, the wicked witch of the west, and many more. The film features one of the most popular songs ever written (by Harold Arlen and E.Y. Harburg), "Over the Rainbow," as well as Herbert Stothart's Oscar-winning score. Whether it's your first time seeing the film or the fiftieth, this wonderous work of art is always a joy to watch.

A WOMAN UNDER THE INFLUENCE (1974)
*** R 2:35
DIR: *John Cassavetes* **CAST:** *Gena Rowlands, Peter Falk, Fred Draper, Katherine Cassavetes*
Gena Rowlands gives a tour-de-force performance as a housewife who is having a nervous break-

down. Peter Falk plays her loving, but powerless husband. Cassavetes allows his actors a lot of room for improvisation and it pays off—Rowlands is alternately funny, tragic, sad, happy, excited, depressed . . . often within the same scene! You'll love her and pity her, laugh with her and cry with her. While some find this film slow and ponderous, others find themselves riveted by one of the great performances by an actress in post-'60s cinema.

WOMEN ON THE VERGE OF A NERVOUS BREAKDOWN (1988)
*** R 1:28
DIR: *Pedro Almodovar* **CAST:** *Carmen Maura, Antonio Banderas, Julietta Sarrano*
Directed by internationally acclaimed filmmaker Pedro Almodovar, this is the bittersweet tale of a woman trying to start her life anew after being deserted one day by her lover of many years. Featuring brilliant performances by an ensemble cast, the movie has some of the most memorable characters in recent years. Funny and warm, it will make you laugh and cry at the same time, and feel happy to be alive.

THE WORLD ACCORDING TO GARP (1982)
*** R 2:16
DIR: *George Roy Hill* **CAST:** *Robin Williams, John Lithgow, Glenn Close, Mary Beth Hurt*

One of the most unusual American films made during the 1980s, *The World According to Garp* is a comedic masterpiece. Funny yet almost unbearably tragic, the film follows the lives of T.S. Garp (Williams), bastard son to a fiercely feminist nurse (Close). As Garp grows older, he hopes to make a career as a writer, but despite rave reviews, he is constantly standing in the shadow of his possessive mother, who has become a famous women's rights advocate. The cast is universally splendid, especially Williams and John Lithgow, who plays a transvestite ex-pro football player! George Roy Hill's direction is solid and biting.

WUTHERING HEIGHTS (1939)
**** NR 1:44
DIR: *William Wyler* **CAST:** *Laurence Olivier, Merle Oberon, David Niven, Geraldine Fitzgerald, Donald Crisp*
Fine film adaptation of classic Emily Bronte romance novel about the doomed love affair between Heathcliff (Olivier) and Cathy (Oberon) in 19th century England. The cast is uniformly excellent, particularly Olivier as the brooding hero, and Ben Hecht and Charles MacArthur's passionate screenplay is sensitively written. Gregg Toland's haunting cinematography won an Oscar.

X

X: THE MAN WITH THE X-RAY EYES (1963)
** NR 1:20
DIR: *Roger Corman* **CAST:** *Ray Milland, Diana Van Der Vlis, John Hoyt, Don Rickles, Harold J. Stone*
Cult science-fiction horror film from the "King of the B's," Roger Corman. Milland plays a scientist who develops a formula which allows him to see through things. This proves to be fatal, however, as he loses his job, becomes a carnival attraction, and goes mad. Fine performance from Milland and appropriately weird cinematography from Floyd Crosby.

Y

YANKEE DOODLE DANDY (1942)
*** NR 2:06
DIR: *Michael Curtiz* **CAST:** *James Cagney, Walter Huston, Joan Leslie, Irene Manning, Richard Whor*
Musical biography features a wonderful Oscar-winning performance from Cagney as the Broadway entertainer George M. Cohan. Patriotic film has several stand-out numbers, including "You're a Grand Old Flag," "Over There," and the title tune. Cagney displays some surprisingly impressive talent as a dancer. Ray Heindorf and Heinz Roemheld won an Academy Award for their musical score.

THE YEAR OF LIVING DANGEROUSLY
(1983)
*** PG 1:54
DIR: *Peter Weir* **CAST:** *Mel Gibson, Sigourney Weaver, Linda Hunt, Michael Murphy, Bill Kerr*
Set in 1965 Indonesia, when that country was heading towards civil war, this atmospheric political drama stars Gibson as an Australian television journalist who finds himself in danger when British embassy worker Weaver tips him off to some top-secret information. Hunt, as the cameraman who shows Gibson the ins-and-outs of the country, steals the film with her Academy Award-winning performance (she's actually playing a man).

YELLOW SUBMARINE (1968)
**** G 1:25
DIR: *George Dunning* **CAST:** *The Beatles*
If you're a fan of the Beatles, then you musn't wait another day to see their fabulous little cartoon, *Yellow Submarine*. Featuring a soundtrack with some of their best and most loved songs, you will follow the Fab Four as they journey into Pepper Land to do battle with the Horrible Blue Meanies. Even if you aren't a fan of the group, you are sure to be entertained by the wisecrack-laden script and psychedelic drawings.

YOU CAN'T TAKE IT WITH YOU (1938)
**** NR 2:06
DIR: *Frank Capra* **CAST:** *Lionel Barrymore, James Stewart, Jean Arthur, Eddie Arnold*
Perhaps Capra's greatest triumph of all time, *You Can't Take it With You* is one of the best and most memorable films ever to come out of Hollywood's golden age. Featuring a smashing group of actors, all of whom were stars in their own right, Capra led this gem with such perfection that it went on to win the Academy Award for Best Picture of 1938. The plot centers on the obstacles to marriage faced by Jimmy Stewart and Jean Arthur, two young and idealistic lovers who want nothing more than to live together blissfully in holy matrimony.

THE YOUNG LIONS (1958)
*** NR 2:47
DIR: *Edward Dmytryk* **CAST:** *Marlon Brando, Montgomery Clift, Hope Lange, Dean Martin*
Many films have examined the potential for human cruelty and human compassion in the midst of war. But what separates *The Young Lions* from most others is its unique perspective: we see World War II through the eyes of both a German and an American officer. Although the entire cast is splendid, Marlon Brando steals the show in his portrayal of a Nazi. Brando's character is utterly reprehensible yet somehow deserving of sympathy, as we see that he has been fooled into adopting his racist beliefs.

Z

ZELIG (1983)
*** PG 1:19

DIR: *Woody Allen* **CAST:** *Woody Allen, Mia Farrow, Garrett Brown, Stephanie Farrow, Will Holt*

Technical masterpiece from Allen and cinematographer Gordon Willis. Allen plays Leonard Zelig, a fictional character who became famous in the 1920s for his chameleonlike ability to transform himself so that he could blend into almost any crowd. Told in a pseudo-documentary style, we see newsreel footage of Zelig standing next to everyone from Hitler to Charlie Chaplin to Herbert Hoover to Babe Ruth! The humorous songs from Dick Hyman recapture the sound of the period.

ZOOT SUIT (1981)
** R 1:43

DIR: *Luis Valdez* **CAST:** *Edward James Olmos, Tyne Daly, John Anderson, Charles Aidman*

This unusual film is certainly different from most of the movies you pick up off the video store shelf. A musical with an audience visible on screen, this fantastical recreation of the true life imprisonment of several Hispanic gangsters in the 1940s is an uneven, yet still highly recommended, story. The music is quite good, even if it doesn't really fit in with the somber theme and tone that the rest of the movie tries to present and create.

ZORBA THE GREEK (1964)
*** NR 2:26
DIR: *Michael Cacoyannis* **CAST:** *Anthony Quinn, Irene Papas, Alan Bates, Lila Kedrova, George Foundas*
Nikos Kazantzakis' highly regarded novel is adapted to film with fine results, thanks in part to the rousing performance by Quinn as the life-loving Greek who refuses to give in to the mores of Greek society. Bates is the uptight English writer who becomes friends with Quinn on the island of Crete. Lila Kedrova won an Oscar for her role as a faded prostitute. The Cinematography and Art Direction were also awarded Academy Awards.

ZULU (1964)
**** R 2:18
DIR: *Cy Endfield* **CAST:** *Michael Caine, Richard Burton, James Booth, Stanley Baker*
Based on the actual events in a British mission in Africa, this film traces the tragic final days before an attack by thousands of Zulu warriors. Told in the familiar style of most disaster films, such as *Towering Inferno*, the script and acting sometimes leave something to be desired. But the action scenes are choreographed so beautifully and extravagantly that they make your heartbeat race. This film, although quite long and slow in parts, is well worth sitting through just for the enjoyment of these action sequences.